Young Muslim Change-Ma

The Muslim charity sector is stronger than ever, attracting thousands of volunteers and millions of pounds in donations. In times of mobile Internet and social media, young people have set up small scale charities in urban areas, providing general social services to Muslims and non-Muslims alike. Breaking away from bureaucratic non-governmental organisations and traditional faith-based charities, these smaller local associations are an attractive alternative to young people.

This book offers an exploration of the Muslim charity sector, from multi-million pound NGOs to discrete grassroots charities who are quietly giving rise to the next generation of Muslim entrepreneurs, scholars, politicians and other influencers. From studies of eleven charities across France, Poland and the UK, it investigates key questions around this young and dynamic movement. What motivates these young Muslim volunteers? What shapes the socially-engaged behaviour of young Muslims? What is the place and the role of Islam in their involvement and commitment to their causes? What social impact do these organisations have in their local area? How do they understand religion, faith, participation and citizenship? What challenges do they face and how do they overcome these? The book also examines how these grassroots are successful in helping to prevent extremism, curb Islamophobia and challenge colonialism.

The analysis of these small, local and original initiatives is fundamental in understanding the role of religiosity for these younger generations who are trying to articulate their multiple identities, cultures and traditions in a modern, secular society. Rich, detailed and vivid, the book sheds new lights on a popular field of research, unveiling exclusive key information on the subject of young European Muslims.

William Barylo is an independent researcher focusing on the articulations between diasporic cultures, religions and hyper-modernity from a decolonial and restorative perspective. He is an awarded photographer and film maker, having directed the internationally released documentary "Polish Muslims: an unexpected meeting".

Routledge Islamic Studies

This broad ranging series includes books on Islamic issues from all parts of the globe and is not simply confined to the Middle East.

For a full list of titles in the series: www.routledge.com/middleeaststudies/series/SE0516

20 **Salafi Ritual Purity**
   In the Presence of God
   Richard Gauvain

21 **Postcolonialism and Islam**
   Theory, Literature, Culture, Society and Film
   Geoffrey Nash, Kathleen Kerr-Koch and Sarah E. Hackett

22 **The Teaching and Study of Islam in Western Universities**
   William Shepherd, Toni Tidswell, Paul Trebilco and Paul Morris

23 **Muslim Active Citizenship in the West**
   Mario Peucker and Shahram Akbarzadeh

24 **Refashioning Secularism in France and Turkey**
   The Case of the Headscarf Ban
   Amélie Barras

25 **Islam, Context, Pluralism and Democracy**
   Classical and Modern Interpretations
   Yaser Ellethy

26 **Young Muslim Change-Makers**
   Grassroots Charities Rethinking Modern Societies
   William Barylo

27 ***Da'wa* and Other Religions**
   Indian Muslims and the Modern Resurgence of Global Islamic Activism
   Matthew J. Kuiper

Young Muslim Change-Makers
Grassroots Charities Rethinking
Modern Societies

William Barylo

LONDON AND NEW YORK

First published 2018
by Routledge

2 Park Square, Milton Park, Abingdon, Oxfordshire OX14 4RN
52 Vanderbilt Avenue, New York, NY 10017

Routledge is an imprint of the Taylor & Francis Group, an informa business

First issued in paperback 2019

Copyright © 2018 William Barylo

The right of William Barylo to be identified as author of this work has been asserted in accordance with sections 77 and 78 of the Copyright, Designs and Patents Act 1988.

All rights reserved. No part of this book may be reprinted or reproduced or utilised in any form or by any electronic, mechanical, or other means, now known or hereafter invented, including photocopying and recording, or in any information storage or retrieval system, without permission in writing from the publishers.

Notice:
Product or corporate names may be trademarks or registered trademarks, and are used only for identification and explanation without intent to infringe.

British Library Cataloguing-in-Publication Data
A catalogue record for this book is available from the British Library

Library of Congress Cataloguing-in-Publication Data
Names: Barylo, William, author.
Title: Young Muslim change-makers : grassroots charities rethinking modern societies / William Barylo.
Description: New York, NY : Routledge, 2018. | Series: Routledge islamic studies series ; v. 26 | Includes bibliographical references and index.
Identifiers: LCCN 2017008261 | ISBN 9781138054158 (hbk) | ISBN 9781315166995 (ebk)
Subjects: LCSH: Islam—Charities. | Charity organization—Europe. | Islamic sociology.
Classification: LCC HV238 .B375 2018 | DDC 361.7/5088297094—dc23
LC record available at https://lccn.loc.gov/2017008261

ISBN: 978-1-138-05415-8 (hbk)
ISBN: 978-0-367-88929-6 (pbk)

Typeset in Times New Roman
by Apex CoVantage, LLC

Contents

List of illustrations	vii
List of tables	viii
Acknowledgements	ix
List of acronyms	xi

Introduction   1
Context 1
Significance and relevance 3
Research questions 4
Theoretical framework 5
Book structure 6

1 **What sociology for Islam?**   11
  Beyond religion 14
  Participating Muslims 19

2 **Muslim grassroots charities and method**   30
  A brief history of European Muslim charities 31
  Study sample: young, skilled and diverse 35
  Methodology, phenomenology and ethics 42

3 **Islamophobia: Countering alienation**   49
  Has Europe alienated its citizens? 49
  Dialogue as a key for contemporaneity 55
  Agents of negotiation, agents of trust 61

4 **The attractive middle way**   66
  Charities as convivial social capital power plants 67
  Building identity, giving a meaning to life 73
  Different, efficient and therefore attractive 77

5	**Crafting an active citizenship** *Staying committed 86* *Shura, the viable chimera of democracy 92*	85
6	**Neoliberal metacolonisation** *Muslims, consumerism and neoliberalism 106* *Metacolonialism and radical monopoly 110* *The paradox of Muslim managerialism 115*	104
7	**From resistance to self-determination** *Coping mechanisms 125* *Emotional theology and alter-system mind-set 129*	123
	Conclusion	137
	Glossary of Arabic terms *Index*	145 147

Illustrations

1.1	Prayer mat in the premises of Amatullah	12
1.2	Circle for consultation and invocations after a soup kitchen at Amatullah	13
2.1	Celebration of the 20th anniversary of Islamic Relief France at la Bastille	32
2.2	Outreach session of Amatullah in Paris	37
3.1	Open day of Amatullah in Bagnolet	56
3.2	Inflatable sumos fight in Jussieu University, during Averroès's open day	57
4.1	Eid picnic in Regent's Park, London	69
4.2	Young volunteers during a soup kitchen of Amatullah in Bagnolet	74
5.1	Volunteers of MADE in a protest for divestment from fossil fuels in London	93
5.2	At JMF's Orientation Forum in La Courneuve	94
6.1	Muslim 'marriage event' event at the GPU in London	105
6.2	Seminar for coaching young Muslim executives	115
7.1	Open canvas at the RAMF in Le Bourget: 'actions for a better world'	124
7.2	Musical performance of Fahad Khalid at Rumi's Cave	131
7.3	People chatting at an event of BARBEDOUN	132

Tables

2.1 Main characteristics of the charities sample 1/3   38
2.2 Main characteristics of the charities sample 2/3   39
2.3 Main characteristics of the charities sample 3/3   40

Acknowledgements

The aim of this book, adapted from my doctoral dissertation in sociology, is to restore a more realistic, objective vision of Muslims, backed by observations, interviews and facts. Rarely do works move beyond sealed categories, such as 'Muslims' as an abstract entity – or sub-groups such as salafis, wahhabis, etc. – and 'the West', 'secularism' or 'democracy'. Such tensions are obscuring the complexity of the lives of Muslims as Europe citizens. The reality is more one of multiple interpenetrations between a variety of subjective appropriations of Islam and different spheres of life. I felt the need to cover a not-so-well known side of the life of Muslims in Europe: the charity sector. Moreover, shifting the focus from the multimillion-pound NGO industry, I wanted to analyse these spontaneous and informal grassroots initiatives, which play a considerable role in reshaping the distribution of wealth, powers and representation of minorities in the public sphere through spirituality. In this regard, I would like to thank my supervisor, Nilüfer Göle, for giving me numerous insights and also for her understanding of my personal journey, which gave me the resources necessary for the completion of this work. I am grateful to Valérie Amiraux, Didier Lapeyronnie and Baudouin Dupret for their assessment of my initial dissertation, Julien Lheureux for the review of the first drafts and Michał Łyszczarz and Katarzyna Górak-Sosnowska for their help in Poland. I would also like to convey my gratitude to Juliette Galonnier and Konrad Pędziwiatr for their support and survival tips in an ever-more volatile and industrial academia. This is not to forget everyone who participated in the fieldwork, volunteers, managers and civil servants whose words and deeds provide the primary material of this book.

From a more personal perspective, this book – and PhD – hides a survival story in which the main protagonists were physical and emotional abuse, divorce, depression, anxiety and self-doubt. To make things more difficult, trying to fight these in our current times is an actual war. The world becomes increasingly volatile: job security, income and social bonds are less guaranteed than ever. How is one supposed to find solace when even love, friendship, joy and hope immediately turn into dust? However, this book is proof that it is possible to navigate between the elements. Society pushes us to conform to certain norms and, moreover, to dwell in dissatisfaction, competitive enmity and self-hatred; therefore, nurturing love and solid friendships are acts of resistance. Life is a long distance hike, and hiking taught me to 'never focus on the wounds but on the people who give you the strength to walk further'. If I am alive today, it would not have happened without the ideas and support of Abbas Zahedi, Asmaa Soliman, Baber Siddiqi, Emmylie Roberts, Fahad Khalid, Fatima Khemilat, Fayet Nsomoto, Jayde Russell, Kamel and Nawal Zine, Marwan Muhammad, Nazra Zuhyle, Raouda Ghenania, Samia Tahraoui, Samra Saeed, Umar Attallah Khan and Uzma Taj, among others.

I would like to express my utmost gratitude to Abdullah Faliq, Engie Salama, Sheila Joy Raymond El Dieb and especially Javayria Masood, for not only the time and effort spent helping me on my writings, but also for their immense personal support.

Acronyms

CCIF	*Collective Contre l'Islamophobie en France* (Collective Against Islamophobia in France)
CEA	*Comité à l'Energie Atomique* (Committee for Atomic Energy)
CERSI	*Centre d'Etudes et de Recherches sur l'Islam* (Centre for Studies and Research on Islam)
CFCM	*Conseil Français du Culte Musulman* (French Council of the Muslim Faith)
FEMYSO	Forum of European Muslim Youth and Student Organisations
GPU	Global Peace and Unity
HEC	*École des Hautes Etudes Commerciales* (School for Higher Commercial Studies)
IERA	Islamic Education and Research Academy
IESH	*Institut Européen des Sciences Humaines* (European Institute of Humanities)
IMAN	Islamophobia Monitoring and Action Network
IRC	International Rescue Committee
JMF	*Jeunes Musulmans de France* (Young Muslims of France)
LM	*Liga Muzułmańska* (Muslim League)
MADE	Muslim Agency for Development and the Environment
MCB	Muslim Council of Britain
MINAB	Mosques and Imams Advisory Board
MZR	*Muzułmański Związek Religijny* (Religious Union of Muslims)
RAMF	*Rencontres Annuelles des Musulmans de France* (Yearly Meetings of Muslims of France)
SPMF	*Syndicat des Professionels Musulmans Français* (French Muslim Entrepreneurs' Trade Union)
UNEF	*Union Nationale des Etudiants de France* (National Union of French Students)
UOIF	*Union des Organisations islamiques de France* (Union of Islamic Organisations of France)

Introduction

Context

Paris, 2008, University of Jussieu.

I was 22 and finishing my Bachelor's in Fundamental Chemistry. I had just come back from my first photo report about the Bushinengue people in West French Guiana[1] and was shocked by the level of inequalities I had seen (it was as if time had stopped during the colonial era). I wanted to dedicate my life to something more connected to people, and especially to building bridges between the mainstream dominant society and diverse ethnic, gender, cultural and religious identities. France was, at the time, clearly violating numerous human rights.[2] The year 2008, especially, was at the dawn of an unprecedented wave of controversy around Islam and Muslims. Since 9/11, the French media had surfed on a wave of sensationalism and the government on one of security, secularism and nationalism. While unemployment, financial crisis and social inequalities were the major problems, politicians orientated the debate about the 'compatibility of Islam and the Republic',[3] or the *hijab* (headscarf) in the public sphere. Some, like Marine Le Pen, compared religious visibility to Nazi occupation. Others, like the 'left-wing' Prime Minister Manuel Valls, explicitly said that 'the fight against the headscarf is essential for the Republic'.[4] While writing this book in 2016, abuses, aggressions and crimes against Muslims did not decrease at all. After the so-called 'burkini ban' in August and with the *État d'Urgence* (state of emergency) indefinitely prolonged, France even seemed to be slowly turning into a totalitarian regime. The last European democracy to have passed a similar law was Nazi Germany in 1933, when the Jews were banned from beaches; history shows us what followed. After each war or genocide during the twentieth century, people vowed 'never again', yet very familiar dynamics have fuelled Brexit and Donald Trump's victory in the US. Who, then, could believe that twenty-first-century Europe and America could forget history? Despite strong global protest movements and awareness campaigns empowered by the rise of cyber-activism, democracy has rarely looked this dark in Europe and America. However, at a grassroots level, dynamic young people and organisations working towards building a more harmonious society show us that perhaps there are still reasons to hope.

2   Introduction

In the climate of 2008, a small charity sparked my curiosity. Working on the premises of the university, the charity was pursuing its unpaid activities in spite of the tense atmosphere. These young Muslim men and women were publishing exam papers corrections for everyone and offering meals to deprived students, and were quite popular amongst the students and the university staff, as if they were living in a microcosm protected from the raging racist hurricane. One year later, I undertook my Master's in Social Sciences of Religions at the EHESS in Paris. While most of my research was done on extremism, immigration or identity, I wanted to understand these young men and women: why and how they get involved as volunteers, what their motivations are, what voluntary social work brings them, what role Islam plays in their activities and what impact they have on their social environment. After seven years of fieldwork, I realised these young Muslims were incredibly resourceful and innovative when it came to living their Islam in a modern and secular society. This book is a summary of my findings.

Two years later, I found myself in Bagnolet, part of the infamous *banlieue*, a peripheral urban area around Paris which came under the spotlight after the 2005 riots. Sarfaraz,[5] a young man in his early twenties, welcomed me into the premises of a charity called Amatullah, on the ground floor of a social housing building. He invited me to take a seat while I waited for the others to come. Later that evening, I would participate in a mobile soup kitchen in some of the most deprived parts of Paris: one entirely managed by Muslims. In the meantime, I contemplated the space around me. Their office was simple: a kitchen, a storage room and a small desk in the corner. A poster of Mecca on the wall, a small Qur'an on a shelf next to a plate bearing a calligraphy of the name of God, *Allah*. A poster of the Taj Mahal. The storage room was full of packs of noodles, oil bottles, cereals, canned vegetables and juice card boxes, which would be brought to the homeless later in the evening. In a corner, some folded prayer mats. A few minutes later, volunteers started arriving. '*Salaam Alaykum*,' people were saying joyfully to one another, shortly followed by the traditional answer '*Alaykum Salaam*'. The sun had just set. While a group prepared to perform the *Maghrib* prayer, some of the team cooked pasta and tomato sauce in huge pots for the soup kitchen. Some others had casual conversations. One talked about holidays, then work, another talked about the results of the last football match . . . discussions were punctuated by traditional '*inshaAllah*' (God willing), '*alhamdulillah*' (praise be to God, used as an expression of satisfaction) or '*MashaAllah*' ('as God wanted', used as an expression of admiration).

Talking to Sarfaraz and some others, waiting for the van to come, I asked about politics. The context was tense. Not long ago, religious signs were banned from high schools and the media were flooded by controversies around Islam and Muslims: *niqab* (face veil), *halal* meat, prayers in the street, terrorism . . . while acts of violence against Muslims were on the rise. However, nobody seemed to really care about the news. 'I don't trust politicians (. . .) it's only a game for power. Here, at Amatullah, we do true politics,' Sarfaraz said. One may share on Facebook an aggression in his neighbourhood or reply to racist words from a minister on Twitter, but casual conversation seemed almost disconnected from context.

People focused more on their personal lives and, most importantly, on voluntary social work. Before each soup kitchen, as a ritual, the volunteers gathered in a circle. Everybody introduced themselves by their first name and their city of residence. Then, the manager read the rules to the volunteers out loud. Rules like 'wear latex gloves at all times, never leave food on the ground' and 'always smile at beneficiaries', on which the speaker commented: 'don't forget that smile is *sunnah*, it's a *sadaqa*' (an alms, an act of worship). After a short invocation in French asking God for help and traditional formulas in Arabic, the soup kitchen began.

The charity itself is small. Ten people at most make up the active core of volunteers. They are young, in their early twenties. They are French, most born and raised in the country. At the same time, their cultural roots reach to North or West Africa, South Asia and the Caribbean, not to mention a few native French people who have chosen Islam and others in the team who are of no faith. However, they call each other 'brothers' and 'sisters'. Some of them are executives in big insurance companies; one is finishing her master's degree in physics; another young woman is a civil servant; the president works as a security agent; another is a businessman. One in the core team left school before getting any qualification. But here, education and career play no role. Everyone is a volunteer. There is no leader, but a rather informal hierarchy in which 'elders', those who have been volunteering for months or years, supervise the 'newcomers', who are not familiar with the environment yet.

The food comes exclusively from private donations. Three years ago, the charity was under the spotlight of French intelligence services. The city council was concerned by potential threats of terrorism or radicalisation. But a few years on, they came to support the charity after observing that their work benefited the whole community. The city council offered them their premises and venues for events and helped them with publicity. These young men and women are Muslims who happen to be volunteers or, conversely, volunteers who happen to be Muslim. Although Islam is a strong frame of reference for most, they offer their food to anyone and work with people from all faiths and none.

Significance and relevance

This is how seven years of work started, the very beginning of my research into faith-based grassroots voluntary organisations in Europe. Although in social sciences the question of Muslims in Europe has been mainly covered from the perspectives of immigration, terrorism or extremism, more recent works have analysed the articulation of religious practice in a secular context, but such works have been limited to rituals such *halal* food, burials, marriage and Islamic education (see Chapter 2, 'A brief history of European Muslim charities'). Thus, non-specifically Muslim charities like Amatullah show a side of the matter barely studied before. Also, most works have analysed dynamics only within Muslim organisations or communities and personal perceptions of concepts such as citizenship, relation to politics, authorities, other faith communities or relations to islamophobia and stigmatisation. This study not only focuses on the personal biographies of the participants but also takes into account external stakeholders, such as the public and the authorities, in order to assess the local impact of these organisations. This work responds to the need for exploring diversity spaces, their involvement in local governance and their engagement in wider civil society (Furbey 2007, 36).

Amatullah is a pioneer in the field of small, local initiatives founded in the late 2000s throughout Europe. Breaking away from traditional non-governmental organisational (NGOs) structures and organisations, these smaller, local associations provide young people with an attractive alternative. They are more flexible and informal and provide an opportunity for many to quickly make a tangible difference, the results of which they can witness themselves. These charities, in the view of many, are the cradle of the coming generation of young Muslim changemakers. Diverse, united, highly skilled and qualified, some of their volunteers are already among the influencers of contemporary European society. At times when crime and aggression related to islamophobia are on the rise, they provide safe spaces in which alternative forms of governance, conflict resolution or democracy are experimented with, such as *shura* (consultation-based decision making). Through this democratic spirit and practice, these charities perform an essential political action in its radical sense, that of the *bios politikos* (the life of the city). They are able to make tangible differences in the areas in which they operate and fight discrimination.

With the power of social media, the younger generation of European Muslims has never been more diverse, creative or quickly changing at the same time. Young, learned and skilled, they break traditional boundaries and redefine society with their own terms and in their own image. Imams, scholars and mosques are not as influential as before. These young volunteers build their own tailor-made interpretation of Islam in a modern secular society. The diverse cultural and spiritual backgrounds of their members are no longer sources of division, but a wealth they use to build bridges throughout the Muslim community. Cohesive, friendly and useful, these charities are a powerful way of smashing the authorities' prejudices against Islam or Muslims and turning the broader public into supporters. Social acts such as feeding the homeless provide a sense of responsibility to young Muslims from deprived areas; they feel safe and helpful in a family-like environment that is key for curbing the frustration and resentment at the roots of religious extremism. Organisations like Amatullah are at a crucial intersection between volunteering and religion. While organisational behaviour, on the one end, and Muslims in Europe, on the other, has been extensively studied, the civil engagement of young Muslims at a grassroots level is a rather new phenomenon in Europe. This raises important questions on theoretical, empirical and analytical levels, which I will try to answer in this book.

Research questions

This work investigates key questions around this young and dynamic movement. First, who are these young Muslim volunteers? Then, what motivates them? What shapes the socially engaged behaviour of young Muslims? What are the place and the role of Islam in their involvement and commitment to their causes? What social impact do these organisations make in their local area and how? How do they understand religion, faith, participation and citizenship? What challenges do they face, and how do they overcome these? The analysis of these small, local and original initiatives is fundamental for understanding the role of religiosity for younger generations who are trying to articulate their multiple identities, cultures and traditions in a modern, secular society. To some extent, this work is about exploring how these change-makers are shaping the new face of twenty-first-century European cosmopolitan society.

Theoretical framework

This work focuses on people working in small-scale, local, not-for-profit organisations on a voluntary basis, commonly named 'charities'. Sometimes called 'voluntary organisations', 'community social organisations' (Amath 2015) or 'associations' (in France), they all fall into the legal category of 'charity' regulated by the Charity Commission in the UK: hence the use of the term 'charity' in this book as a synonym of the aforementioned appellations, for a matter of convenience.

This work is about exploring a reality and subjects under the radar in their different aspects and challenges, their different approaches to their social environment and their group dynamics through their different individual trajectories and stories. It appeared to me that the best way to understand these questions was to start at a microscopic level within the groups themselves, taking into account the personal stories, biographies and subjective understanding of religion as lived in daily life. For this purpose, this work takes an ethnographic approach based on descriptive phenomenology, a choice explained further in this book (see Chapter 1, 'Participating Muslims'). This very methodological choice influenced the theoretical framework, in the sense that I did not use any theory before my fieldwork and therefore analyse the subjects through the lens of specific concepts, but rather the fieldwork and the participants shaped the theoretical choices I made (similar to works such as Amath 2015, Englander 2012 or Giorgi 2008). This method allowed me to critically examine and discuss existing concepts and categories such as 'religion', 'identity' and 'citizenship' (see Chapter 1, 'Participating Muslims', and Chapter 5), depending on how they fit my observations.

Being a European Muslim in the twenty-first century is not as simple as belonging to simplistic, hermetic ideal-types such as 'traditionalists' or 'political activists'. While sociological literature about Muslims in Europe, especially French studies (Frégosi 2008; Lamchichi 1999; Kepel 1991), have extensively used similar categories, I found more nuanced approaches more faithful to my field observations (Amath 2015; Peucker and Akbarzadeh 2014; Pędziwiatr 2010; Amiraux 2006 and 2007; Fadil 2006): hence my choice to avoid categorising the participants. The act of classifying subjects as part of certain ethnic groups, categories or types of behaviour means that we see only these categories instead of seeing people and thus reduce complex subjects to mere labels. The volunteers in this study are young men and women from different socio-economic classes, different political opinions, different professional backgrounds and different understandings of Islam who are not necessarily vocal in the public sphere or on social media, but who beyond the differences of class, ethnicity, gender, age or opinions unite and try to make a difference at a local level. As the reader will find more extensively in the following chapters, whether they are drawn to some more rigorous practice of Islam or do not practise at all, these young Muslim volunteers all participate in the social life of their environment and thus are 'active citizens' in a sociological sense (Peucker and Ceylan 2016 and Peucker and Akbarzadeh 2014; see also Chapter 5). They are active agents of social capital (Amath 2015; Pędziwiatr 2010), relying on a form of 'thick trust' and developing a microscopic form of 'primary democracy' (Newton 1999). This work answers the questions of how they build their social capital, how they develop this thick trust and what the consequences are of these on their own experience of democracy. How do they find a balance between engagement within the system while being against the dominant system (Gest 2010; see also Chapter 7)? The reasons for getting involved in and committing to these charities are various and overlapping. These cannot be limited to questions of money, power or charisma, or more generally material factors (see Chapters 1 and 5). Nor are Islam or any reward in the afterlife the answers; even if they are present, they do not explain everything. For the sake of depicting the complexity of the fieldwork faithfully, I use French sociologists Alain Caillé's (2009) anti-utilitarian theory for action and subject and Edgar Morin's (1977 and 1986) theory of complex systems as applied to culture to explore how the economy of gift, emotions and feelings works in an ecosystem with beliefs and their social environment to shape the volunteers' behaviour. This allows me to try to bridge the gap that exists between Francophone and Anglophone social sciences theories. Eventually, studying participants from diasporic backgrounds under a dominant society led me to explore the concept of metacolonialism (Bulhan 2015; see also Chapter 6), to analyse how dominant cultural norms and conventions shaped the subjects of this study. Finally, I do not claim that this work is a thorough sociological study. I started this research with little knowledge about Islam, and I was not familiar at all with Muslims at the very beginning; I had to start from scratch. Seven years is a very short time to take distance from a given subject, especially when studying an emerging phenomenon. Here, I do not claim to find all of the answers; I rather document my fieldwork, cross-compare and analyse my observations and interviews and eventually draw trends from them. Therefore, this book is more of a preliminary work with rich empirical material, perhaps for future research to be undertaken.

Book structure

This work starts with a reflection on how to study Islam, Muslims and, more generally, religion. Can Islam be considered only as a 'religion'? What does it mean to be Muslim in twenty-first-century Europe? What place do faith, spirituality, rituals and ethics have in the daily life of these volunteers? The way Muslim volunteers practise their Islam is not limited to ritual performance; they try to find practical implementations of the ethics of Islam in areas like banking, charity, consumerism or democracy. Then, these volunteers blur the boundaries of the concepts of 'sacred' and 'mundane', thereby redrawing the limits of what is 'religious' and what is not. In this regard, I will be questioning contemporary considerations of Islam as a 'religion' and the damage of traditional Eurocentric epistemology on the study of Islam. I will attempt to define more accurately Islam as a complex system, using Edgar Morin's (1977 and 1986) work on complexity and the anti-utilitarian theory of action and subject developed by Alain Caillé (2009) to analyse collective and individual trajectories explaining social participation. I will try to answer these questions in the first chapter, which serves as a theoretical foreword, and will also touch on the issues of sociological studies on Muslims and social participation.

Concerning the context: as most of the charities studied in this work were founded in the 2000s by people in their early twenties, many differ in various ways from older organisations. They do not care much about differences of cultural, spiritual or professional background. They do not care about building just mosques – they want 'eco-friendly' mosques; they do not seek mere *halal* meat – they look for 'organic' *halal* meat (Pettinato 2016; Corbet 2015). They do not aim to make a huge difference but rather do what they feel is a 'duty'. While making the best of a world that was not built for them, and now empowered by globalisation and the ease of access to knowledge and social media, they exhibit a sense of confidence in building a better society according to the vision they have. In what context have they been set up? Who volunteers for these charities, and what do they do? What approach to volunteerism does this work take? Following a short history of the development of Muslim charities in Europe, this section will explain the methodology used for this study and finally paint a portrait of the different charities studied and their volunteers, which exhibit a diversity of cultural, religious and professional backgrounds.

The third chapter assesses one of the major impacts of these charities. By engaging with matters of general interest (poverty, education, alternative media, etc.) in a climate of rampant and institutionalised islamophobia, these young Muslim men and women are able, at a local level, to change mind-sets and turn public services into supporters. They do not only criticise the system or stay stuck in reactive attitudes; rather, they bring the solutions themselves. What are their attitudes towards islamophobia? How do these small grassroots initiatives manage to bring positive attitudes towards Muslims and Islam? In the third chapter of this book, I focus on the relationships between Muslim organisations, the public and the authorities they depend on and how these initiatives eventually become agents of negotiation in the public sphere, building bridges through trust and thus planting seeds for a harmonious plural society.

From traditional large structures working in a bureaucratic system and at an international level, this younger generation of Muslims has set up effective initiatives by responding to concrete social needs at a local level. Moreover, the extreme attractiveness of these charities makes them power plants of social capital. The informal governance, family-like environment and work beneficial for the whole community make a cohesive environment that appeals to volunteers of all faiths and none, enabling the building of solid bonds of trust between the various stakeholders. Mixing people from various levels of understanding in Islam and different levels of orthopraxy, these charities happen to be at the same time a powerful way to discourage young people from getting trapped in the pitfalls of religious extremism. What is their recipe for becoming so attractive and managing social capital? Can they be more efficient than any government programme? The fourth chapter of this book unveils the effective, natural means of these charities for spreading a balanced understanding of Islam to volunteers and giving them meaning and a sense of responsibility.

The particular, subjective understanding of Islam present in these charities smashes the long-supposed antagonistic relation between Islam and citizenship in a Western context. For the volunteers, being Muslim implies being a 'good' citizen and actively contributing to their neighbourhood, their university or their town. While citizenship is often presented in schools as a passive status, limited to belonging to and voting and paying taxes in a given country, the volunteers share a perception of the citizen as someone active and working for the betterment of society. This understanding is underpinned by their explicit reference to the Qur'an, in which the human being is described as a guardian of creation. The fifth chapter of this book explores, from the perspective of governance, how these charities become spaces for the experimentation of democracy.

More skilled, more vocal, attaining higher education levels and higher positions in large companies, some of these young Muslims try to articulate modernity and religiosity in various ways, whether they revolve around food certification, finance, education, or newly founded businesses that try to provide products and services compliant with religious prescriptions. Inspired by the financially successful methods of big multinational companies, some charities try to design modes of action that emulate corporate culture. Driven by results and figures such as 'likes' on Facebook, retweets on Twitter and 'views' on YouTube, they adapt their interpretation of the Qur'an and the *hadith* to justify material success as a means to achieve happiness. Conforming their Islam to the norms of a white-dominated, secular, hyper-modern and neoliberal society and methods of large multinationals, they undergo the phenomenon of metacolonisation (Bulhan 2015). The sixth chapter of this book analyses how some Muslim charities develop a utilitarian mind-set and how corporate culture impacts the not-for-profit sector.

However, more among these young Muslims are becoming aware of the excesses and unsustainability of the hyper-modern (see p. 99) West. They realise that the world is undergoing a global and total crisis, that financial systems are the furthest from stability, that politicians are failing to address the main social issues, that the damaging effects of climate change are beginning to manifest and, slowly, that dominant societies are waking up to the complexity of race, class and gender struggles. This young generation realises that the current struggles against racism and islamophobia and for social justice and the environment are only symptoms of a global race for profit and power. The mid-2010s mark a turning point at which more people realise that decolonial struggles are not solely a matter of cultures and identities but essentially a fight against the human ego. By raising awareness of the excesses of consumerism, offering various activities and reviving Islamic culture and traditions through artistic expression, they not only reject modern models, but create safe spaces and design alternatives and, ultimately, provide hope for independence and self-determination. The last chapter of this book focuses on how these charities become spaces and times of socialisation more focused on emotions, feelings, bonds of friendships, conviviality and faith.

The overall aim of this book is to show an original glimpse of what future generations of twenty-first-century Muslims will look like, and why it is important to acknowledge and understand their diverse and dynamic universe. These young Muslim change-makers, refreshing the fundamental concept of democracy in light of Islamic ethics and redefining modernity through traditions (and traditions through modernity) are meant to become key stakeholders in modern European societies.

Notes

1. Barylo, W. Bushinengue Of French Guiana. hbushinengue.light-inc.org/ [last accessed on 18 April 2017].
2. Amesty International (2014). France: submission to the European Commission against Racism and Intolerance. www.amnesty.org/download/Documents/8000/eur210012014en.pdf [last accessed on 15 Jan. 2017].
3. BFMTV. la compatibilité de l'islam et de la République reste à démontrer. http://www.bfmtv.com/politique/pour-valls-la-compatibilite-de-l-islam-et-de-la-republique-reste-a-demontrer-966406.html
4. Le Point, online edition. Manuel Valls : "La question du voile relève d'un combat sur la condition des femmes". www.lepoint.fr/politique/manuel-valls-la-question-du-voile-releve-d-un-combat-sur-la-condition-des-femmes-10-04-2013-1652945_20.php [last accessed on 15 Jan. 2017].
5. Names of volunteers have been changed.

References

Amath, N. (2015). The Phenomenology of Community Activism: Muslim Civil Society Organisations in Australia. Melbourne: Melbourne University Press.
Amiraux, V. (2006). Speaking as a Muslim: Avoiding Religion in French Public Space. In: Jonker, G. and Amiraux, V. (eds.) *Politics of Visibility: Young Muslims in European Public Spaces*. Bielefeld: Transcript Verlag, pp. 21–52.
Amiraux, V. (2007). The Headscarf Question: What Is Really the Issue? In: Amghar, S., Boubekeur, A. and Emerson, M. (eds.) *European Islam: The Challenges for Society and Public Policy*. Bruxelles: CEPS, pp. 124–43.
Bulhan, H. A. (2015). Stages of Colonialism in Africa: From Occupation of Land to Occupation of Being. *Journal of Social and Political Psychology*, 3(1), 239–56.
Caillé, A. (2009). Théorie Anti-Utilitariste de l'Action et du Sujet [Anti-Utilitarian Theory of Action and Subject]. Paris: La Découverte.
Corbet, R. H. (2015). Tayyib: British Muslim Piety and the Welfare of Animals for Food. In: Suleiman, Y. (ed.) *Muslims in the UK and Europe*. Cambridge: Centre of Islamic Studies, pp. 67–75.

Englander, M. (2012). The Interview: Data Collection in Descriptive Phenomenological Human Sciences Research. *Journal of Phenomenological Psychology*, 43(1), 13–35.

Fadil, N. (2006). We Should Be Walking Qurans, the Making of an Islamic Political Subject. In: Jonker, G. and Amiraux, V. (eds.) *Politics of Visibility: Young Muslims in European Public Spaces*. Bielefeld: Transcript Verlag, pp. 53–78.

Frégosi, F. (2008). Penser l'islam dans la laïcité [Thinking Islam Within Secularism]. Paris: Fayard.

Furbey, R. (2007). Faith, Social Capital and Social Cohesion. In: Jochum, V., Pratten, B. and Wilding, K. (eds.) Faith and Voluntary Action. London: National Council for Voluntary Organisations, pp. 34–8.

Gest, J. (2010). Apart: Alienated and Engaged Muslims in the West. London: Hurst.

Giorgi, A. (2008). Difficulties Encountered in the Application of the Phenomenological Method in the Social Sciences. *The Indo-Pacific Journal of Phenomenology*, 8(1), 1–9.

Kepel, G. (1991). Les Banlieues de l'islam: naissance d'une religion en France [Peripheral Urban Areas of Islam: Birth of a Religion in France]. Paris: Seuil.

Lamchichi, A. (1999). Islam et musulmans de France: pluralisme, laïcité et citoyenneté [Islam and Muslims in France: Pluralism, Secularism and Citizenship]. Paris: L'Harmattan.

Morin, E. (1977). La Méthode: La nature de la Nature. [Method: The Nature of Nature]. Paris: Seuil.

Morin, E. (1986). La Méthode: La vie de la Vie. [Method: The Life of Life]. Paris: Seuil.

Newton, K. (1999). Social Capital and Democracy in Modern Europe. In: Van Deth, J. W., Maraffi, M., Newton, K. and Whiteley, P. F. (eds.) *Social Capital and European Democracy*. London: Routledge, pp. 3–24.

Pędziwiatr, K. (2010). The New Muslim Elites in European Cities: Religion and Active Social Citizenship Amongst Young Organized Muslims in Brussels and London. Saarbrücken: VDM Verlag.

Pettinato, D. (2016). 'MADE a Difference?' – British Muslim Youth and Faith-Inspired Activism Between Post-Conventional Politics', 'Post-Secularity', and 'Post-Immigration Difference'. In: Suleiman, Y. and Anderson, P. (eds.) *Muslims in the UK and Europe II*. Cambridge: Centre of Islamic Studies, pp. 100–13.

Peucker, M. and Akbarzadeh, S. (2014). *Muslim Active Citizenship in the West*. Oxon and New York: Routledge.

Peucker, M. and Ceylan, R. (2016). Muslim Community Organizations: Sites of Active Citizenship or Self-Segregation? *Ethnic and Racial Studies*, doi: 10.1080/01419870.2016.1247975

1 What sociology for Islam?

'Smile, it's s*unnah*', Amena's flashy t-shirt read. In this context, *sunnah* refers to a recommended action, because it is often practised by the prophet of Islam. Ironically, Amena's face was showing everything but a smile. She was probably exhausted after a whole day running all over the place at Birmingham University, where she was volunteering at a major event. Today was the yearly general meeting of the Federation of Students Islamic Societies (FOSIS), an event gathering hundreds of young Muslim students from all over the UK. Some gifts given to participants comprised conventional items such as *attar* (oil-based perfumes) sticks and *siwak* (sticks for cleaning teeth), but it was Amena's t-shirt that intrigued me most, especially because I had seen this reference to smiling as a religious duty somewhere before. Back in Paris, before each soup kitchen, volunteers at Amatullah are reminded to smile to the beneficiaries. This duty of smiling is explicitly written in the rules and guidelines for the outreach sessions. When the outreach supervisor reads these rules out loud, he or she often reminds the volunteers that 'smiling is a *sadaqa*',[1] which translates as an 'alms' and an 'act of worship'. The way an apparently mundane action (a smile) was elevated to a ritual was curious. In another charity, prayer mats are part of the premises' furniture (see Figure 1.1), and after every outreach session, volunteers gather in a circle for performing invocations (see Figure 1.2; this will be further described in Chapter 4). In another charity, a poster on the premises read: 'please leave the premises clean and tidy, cleanliness is part of faith', the second part being a *hadith*, or saying attributed to the prophet Muhammad.[2] Thus, in the discourse and actions of these volunteers, seemingly ordinary and common actions of smiling or cleaning embrace a whole spiritual dimension. So, where does religion start, and where does it end? This poses, then, a conceptual question: can social sciences distinguish between the 'sacred' and the 'mundane' when observing Islam? What can be considered as religious, and what cannot? Eventually, how can faith and beliefs be taken into account when explaining social participation? Following a phenomenological approach, the researcher is 'in debt of the meaning of [the cultural systems'] members' (Cefaï 2010, 14). This is why this study takes into account the opinion of the participants and other data from the fieldwork to shape its theoretical framework.

Figure 1.1 Prayer mat in the premises of Amatullah

What sociology for Islam? 13

Figure 1.2 Circle for consultation and invocations after a soup kitchen at Amatullah.

Muslims from the younger generations rely on Islamic traditions in a complex way to shape their societal behaviour, through their approaches to various topics such as consumerism, finance education, identity, citizenship and democracy. In her observations, Saba Mahmood (2004, 122) notices similarly how women give religious meaning to everyday life: the mundane becomes sacred and *vice-versa*. Daily life is religious, and religion is lived daily (Fadil 2006, 72) and takes a political dimension: 'active citizenship stands for being a good Muslim, and being a good Muslim becomes synonymous with active citizenship (in the discourses)' (Fadil 2006, 69–70). Thus, the usual sealed boundaries between 'religious' and 'non-religious' actions tend to become blurred, making it almost impossible to entirely describe and analyse those social phenomena.

Although it may seem obvious that Islam is an all-encompassing system and that most participants share this perspective – also widespread among Islamic scholars (Al Ghazali, Al Qaradawi, Ramadan, etc.) – studies on Islam and Muslims have been operating clear dichotomies between the realms of 'religious' and 'non-religious' actions and discourses. Major works about Muslims (such as Frégosi [2008], Lamchichi [1999] or Kepel [1991]) analysed Islam mostly from a ritualistic perspective and classified their ideal-types in relation to their respective levels of orthopraxy (prayers, fasting or clothing preferences, etc.). Using terms and concepts rooted in Latin and Greek languages to describe spiritual systems which are not native to them, holding to Eurocentric concepts and visions and performing a binary segregation between what is 'religious' and what is not, puts research at risk of major simplification.

Following a critical discussion about the relevance and limitations of contemporary, widely used concepts gravitating around that of 'religion,' this chapter uses Edgar Morin's (1977 and 1986) work about complex systems applied to culture in an attempt to depict more accurately the ensemble of ideas, beliefs, ethics and practices that make up Islam. The second point of this chapter is defining a framework for the study of socially engaged Muslims living in twenty-first-century Europe, trying to determine what place to give to beliefs in social participation. While most past work has been widely based on using hermetic ideal-types, siloed classifications and analysing dynamics from the perspective of money and power, this work analyses its subjects from the Maussian perspective of gift (2007 [1924]) and French sociologist Alain Caillé's (2009) anti-utilitarian theory for subject and action. In a world becoming more complex, with traditional cultures and spiritualities quickly adapting to a hyper-modern, secular environment (see p. 99), research needs to rethink the way people and movements are analysed in order to truly understand what is unfolding. As a result, I hope to offer through this chapter a new, more nuanced, balanced and faithful perspective about the social study of religions in general and Islam particularly.

Beyond religion

A binary differentiation between 'religious' and 'non-religious' actions or discourses makes the analysis of social phenomena easier. However, the complexity of human cultural systems and behaviours questions the very possibility of this dichotomy. Declaring that actions can be 'religious' at one moment and 'non-religious' at another would be the same as declaring that humans behave individually at a certain time and socially at another, or that matter follows the laws of chemistry at a certain time and the law of physics at another (Sapir 1927, 36). As in the introduction of this chapter and in the fifth chapter of this book, the reader will see that the interviewees show a complex and subjective understanding of their behaviour, where mundane actions can be perceived as religious and *vice-versa* depending on the circumstances and the individual. As a consequence, trying to differentiate religious from non-religious actions in social sciences seemed to me like trying to know if Schrödinger's cat is dead or alive. Quantum physics teaches us that for scholarly purposes, we need to consider the aforementioned cat in both states simultaneously. Advocating a dialogic approach for cultural and religious systems, Edgar Morin (1995) advocates that in the same way as in quantum physics, where the photon is wave and particle at the same time, observing religious actors requires the researcher to consider that things, actions, discourses, objects, etc., can be religious and non-religious at the same time. Fortunately, sociology is not quantum physics and the researcher can know accurately the answer to this question through descriptive phenomenology: the interviewees can provide their subjective perspective about how they interpret their experience (Denscombe 2003).

Finding a methodology for the individuation of rituals (Seaquist 2009) or demarcating religious fields of discourse (Von Stuckrad 2010) have been discussed, when actions are named as such by participants. However, for a large sample of participants, there is no limit to what can be considered as sacred. For example, Sana states:

> You can make everyday actions sacred. (. . .) Every single action can be an act of worship if you do it, with the intention of doing it for God.

As a consequence, it puts any external observer in a difficult situation: to determine which actions are rituals or not, one would have to ask every participant individually about every single one of their actions. Also, how does this apply for actions such as smiling that are performed as religious actions, but the meaning of which can differ from one participant to another? In Islam, where religious practice is linked to decision making, education, professional environment and political and social participation, belief takes on a social and thus sociological dimension (Amiraux 2006, 34–6). Not only beliefs have to be noticed in a wider range of action than those clearly labelled as 'religious' (Amiraux 2006, 34–6), but the realms of what is 'sacred' and 'mundane' exist in a complex situation, from the Latin *complexus*, meaning that faith, practice, rituals and daily life are interwoven (Morin 1995, 105). However, this level of understanding and analysis requires first a clear definition of Islam as a sociological object of study and determine if it fits the categories usually applied to it, such as 'religion'.

The disciplinary term of 'religion' lacks the flexibility needed to 'perform all the work scholars demand of it' (Tweed 2006, 39). The legacy of history also contributes to giving the word a Eurocentric bias, to the point that 'the terms of religion and religious are so damaged by their colonial, imperial and globalizing legacy that they should be abandoned in cultural analysis' (Chidester 2005, 27). Some others, such as Nongbri (2013), Masuzawa (2005), Dubuisson (2003) or Saler (1993), acknowledge the impact of ethnocentrism and especially European universalism on categories. Benson Saler (1993) has described 'religion' as a Western folk category. The answer to the question 'how do I know this is a religion?' would be 'because I speak English'. Indeed, to quote Edgar Morin (1977, 10; my translation), 'any concept refers not only to the conceived object, but also to the conceiver subject'. Jonathan Smith (1998, 281–2) criticises the term as being 'a generic concept', similar to what 'language' is to linguistics, thus being 'irrelevant', for the social sciences. Moreover, the 'religion' bears a heavy legacy of ideological opposition to modernity and secularism (Touraine 1992, 354), and attempts to study Buddhism, Chamanism or Dharmic spiritualities through the lens of religion shows that the category is not free from an Eurocentric bias, knowing that 'every civilisation tends to overestimate the objective orientation of its thought' (Lévi-Strauss 1962, 13; my translation).

'Religion', as a term and a concept, has emerged from Greek and Latin cultural areas and has been mostly shaped by Christianity. Research found one of its very first appearances in Cicero's works.[3] Etymologically, 'religion' comes from the

Latin word *religare* (to bind), which can be understood in different and imprecise ways (Smith 1978). Islam, which ties relative bonds between humans, God and objects, fits the definition of religion according to the functionalist tradition, especially Tylor (religion as a form of communication), Durkheim (religion as a function for social cohesion) or Geertz (religion as an orientation). Durkheim draws a clear division between individual occupations of the aboriginals and common religious ceremonies (1975 [1912], 214–16). However, Muslims in this work do not draw such divisions, and religious life is a continuum which is not limited by space or time: 'The charity is the continuation of the mosque,' said Fatima, talking about her reasons to get involved in a Muslim charity. Tanzila, another volunteer, expresses a similar point of view: 'Practice, faith, ethics, it's a whole [. . .] they are united.'

Although functionalist approaches, such as Geertz's Cultural Systems (1973, 90) provide a comprehensive framework, they focus on cultural functions and representations, leaving other aspects of religion unconsidered (Platvoet 1990; Hofstee 1986). Religion is an ensemble of several interrelated and connected components which comprise not only the ritual or practical, doctrinal or philosophical, or mythic or narrative dimensions, but also the experiential, emotional, ethical, legal, organisational, material and artistic dimensions (Smart 1996, 9–11; see also Chapters 5 and 7).

Second, Islam undergoes a process of subjectification and objectivation (Hałas 1991, quoted in Pędziwiatr 2010). The subjective understanding of Islam is perpetually redefined by the participants according to their experiences (family, friends, media, school, books, Friday sermons) that modify their perception of life and affinities to social groups, which eventually reconstruct normative objects (see Chapter 4). We need to understand religion as a 'dynamic, changing process, rather than a static, unchanging ideal' (Cort 1990, 63). Morin (1995) suggests that Western modern social sciences do separate instead of binding and linking elements in an 'autoproductive looped connection'. Göle (2005, 25) writes: 'Islam becomes a movement; . . . subject to a discursive and performative interpretation and this, at a personal and collective level at the same time'. The functional concepts of 'system of symbols' (Geertz 1973), producing 'conceptions', 'moods and motivation', lack the perspective that this very system does not only 'establish' and 'formulate', but at the same time is constantly re-established and re-formulated.

However, contrary to Asad's (2001) or Cantwell Smith's (1978) position of abandoning or replacing, it is unrealistic to get rid of the category 'religion'; instead, we need to look beyond and submit it to a utility test (Strenski 2010, 142). All of the above definitions fit the data of my fieldwork, up to a certain limit. The term 'religion' and the typologies gravitating around it are still useful as tools with which to conduct research (Nongbri 2013, 155; Cox 1998), as there are no universal concepts. In Saler's (1993) terms, they are 'cultural bridges' or starting points for research, which have to be explained by the researcher through a 'dialogue with the adherents' (Cox 1998, 261). As the word is polythetic (Martin 2009) and has variable uses, I would agree that the most important is how one defines 'religion' for one's own use (Martin 2009; Saler 1993). Therefore, the main question here is not whether Islam is a religion or not, but rather what I am talking about when I am talking about Islam.

Because Islam is more of a personal choice, practised collectively and individually at the same time (Amiraux 2006; Fadil 2006; Khosrokhavar 1997), a religion of the world rather than a religion rejecting the world (Weber 1958), Islam becomes a hybrid between 'religion' in the sense of an organised, institutionalised cult around rituals, myths and practices and a 'spirituality', which is a relationship between the self and a transcendent deity and a quest for self-transformation (Roof 2003).

As King (1999) and Saler (1993) suggested, there is a need for native perspectives. Whereas '*dîn*' is the word in the Qur'an most often translated as 'religion', most participants describe Islam in French, English or Polish as 'faith'. 'Faith' in the Arabic language is called *imân*, from *amana* (deposit, responsibility). Thus, the one who has faith is a depository of knowledge. Indeed, this is an idea found in the Qur'an, where the human being is called the *khalifat* (caliph) of God on Earth (Qur'an 2, 30), meaning the steward or the entrusted of God on Earth, and is thus in the duty of safekeeping the creation. Many volunteers tightly link the idea of caliph to their perception of the protective role of the human being on Earth (as with the charity MADE[4] in Europe, which prints the verse on commercial merchandise). 'Faith' is a category used along with 'tradition' by Cantwell Smith (1978, 175), but does not embody the diversity of elements and phenomena observed. In the Indian subcontinent, Islam is described by the Urdu word *nizam* (Mawdudi 1948; Zuhuri 1946). Trying to define complex religious systems, Corless suggested that what we call Buddhism might be defined as a 'universal system' (Corless 1990). Borrowing from contemporary Muslim thinkers, Islam is a set of constant elements (as the uniqueness of God) but also variables (context-related prescriptions) that allow the human being to have a critical view of the world, aiming for symbiosis between the believer and his environment (Ramadan 2008). As a result, 'no one believes in the same way as another even within the same realm of significations and symbols' (Amiraux 2006, 35). This is what Edgar Morin (1995) calls the hologrammatic dimension of systems: whereas cells of a given living creature hold a similar genome but express it in different ways, Islam and Islamic identity comprise a set of invariable elements but different, evolutive expressions in permanent building and renewal (Vermeersch 2004, 695).

Moreover, Morin (1995) considers cultural and religious systems as part of a wider, evolving ecosystem. Like living creatures, Islam is auto-organisational, autonomous and capable of interacting with its environment. In the same way a living creature is able to extract energy from its environment, Islam is capable of extracting information from different contexts, which reshape its organisation and make it integrate into its environment differently. Similarly to evolutionary theories, each system of values, cultural system or subjective spiritual frame of reference is the outcome of 'a selection and a combination' (Descola 2001, 82), 'built one on another, by each other, with each other, over another' (Morin 1977, 99). Morin stresses that their relation is 'permanent and simultaneous' (Morin 1977, 36). He presents a way to conceive complex systems through the paradox of '*Unitas Multiplex*' first stated by Angyal (1941) to describe the complexity of the human personality. *Unitas Multiplex* allows for the conception of the simultaneous plural identity of a given system and its unity through the diversity of declinations. 'Considered from the perspective of the Whole, it is one and homogeneous; considered from the perspective of its constitutive elements, it is diverse and heterogeneous' (Morin 1977, 105). Then, new properties do emerge from its original organisation and global unity; this is what he called 'emergence', which gives a specific distinctive tone to systems. Just as a given person might refer to the result of a combination of several systems, Islam is only an emerging brick among others.

More precisely than a system, Islam is a referential, an analysis grid allowing a person to read the world and more, an environment enabling the creation of ideas and generating practices in everyday life, as for a uterine matrix enabling the development of the human being. Describing dynamics of commitment, Grollemund and LeFloch (2004) presented the concept of 'ideological matrix' as one of the essential elements found in altruistic behaviour. Using Morin's theory and following Saler's (1993, 23) suggestion to delimitate a pool of elements, I understand that Islam is a matrix: a generative environment of visible or invisible references, from which personal thoughts develop and eventually take shape of observable actions and which:

1 Provide a critical analysis of fundamental matters regarding action and human knowledge, within which assumptions or beliefs originate;
2 Inspire an effort to give a place to the human being and the universe in a particular cosmology (following Dubuisson's [2003] cosmographic formations).

These references include, but are not limited to: beliefs, scriptures, written and oral traditions, rituals, actions, values, ethics, a vision of life, people (whether they are scholars or family members influential to the subjects), places of worship, spaces, times, symbolic items (prayer mats, perfume), items conferred with religious meaning and, most importantly, all of the subjective interpretation of the aforementioned. However, for scholarly purposes this pool of elements has to remain open (Saler 2000, 323), especially as, following Morin, it is an ever-changing, ever-subjectively redefined environment. As opposed to single-sided and linear approaches (cultural systems define societies), the idea of a matrix is double-sided and cyclic (it defines the society, which redefines it in return and so on . . .). This matricial concept does not reject previous definitions and conceptualisations of 'religion', but rather expands and complements them, taking into account the malleability of such a system, the instability and multiplicity of its various subjective interpretations and that such a system is not given once and for all.

However, describing Islam as a religious 'matrix' is perhaps only defining 'religion' with my own terms (which has been suggested by Saler [1993] and Martin [2009]). As for its limitations, some behaviours may be not entirely the result of rationally decided choices, but a replication of the behaviour observed in some social circles as per the concept of Habitus, conceptualised by Bourdieu (1972). How, for example, to define Islam in relation to subjects for whom Islam is a mere inheritance, or cultural distinction, detached from any spiritual dimension? Is the pool of elements I have selected relevant for more various uses, or is it something to be refined? The question remains open. Conceptualising Islam as a matricial system in perpetual evolution helps to grasp its interactions with various other cultural, religious and social systems. Europe and Islam are in a process of 'interpenetration' (Amiraux 2007, 134) or 'mutual copenetration' (Göle 2005, 25), which shape each other by each other. Helped by a higher level of education and better social insertion than in the past decades (Lamchichi 1999), this encounter or fusion produces a new relation to society, new and original modes of action and discourse which will be discussed further in this book and, more precisely, the issue of Muslims and political and social participation in the next section.

Participating Muslims

Now that we have set the theoretical framework for understanding Islam as appropriated by the subjects, through a phenomenological approach, we need to determine how to take into account Islam in the process of engagement.

Researchers on the topic of Muslims in Europe have been labelling their subjects in various ways: Godard and Taussig (2007), Frégosi (2008), Lamchichi (1999) and Kepel (1991) are using precise categories such as 'neo-orthodox', 'liberal Muslim', 'puritanist', and 'pious devout'. For example, according to Franck Frégosi (2008), the young volunteers I have been studying can be labelled as 'practising activists'. The problem is that such a category is not accurate; not every participant in this study is (or would describe themselves as) 'practising'. Valérie Amiraux (2006) classifies three major traditional tendencies of studying European Muslims in Social Sciences. First are the researchers who study the regulation of religious pluralism and particularly Islam as a religion. Second are those who observe the articulation between Muslim identity and the performance of citizenship. Third are those who analyse the living conditions of Muslims in France within the framework of the established law. Adding to these, many works have addressed issues like generation gaps, questions of religious authority and controversies around the headscarf or *halal* meat, or have focused on immigration and extremism, especially in deprived area such as the French *banlieue* (Kepel 1994 and 1991). Muslims in Europe are still studied from the remains of an orientalist perspective, as is shown in research on marginal phenomena such as conversions in general, but especially related to salafism or Shi'a Islam and conservative gender-related phenomena (male guardianship, forced, arranged or intra-family marriages, women's freedom of movement and sexual life): the more behaviours differ from modern Western norms, the more they draw interest.

More generally, the vision of having to be part of a category is characteristic of an assimilationist perspective (Pędziwiatr 2010), which is explicitly prevalent in France and is more subtly present in the United Kingdom under the label of political multiculturalism. However, for Muslims living in twenty-first-century Europe, the logic of assimilation is no longer relevant (Göle 2005). For researchers such as Bouzar (2004) and Babès (1997), a categorisation of Muslims is not representative of the diversity of religious interpretations, behaviours, thoughts or opinions and implies a consideration only of actors and categories instead of people (Amiraux 2006, 26). As seen in the previous section, describing a complex universe where elements work in a symbiosis is conceptually impossible with binary categories, just as one would describe quantum physics with a binary computer.

The fieldwork shows that categorising the volunteers involved in charities would seem difficult. They do not share the same social conditions, same age, same level of education, same culture, same family background and religious practice, same understanding of Islam . . . Their only commonalities are Islam as a moral and ethical reference, and the frequentation of charities. The variety of their past experiences, their childhoods and their families gave birth to diverse personalities and characters. Therefore, this work does not classify charities or volunteers according to their religious orientation or level of orthopraxy. With the power of virtual social networks, the younger generation of European Muslims has never been more diverse, creative and quickly changing at the same time. Young, learned and skilled, they break traditional boundaries and redefine society with their own terms. These volunteers show a perfect articulation between Islam and democracy; Amiraux (2006, 21) stressed the need to study Muslims as 'an issue tied to the politics of citizenship' and Islam as 'an individual choice' rather than an 'inheritance'. This perspective has been extensively highlighted in works such as Yasir Suleiman's (2015) and Suleiman's and Anderson's (2016) annual report *Muslims in UK and Europe*, Nilüfer Göle's (2015) *En-quête de l'islam Européen* (*In Quest for European Islam*, in French only), Konrad Pędziwiatr's (2010) *The New Muslim Elites in European Cities* and, more specifically, in Peucker's and Akbarzadeh's (2014) and Amath's (2015) works on social and political participation.

Besides analysing how Muslims articulate ritual practice in a secular environment, most aforementioned works about Muslim organisations have focused on internal dynamics within Muslim communities and give outlines about the cohesive role of Muslim organisations in a given neighbourhood, but do not focus on the personal journeys of their members or how Islam reshapes dominant norms. There is a need for answering questions about the role of Islam in the organisations' governance or in the volunteering process, and, most importantly, there is a need for taking distance from a linear analysis from within and take into account external stakeholders such as the general public, beneficiaries and the authorities.

The study of the articulation of Islam and political or social participation is challenging; first, the secularisation of European and its process of 'privatisation of beliefs' (Amiraux 2007, 132) leads to the idea that 'practices can be restrained to choices and preferences' (Amiraux 2007, 133). As an example, the French concept of secularism, *laïcité*, 'is built upon the notion that nobody knows who you are or in what you believe in (or if you believe in anything)' (Amiraux 2007, 134). Second, studies around the topic are impacted by a presumption in favour of secularism for talking about religious minorities (Pędziwiatr 2010). However, research has observed that not only can religion not be a solely private or individual matter, but religion can drive and contribute to remarkable changes within communities. Religion serves as a powerful, unifying force on the level of identity (McAndrew and Voas 2014; Pędziwiatr 2010), provides an institutional basis for political mobilisation (Pędziwiatr 2010; Verba et al. 1995) and contributes to the normative dimension of citizenship by inspiring emancipatory movements and giving life a philosophical and spiritual depth (Pędziwiatr 2010). More than having an associative effect, religiosity mobilises, encourages socio-economic participation and reinforces values promoting social order (McAndrew and Voas 2014).

Babès (1997) and Khosrokhavar (1997) analysed the spiritual revival among 'second generation' young Muslims who consciously chose to practise Islam, as opposed to their parents, who inherited a set of practices and beliefs. The Muslims interviewed and observed in this work perceived Islam as a parallel or alternative way to citizenship (Frégosi 2008), understanding active citizenship and contributing to positive social dynamics as part of Islam distinctive to the 'Positive Islam' (Babès 1997) they are practicing. As they rely on their local initiatives rather than the State to solve social matters, they even become 'gravediggers of the welfare State' (Haenni 2005). Haenni depicts an action-oriented Islam which gives birth to collective projects in areas such as financial alternatives, environment protection, charities, fundraising campaigns, etc. These actors short-circuit the State bureaucracy with the help of 'traditional mechanisms of solidarity' (2005, 92). Most of the volunteers do not trust politicians to relieve social inequalities; instead, they find in the charities a means to concretely make a difference by themselves at a local level. Engaging in ways different from traditional forms of participation, these Muslim volunteers practise their citizenship beyond legalistic definitions; they form a new category of 'active citizens', demonstrating positive and proactive engagement at different levels of politics and society (Peucker and Akbarzadeh 2014; see also Chapter 5).

Furthermore, religion provides strong social capital and democratic skills (Wood 2002; Verba et al. 1995; Putnam 1993). The power of small, faith-based organisations resides in their ability to provide trust (through subjective social norms), social networks (objective features) and effectiveness or efficiency (there are outcomes) (Newton 1999; Putnam 1993). In Chapters 3 and 4, this study explores in what shape this social capital comes and how is it built, and analyses the specificities of trust, social networks and outcomes in the case of Muslim voluntary organisations. In *Voice and Equality*, Verba et al. (1995) explain civic voluntarism with capacity (which comprises social capital, among others) and motivation.

The question of political or social motivation for participation has been approached from different angles. Rational choices theories, such as in Pattie et al. (2004), Whiteley and Seyd (2002) or Rosenstone and Hansen (1993), suggest material or outcome incentives (such as employment opportunities), solitary motivations (being a leader) or purposive participation (the sense of having done duty). Some others, such as Tullock (1971) or Opp (1990), put forward self-interest motivations because of the psychological benefits or therapeutic or thrilling effects of participation. Other theories suggest that participation is related to risk and appears more accessible to people who have reached a certain level of material security in a post-materialist environment (Dalton 1996; Inglehart 1981). Finally, some works mention value, moral and quality-based motives, which, however, are distinct from self-interested and rational ones (Pattie et al. 2004; Whiteley and Seyd 2002; Teske 1997; Rootes 1991; Müller-Rommel 1989; Heath 1985). However, most of these theories assume that actors are driven by utilitarian motives; the aforementioned motives respond to the question: 'how can I benefit from participation? How is it useful for me?' (Caillé 2011, 11). When it comes to the question of motivation related to political or social participation among Muslims, Asma Mustafa (2015) introduces a more nuanced approach, arguing that even if it is a matter of choice, various experiences can trigger political interest, especially the environment, personal experiences, incidents or a value system (Mustafa 2015, 86), which echo the findings in this book. Also, the process can be driven by opportunity when the subjects see the democratic system as their 'prerogative and privilege' (Mustafa 2015).

Participants in my study show more complex and less rational reasons (see Chapter 5), which are not necessarily utility-driven or opportunistic. For the purpose of revealing these reasons, this work follows the analysis of organisations from a gift perspective (Chanial 2001 and 2008) and the anti-utilitarian analysis of actions developed by Alain Caillé (2009). Without completely overlooking the presence and influence of interests and rational or quantifiable motives, Caillé's theory suggests taking into account non-rational or non-quantifiable motives. Caillé's works allow us to conceive of social interactions as not solely driven by interest, but rather to take into account bound-free generosity, gift, friendship, love and emotions.

Indeed, social relations are not limited to the sole relations of economic and power interests (Chanial 2011, 10). The subjects of this research are the polar opposites of '*Homo oeconomicus*' (Humbert 2011, 121), which earns, possesses and consumes, a 'calculating machine' (Chanial 2011, 10), or economic humans led only by their own personal interests and the increase of their own individual well-being. Gift can have an utilitarian or even agonistic function, but volunteers in this work show that their actions are not necessarily performed while expecting something in return. Granovetter points out that the matter of motivation is indeed complex: 'in social interactions, individuals have mixed motivations, as a consequence, they act in a manner which is hard to describe only in terms of personal interest' (Hoarau and Laville 2008, 12; my translation). Their action exists at a crossroads where the quest for interest and its absence both coexist in a complex reality (Caillé 2009).

Based on previous work around organisations and gift (Chanial 2001 and 2008), getting involved in a charity as an unpaid volunteer is mainly based on a personal quest of realising one's beliefs or personal or social aspirations and convictions, rather than a quest for money, career or a default option to sustain one's family, which are the case for paid jobs. In theory, because charities provide non-material elements, and getting involved is a voluntary act, this work assumes it provides a more relevant environment from which to extract various social, cultural or psychological reasons for commitments. By selecting charities led by unpaid volunteers, this work makes the assumption that hierarchical relations and financial interest will play a minor role in explaining volunteers' motivations and that volunteering is able to reveal more effectively social bonds, as well as psychological and spiritual elements. Caillé stressed the extent to which charities employing volunteers offer an alternative: volunteers' actions bear importance and social efficiency just because they have a certain logic of bound-free generosity, or spirit of gift. Or even because they actively and generally refuse to be merchandised or monetised, 'there is therefore a problem wanting at any cost to stick a price on the priceless' (Chanial 2001 and 2008; my translation). As 'we never were completely modern', gift is therefore a 'positive standard for human relations' (Chanial 2011, 10; my translation). According to Chanial (2011, 10), gift has a real social power:

> it can be utilitarian, it can be the result or be as a tool for a strategy. It can be made to 'oblige' through the reciprocity it induces; to submit, to impress or free when it is made first, it is at the borderlines of corruption and traffic of influence.
>
> (Godbout 2008, 85)

Furthermore, it can sustain or pacify social relations by getting a situation out of the vicious circle of the talion (Godbout 2008, 10). Although charitable gift is present in sacred texts, it does not remove injustices, as in Mauritania where some deprived people can live only through the gift they receive (Latouche 2011, 206), while modernity condemns what it sees as a form of parasitism. The act of gracious gift questions social sciences: 'the wanton impetus, the oblation without ulterior motive, the gift as an ethical expectation would not exist according to social sciences: we give to give back or to receive' (Crochet 2008, 381; my translation).

However, how is it possible to take beliefs into account? Volunteers link their gift to their belief that time on Earth is itself a gift from God, such as Abdelkarim, voluntary CEO of a small charity:

> some people give to avoid paying taxes. I, for one, give without expecting anything in return. We don't have much time left, but time is precious for God. A little time well used, is in sum very huge.

Also, the charities' work itself is perceived as a gift for most volunteers, like Abdallah:

> we are giving, but in fact, it's us who receive. It's an incredible life lesson. (. . .) In fact, the meal [for the homeless] is just an accessory.

The participants give their time, their energy and sometimes their own money, but do not perceive their actions as giving. According to Mauss (2007 [1924]), gift comprises three times: giving, receiving and giving back. Most perceive being given something through their work. What do the volunteers receive in return, and what do they give back? Volunteers speak about 'getting closer to God', 'mak[ing] as many people as I can around me feel the Love of God' and 'understand[ing] my religion better', etc.; All of these are related to transcendental expectations: the work accomplished on Earth is done in the perspective of the afterlife. People do not act towards a goal under specific conditions, as in a commercial exchange, and volunteers do not necessarily expect any return . . . even if it happens. Volunteers give for the sake of giving and give to 'give back', in some cases, what they feel God has given to them, as an expression of gratitude or acknowledgement. They also give back what they feel they owe to society, as believers, citizens or human beings. They expect a return in the afterlife, or sometimes something more immediate such as social bonds, but they always eventually receive something through experiences, meetings or questions. The volunteers personify a hub in which Mauss's three times coexist: giving, receiving and giving back.

Descola states that 'the analysis of the interactions between inhabitants of the world cannot be restricted to the sole field of institutions ruling human lives' (2005, 15), therefore inviting sociologists to include in their research something 'more than the *anthropos*'. Works such as Marcel Mauss's (2007 [1924]) on the concept of gift invite researchers to understand and comprehend that, for some subjects, the 'borders of humanity never stopped at the human species' (Descola 2005, 15). The volunteers in this study give and receive in various ways. They give their time to beneficiaries and to their colleagues, but also to God. Similarly, they receive, whether it is experience, emotions or bonds from the other volunteers or from the beneficiaries; they also believe they receive from God. In summary, there is a need to understand the empirical consequences of the subjective bonds between humans and the empirically inaccessible world of their own beliefs, taking into account the *anthropos* (human) and the *theos* (divine, transcendental) and their relations. Muslims do not perceive themselves as living in an empirical and tangible terrestrial world; they live partly in the hereafter at the same time and their worldly actions are a means to prepare for the afterlife. They do not perceive themselves as a mere body, but as a soul living under the presence of God on a daily basis. Following the Thomas Theorem,[5] we need to conclude that God, in the social sciences, is therefore a real actor with a relative existence (Day 2010).

Moving beyond 'religion', Edgar Morin's works on complex systems applied to culture provided a more flexible and dynamic way of conceiving Islam as a sociological object; this is more of an evolutive matrix of elements interacting as a living being with a wider ecosystem in a complex manner. Islam does not only define the subjects' behaviour; the subjects also define Islam. Talking about the subjects – Muslim volunteers participating in voluntary organisations – these considerations led to a movement away from traditional categorisations and the consideration of Muslims as full stakeholders in European societies. Creating original modes of action and discourses by a phenomenon of copenetration (Göle 2005), there is a need for a framework that takes into account new forms of motives.

Therefore, Caillé's (2009) anti-utilitarian approach and Chanial's (2008) analysis through the lens of gift can complement the study of organisations through the lens of social capital, capacity and motivations. These frameworks allow taking into account non-numerable variables: feelings, emotions, friendship and beliefs. At the very intersection of charitable works, theory of action and religion, I am aware that I am undertaking a difficult and challenging work. However, these very challenges are what make it more stimulating to understand these grassroots Muslim charities in the hyper-modern, twenty-first-century Europe, which will be presented with more detail in the following chapter.

Notes

1 Etymologically, sadaqa comes from the Arabic root S-D-Q, meaning 'wisdom'. It is an act of worship which derives from the principle of zakat – required alms and third pillar of Islam – and sadaqa is defined in the Sunnah as "any act of kindness" (Sahih Muslim, Book 2, n°2197) and it is a 'daily duty' (Sahih Bukhari, Book 52, n°141), Hadith from The Center for Muslim-Jewish Engagement, University of Southern California www.usc.edu/org/cmje/religious-texts/hadith/ [last accessed on 15 Jan. 2017].
2 Sahih Muslim, Book 2, n°432. Hadith from The Center for Muslim-Jewish Engagement, University of Southern California www.usc.edu/org/cmje/religious-texts/hadith/ [last accessed on 15 Jan. 2017].
3 Cicero, De Natura Deorum, 2, 28, 71.
4 Muslim Action for Development and the Environment.
5 "If men define situations as real, they are real in their consequences", Merton (1995, 379–424).

References

Amath, N. (2015). *The Phenomenology of Community Activism: Muslim Civil Society Organisations in Australia*. Melbourne: Melbourne University Press.
Amiraux, V. (2006). Speaking as a Muslim: Avoiding Religion in French Public Space. In: Jonker, G. and Amiraux, V. (eds.) *Politics of Visibility: Young Muslims in European Public Spaces*. Bielefeld: Transcript Verlag, pp. 21–52.
Amiraux, V. (2007). The Headscarf Question: What Is Really the Issue? In: Amghar, S., Boubekeur, A. and Emerson, M. (eds.) *European Islam: The Challenges for Society and Public Policy*. Bruxelles: CEPS, pp. 124–43.
Angyal, A. (1941). *Foundations for a Science of Personality*. New York: The Commonwealth Fund.
Asad, T. (2001). Reading a Modern Classic: W. C. Smith's *The Meaning and End of Religion*. *History of Religions*, 40(3), 205–22.
Babès, L. (1997). *L'islam positif: La religion des jeunes musulmans en France* [*Positive Islam: The Religion of the Young Muslims in France*]. Paris: L'Atelier.
Bourdieu, P. (1972). *Esquisse d'une Théorie de la Pratique Précédé de Trois Études d'Ethnologie Kabyle* [*Draft of a Theory of Practice Preceded by Three Studies in Kabyle Ethnology*]. Genève: Droz.
Bouzar, D. (2004). *Monsieur Islam n'Existe Pas: Pour une Désislamisation des Débats* [*Mr. Islam Doesn't Exist: For a De-Islamisation of Debates*]. Paris: Hachette.
Caillé, A. (2009). *Théorie Anti-Utilitariste de l'Action et du Sujet* [*Anti-Utilitarian Theory of Action and Subject*]. Paris: La Découverte.

Caillé, A. (2011). *Du Convivialisme vu comme un Socialisme Radicalisé et Universalisé (et Réciproquement)* [On Convivialism as a Radicalised and Universalised Socialism and Reciprocally]. In: Caillé, A., Humbert, M., Latouche, S. and Viveret, P. (eds.) *De la convivialité, dialogues sur la société conviviale à venir*. Paris: La Découverte, pp. 73–98.

Cantwell-Smith, W. (1978) [1962]. *The Meaning and End of Religion*. London: SPCK.

Cefaï, D. (2010). L'Engagement Ethnographique [The Ethnographic Engagement]. Paris: Editions de l'EHESS.

Chanial, P. (2001). *Justice, Don, Association* [Justice, Gift, Charity]. Paris: La Découverte.

Chanial, P. (2008). *La société vue du don* [Society From a Gift Perspective]. Paris: La Découverte.

Chanial, P. (2011). *La sociologie comme philosophie politique et réciproquement* [Sociology as a Political Philosophy And Reciprocally]. Paris: La Découverte.

Chidester, D. (2005). *Authentic Fakes: Religion and Popular American Culture*. Berkeley and Los Angeles: University of California Press.

Corless, R. (1990). How Is the Study of Buddhism Possible? *Method and Theory in the Study of Religion*, 2(1), 27–41.

Cort, J. E. (1990). Models of and for the Study of the Jains. *Method and Theory in the Study of Religion*, 2(1), 42–71.

Cox, J. L. (1998). Religious Typologies and the Postmodern Critique. *Method and Theory in the Study of Religion*, 10(3), 244–62.

Crochet, S. (2008). Le sacrifice: contradictions de l'action humanitaire [Sacrifice: Paradoxes of Humanitarian Action]. In: Chanial, P. (ed.) *La société vue du don*. Paris: La Découverte, pp. 381–98.

Dalton, R. J. (1996). *Citizen Politics: Public Opinion and Political Parties in Advanced Western Democracies*. London: Chatham House.

Day, M. (2010). How to Keep It Real. *Method and Theory in the Study of Religion*, 22(3), 272–82.

Denscombe, M. (2003). *The Good Research Guide: For Small-Scale Social Research Projects*. Buckingham: Open University Press.

Descola, P. (2001). *L'écologie des autres* [The Ecology of Others]. Paris: Quae.

Descola, P. (2005). *Par-delà nature et culture* [Beyond Nature and Culture]. Paris: Gallimard.

Dubuisson, D. (2003). *The Western Construction of Religion*. Baltimore: The John Hopkins University Press.

Durkheim, E. (1975) [1912]. *The Elementary Forms of Religious Life*. New York: Allen and Unwin.

Fadil, N. (2006). We Should Be Walking Qurans: The Making of an Islamic Political Subject. In: Jonker, G. and Amiraux, V. (eds.) *Politics of Visibility: Young Muslims in European Public Spaces*. Bielefeld: Transcript Verlag, pp. 53–78.

Frégosi, F. (2008). *Penser l'islam dans la laïcité* [Thinking Islam Within Secularism]. Paris: Fayard.

Geertz, C. (1973). Religion as a Cultural System: *The Interpretation of Culture*. New York: Basic Books, pp. 87–125.

Godard, B. and Taussig, S. (2007). *Les Musulmans en France. Courants, institutions, communautés: un état des lieux* [Muslims in France: Trends, Institutions, Communities. Situation]. Paris: Robert Laffont.

Godbout, J. (2008). Don et stratégie [Gift and Strategy]. In: Chanial, P. (ed.) *La société vue du don*. Paris: La Découverte, pp. 70–84.

Göle, N. (2005). *Interpénétrations: L'Islam et l'Europe* [*Interpenetrations: Islam and Europe*]. Paris: Galaade.
Göle, N. ed. (2015). *En-quête de l'Islam Européen* [*In Quest for European Islam*]. Paris: Halfa.
Grollemund, C. Le Floch, R. (2004). *Les jeunes et les associations: entre participation et engagement* [*Youth and Charities: Between Participation and Involvement*]. Paris: CREFAD.
Haenni, P. (2005). *L'islam de marché: l'autre révolution conservatrice* [*Market Islam, the Other Conservative Revolution*]. Paris: Seuil.
Hałas, E. (1991). *Znaczenia I wartosci spolezne: O sociologi Floriana Znanieckiego* [*Meanings and Social Values: On Florian Znaniecky's Sociology*]. Lublin: University of Lublin.
Heath, A. (1985). *How Britain Votes*. Oxford: Pergamon Press.
Hoarau, C. and Laville, J-L. eds. (2008). *La gouvernance des associations* [*Governance of Charities*]. Paris: Eres.
Hofstee, W. (1986). The Interpretation of Religion: Some Remarks on the Work of Clifford Geertz. In: Hubbeling, H. G. and Kippenberg, H. G. (eds.) *On Symbolic Representation of Religion*. Berlin: Gruiter, pp. 70–83.
Humbert, M. (2011). Convivialisme, politique et économie. Ivan Illitch et le 'bien vivre ensemble' [Convivialism, Politics and Economics: Ivan Illitch and the 'Well Living Together']. In: Caillé, A., Humbert, M., Latouche, S. and Viveret, P. (eds.) *De la convivialité, dialogues sur la société conviviale à venir*. Paris: La Découverte, pp. 99–130.
Inglehart, R. (1981). Postmaterialism in an Environment of Insecurity. *American Political Science Review*, 75(4), 880–900.
Kepel, G. (1991). *Les Banlieues de l'islam: naissance d'une religion en France* [*Peripheral Urban Areas of Islam: Birth of a Religion in France*]. Paris: Seuil.
Kepel, G. (1994). *À l'Ouest d'Allah* [*To the West of Allah*]. Paris: Seuil.
Khosrokhavar, F. (1997). *L'islam des jeunes* [*Islam of the Youth*]. Paris: Flammarion.
King, R. (1999). *Orientalism and Religion: Postcolonial Theory, India, and 'The Mystic East'*. Oxford: Routledge.
Lamchichi, A. (1999). *Islam et musulmans de France: pluralisme, laïcité et citoyenneté* [*Islam and Muslims in France: Pluralism, Secularism and Citizenship*]. Paris: L'Harmattan.
Latouche, S. (2011). La voie de la décroissance, pour une société d'abondance frugale [The Way of Degrowth, for a Society of Frugal Abundance]. In: Caillé, A., Humbert, M., Latouche, S. and Viveret, P. (eds.) *De la convivialité, dialogues sur la société conviviale à venir*. Paris: La Découverte, pp. 43–72.
Lévi-Strauss, C. (1962). *La pensée sauvage* [*Savage Thought*]. Paris: Plon.
McAndrew, S. and Voas, D. (2014). Immigrant Generation, Religiosity and Civic Engagement in Britain. *Ethnic and Racial Studies*, 37(1), 99–119.
Mahmood, S. (2004). *Politics of Piety: The Islamic Revival and the Feminist Subject*. Princeton: Princeton University Press.
Martin, C. (2009). Delimiting Religion. *Method and Theory in the Study of Religion*, 21(2), 157–76.
Masuzawa, T. (2005). *The Invention of World Religions: Or, How European Universalism Was Preserved in the Language of Pluralism*. Chicago: Chicago University Press.
Mauss, M. (2007) [1924]. *Essai sur le don* [*Essay on Gift*]. Paris: Presses Universitaires France.

Mawdudi, A. (1948). *Islam ka Niza-I Hayat*. Lahore.
Merton, T. (1995). The Thomas Theorem and the Matthew Effect. *Social Forces*, 74(2), 379–424.
Morin, E. (1977). *La Méthode: La nature de la Nature* [*Method: The Nature of Nature*]. Paris: Seuil.
Morin, E. (1986). *La Méthode: La vie de la Vie*. [*Method: The Life of Life*]. Paris: Seuil.
Morin, E. (1995). La stratégie de reliance pour l'intelligence de la complexité [Linking Strategy for the Complexity Intelligence]. *Revue Internationale de sytémique*, 9(2), 105–22.
Müller-Rommel, F. (1989). *New Politics in Western Europe: The Rise and Success of Green and Alternative Lists*. Boulder: Westview Press.
Mustafa, A. (2015). *Identity and Political Participation Among Young British Muslims*. London: Palgrave.
Newton, K. (1999). Social Capital and Democracy in Modern Europe. In: Van Deth, J. W., Maraffi, M., Newton, K. and Whiteley, P. F. (eds.) *Social Capital and European Democracy*. London: Routledge, pp. 3–24.
Nongbri, B. (2013). *Before Religion: A History of a Modern Concept*. Yale: Yale University Press.
Opp, K-D. E. (1990). Postmaterialism, Collective Action and Political Protest. *American Journal of Political Science*, 34(1), 212–35.
Pattie, C., Seyd, P. and Whiteley, P. (2004). *Citizenship in Britain: Values, Participation, Democracy*. Cambridge: Cambridge University Press.
Pędziwiatr, K. (2010). *The New Muslim Elites in European Cities: Religion and Active Social Citizenship Amongst Young Organized Muslims in Brussels and London*. Saarbrücken: VDM Verlag.
Peucker, M. and Akbarzadeh, S. (2014). *Muslim Active Citizenship in the West*. Oxon and New York: Routledge.
Platvoet, J. (1990). The Definers Defined: Traditions in the Definition of Religion. *Method and Theory in the Study of Religion*, 2(2), 180–212.
Putnam, R. (1993). *Making Democracy Work: Civic Traditions in Modern Italy*. Princeton: Princeton University Press.
Ramadan, T. (2008). *Islam, la réforme radicale: Ethique et libération* [*Islam: Radical Reform: Ethics and Liberation*]. Paris: Presses du Châtelet.
Roof, W. C. (2003). Religion and Spirituality: Towards Integration of Religion and Spirituality. In: Dillon, M. (ed.) *Handbook of the Sociology of Religion*. New York: Cambridge University Press, pp. 137–50.
Rootes, C. A. (1991). The Greening of British Politics. *International Journal of Urban and Regional Research*, 15(2), 287–97.
Rosenstone, S. J. and Hansen, J. M. (1993). *Mobilization, Participation and Democracy in America*. New York: Palgrave Macmillan.
Saler, B. (1993). *Conceptualizing Religion*. Leiden: Brill.
Saler, B. (2000). 'Conceptualizing Religion': Responses. *Method and Theory in the Study of Religion*, 12(1), 323–38.
Sapir, E. (1927). The Unconscious Patterning of Behavior in Society. In: Dummer, E. S. (ed.) *The Unconscious: A Symposium*. New York: Knopf, pp. 114–42.
Seaquist, C. (2009). Ritual Individuation and Ritual Change. *Method and Theory in the Study of Religion*, 21(3), 340–60.
Smart, N. (1996). *Dimensions of the Sacred: An Anatomy of the World's Beliefs*. Berkeley: University of California Press.

Smith, J. Z. (1998). Religion, Religions, Religious. In: Taylor, M. (ed.) *Critical Terms for Religious Studies*. Chicago: University of Chicago Press, pp. 269–84.
Strenski, I. (2010). Talal Asad's 'Religion' Trouble and a Way Out. *Method and Theory in the Study of Religion*, 22(2), 136–55.
Suleiman, Y. (2015). *Muslims in the UK and Europe*. Cambridge: Centre of Islamic Studies.
Suleiman, Y. and Anderson, P. eds. (2016). *Muslims in the UK and Europe II*. Cambridge: Centre of Islamic Studies.
Teske, N. (1997). *Political Activists in America: The Identity Construction Model of Political Participation*. Cambridge: Cambridge University Press.
Touraine, A. (1992). *Critique de la Modernité* [*Critique of Modernity*]. Paris: Fayard.
Tullock, G. (1971). The Paradox of Revolution. *Public Choice*, 11(1), 89–99.
Tweed, T. A. (2006). *Crossing and Dwelling: A Theory of Religion*. Cambridge: Harvard University Press.
Verba, S., Schlozman, K. and Brady, H. eds. (1995). *Voice and Equality: Civic Voluntarism in American Politics*. Cambridge: Harvard University Press.
Vermeersch, S. (2004). Entre individualisation et participation: l'engagement associatif bénévole [Between Individualisation and Participation: Voluntary Involvement in Charities]. *Revue Française de Sociologie*, 45(4), 681–710.
Von Stuckrad, K. (2010). Reflections on the Limits If Reflection: An Invitation to the Discursive Study of Religion. *Method and Theory in the Study of Religion*, 22(2), 156–69.
Weber, M. (1958). Religious Rejections of the World and Their Direction. In: Gerth, H. H. and Wright Mills, C. (eds.) *From Max Weber: Essays in Sociology*. New York: Oxford University Press, pp. 323–58.
Whiteley, P. and Seyd, P. (2002). *High Intensity Participation: The Dynamics of Party Activism in Britain*. Ann Arbor: University of Michigan Press.
Wood, R. L. (2002). *Faith in Action: Religion, Race and Democratic Organizing in America*. Chicago: University of Chicago Press.
Zuhuri, A. (1946). *Islam ka Nizam-I Hayat*. Hyderabad.

2 Muslim grassroots charities and method

How can an NGO like Foul Express evidently be so successful without even possessing a physical office to operate from? In the first decade of the twenty-first century, the answer to this question would appear to be obvious: its volunteers work on the project and its online blog with the help of a mailing list and cloud-shared documents and stay in touch on social media, a strategy which helps it reach out to wider audiences and communities. One may also be surprised at how a core team of less than ten volunteers can keep the organisation running for nearly a decade with barely any funds and find members as eager and motivated as in the first year of its launch. What struck me during the tenure of conducting fieldwork for this research was the repetitive pattern that is observable through these different small, local organisations, whether they were in France, Poland or the UK. Contrary to large structures in the NGO industry (which offer well-paid and high-end posts such as CEO), they largely appear as financially unattractive and do not seem to offer any career opportunities or prestigious or influential positions. Contrary to humanitarian NGOs, these small organisations do not offer the opportunity to volunteer in distant countries. Paradoxically, this is what most of their members admire and seek: they value working in a small team, believe in providing basic services, find no sense or need in hierarchy and bureaucracy or prefer to stay in their local area. Moreover, they are happy doing it for years while doing busy jobs or studies, and even after getting married or raising children. Some volunteers still come back years after they left.

This work focuses on small-scale, local, not-for-profit organisations, designated legally as 'charities' in the UK and regulated by the Charity Commission. Although these NGOs bear various names depending on the country, language or researcher ('voluntary organisations' or 'social organisations', as in Amath 2015), this work will use the term 'charity' as a synonym of the other appellations. These charities are rooted in two major contexts: the first is the general social, economic and political context of the charity sector in Europe. There is a need for understanding the particular history and situation of Muslim charities in Europe: when and how did these charities emerge? Second, it is the evolution of social movements in a diverse, modern Europe in a global diasporic context: in a globalised world in the age of social media, forms of political and social participation are evolving faster than ever (taking the shape of movement such as Occupy or Black Lives Matter). Both of these contexts are the object of the first section of this chapter. The second section introduces the different charities included in this study, their volunteer base and how they are becoming key figures in their social or political landscape. Finally, because defining, identifying and studying these organisations can be challenging, as they are 'so all-pervasive, loose-knit, changeable, amorphous and numerous' (Newton 1999, 11), the third section will present the methodology employed in this work.

A brief history of European Muslim charities

Although the first mosques were built in the early twentieth century in France and the UK (if we focus on these two countries especially), Muslim organisations were set up decades later. Until the 1960s and the 1970s, both countries experienced decades of 'invisible' migrant workers (Frégosi 2008; Etienne 1989 and 1991) and the emergence of the first significant generation of Muslims born in Europe, most adopting ways of practising Islam differently from their parents, with a more religious practice (Frégosi 2008; Etienne 1989 and 1991). Researchers set the late 1980s and 1990s as a turning point for Muslims in Europe (Fitzgerald 2015; Frégosi 2008; Etienne 1991 and 1989). This decade included the first headscarf issue in France and Salman Rushdie's *Satanic Verses* in the UK as well as the foundation of major Muslim representative organisations, especially the *Union des Organisations Islamiques de France* (UOIF, Union of Islamic Organisations in France, still the biggest to date) and the Muslim Council of Britain (MCB). This decade marks the beginning of the spreading of religious education in faith-based schools or Madrassas, the settlement of migrant families, the beginning of political activism and the emergence of 'Muslim elites' (Pędziwiatr 2010).

The late 1980s and 1990s were also when the major European humanitarian NGOs were founded: Islamic Relief Worldwide was established in 1984; Muslim Aid in 1985; Human Appeal in 1991; Muslim Hands in 1993; and Islamic Relief France in 1990. Islamic Relief France was founded in 1991 and celebrated its twentieth anniversary in 2001 with a public event gathering hundreds of volunteers at one of the most iconic places in Paris (see Figure 2.1). Generally, Muslim NGOs came decades after the foundation of mainstream humanitarian NGOs, mostly in the aftermath of the World War II: Oxfam was set up in 1942, the same year the International Rescue Committee (IRC) settled in the UK, and Christian Aid in 1945. In France, the *Secours Populaire* (People's Relief) was established in 1945 and the *Secours Catholique* (Catholic Relief) in 1946. Only NGOs with a more local focus were founded in the 1980s and 1990s, such as *Restos du Coeur* (1986) and *Fondation Abbé Pierre* (1992), both of which worked around the issue of homelessness.

However, whereas the British government started to actively work with organisations like the MCB or the Al-Khoei Foundation, France had to wait until 2003 to create the *Conseil Français du Culte Musulman* (CFCM, French Council of Muslim Faith). The CFCM, supported by the French Home Office, is comparable to the Mosques and Imams Advisory Board (MINAB) founded in the UK in 2006

Figure 2.1 Celebration of the 20th anniversary of Islamic Relief France at la Bastille

and supported by the British Home Office. As a direct consequence of the wars in Afghanistan and Iraq in the 2000s in Britain, and the rise of far-right discourse and the ban of the *hijab* from high schools in France, these representative bodies either severed major links with the government or, as in the case of the CFCM, Muslims did not trust it. Whereas French Muslim organisations in general experienced a slowdown in the 2000s, the late 2000s and early 2010s were when a new generation of activists in their early twenties began to emerge; at the same time, the start of more liberal modes of governance, religious opinions and niche businesses paralleled the rise of individualism in a context of political and social tensions with an unprecedented wave of popularity of far-right groups.

Nowadays, the Muslim charity sector in Europe has mushroomed dramatically. With an average of £371 in donations per head per year, multiplied by an estimated 2.7 million Muslims in the UK,[1] the total in donations comes to just over £1 billion, which is staggering. According to the statistics of the Charities Aid Foundation, based on official data of the Charities Commission,[2] large Muslim humanitarian NGOs such as Islamic Relief can receive on average millions of pounds in voluntary donations per year (Islamic Relief recorded more than £50 million in 2012).

On the eastern side of Europe, Muslim families have settled since the fourteenth century (Tatars) and are an officially recognised community in Poland. With no more than 3,000 individuals, they are a minority within the 40,000 Muslims living in the Polish territory (Górak-Sosnowska 2011). Poland is among the countries with the lowest proportion of Muslims citizens in the world, estimated to be no more than 0.1%. Most of them are immigrants. Although Muslims (especially through Tatars) were officially recognised by the government, and politicians attend yearly commemorations of the historical military services offered by Tatar officers, Poland had for a long time only two Muslim representative organisations: the *Muzułmański Związek Religijny* (MZR, Religious Union of Muslims), a historical Tatar organisation founded in 1925, and the *Liga Muzułmańska* (LM, Muslim League), founded in 2001 by Muslims from a migrant background. Charities emerged in Poland in 2000 and 2010, notably through the Hizmet movement (*Dunaj Instytut Dialogu*, established in 2008) and smaller charities like *Alajkumki* and *Fundacja Iqra* (2011) – female-led social services charities.

The charities studied in this work engage with issues of local poverty, protection of the environment, homelessness, diversity, objectivity in the media and much more. They have been set up and started as informal groups of young Muslims as a response to issues in their local area (homeless people in the neighbourhood, deprived students, etc.). Among the pioneering work on this new kind of Muslim charity is Davide Pettinato (2016), who suggests these are characterised by a trinitarian convergence of social and political conditions: post-conventional politics, post-secularity and post-immigration difference. Post-conventional politics mark the era of the late third of the twentieth century, whereby concepts such as nation-state and party politics lose their relevance and more personalised, flexible and informal forms of engagement emerge (Keck and Sikkink 2014; Langman 2013; Kennelly 2011; Feixa et al. 2009; Blühdorn 2006; McDonald 2006;

Wieviorka 2005; Meyer and Tarrow 1998). They use extra-institutional channels (e.g., campaigns and social media) and are usually based on identity criteria such as age, gender and ethnicity (Blühdorn 2006; McDonald 2006; Meyer and Tarrow 1998; Offe 1985). Some contemporary illustrations can be seen in the Occupy Wall Street, Indignados, 99 Percenters, or Black Lives Matter movements, all of which are characteristic of a 'social movement society' (Meyer and Tarrow 1998). These forms of engagement seem attractive to young Muslims as an alternative to mainstream politics, which are often exclusionary to minorities (O'Toole and Gale 2010). Although their action is political in the sense that they take part in the public life of the city, these charities do not take part in party politics nor are they linked to any political movements. They are political, but are not followers of any party. As Chanial states, 'the charity field is not able to develop itself if it is instrumentalised' (Caillé 2008, 349; my translation). The structures studied in this work are also independent from larger structures in the Muslim community (e.g., UOIF, MCB). They do not take part in the management of their local towns or neighbourhoods, although they are essential components for the life of these. They do not replace public services, but have their place in a democratic environment where collective responsibility is expressed. In that sense, they are 'infrapolitical' structures (Chanial 2003). Duclos and Nicourd (2005, 17) label them as '*collectifs d'engagement*'. The French '*engagement*' means, at the same time, to get involved and to act. The verb '*engager*' is similar to the English verb 'to engage': it means to 'give one's word, tie a bond with a promise' (first occurrence in 1595); since the twentieth century, '*engager*' has come to mean 'tak[ing] position on matters',[3] which derives from the 1694 sense of to 'enter at the service of'. Therefore, 'engager' is to tie bonds in the service of a cause, or to act (Bobineau and Seraïdari 2010, 13), just as these charities take positions on social issues.

Pettinato (2016) also posits that the increasing presence of Muslims in the public sphere is blurring the very boundaries between private and public spheres (Salvatore 2004), and that this in turn challenges the established separation between faith or religion as well as the secularised structures of modern European societies (Beaumont 2010). Emanating from this is the formation of 'hybrid spaces', in line with the concept of heterotopias and counter-spaces, as suggested by Göle (2005). Finally, the 'post-immigration difference' refers to the diasporic dimension of young Muslims in Europe and how they are perceived as outsiders by both mainstream European societies and elder Muslim generations (Modood 2012, 25), 'from the outside in and from the inside out' (Modood 2012, 29). While one may agree that such a 'post-immigration difference' could be relevant between 2000 and 2010, it is suggested here that this difference is likely to disappear with the acceptance and acknowledgement of this new face of European society, especially for large metropolitan cities.

Until the late 2000s, most Muslim charities were either large representative organisations and humanitarian NGOs, or smaller, local organisations managing mosques and prayer spaces. This is when we see the development of a new type of organisations emerging. These organisations originated from the same generation as social welfare organisations like *Les Enfants de Don Quichotte* (established in

2006 to help homeless people in Paris with finding better living conditions) or the *Mouvement Colibris* (established in 2007 to campaign and promote sustainable housing, food and environmentally friendly practices). They were founded at the peak of mobile Internet, virtual social networks such as Facebook and Twitter and a global awareness of environmental and social challenges as consequences of globalisation. This young generation of European Muslims is characteristic of a larger, more important European social singularity, marking the irreversible shift from a traditionally White Christian (or secular) society to a more diverse one in terms of cultures, ethnicities, beliefs and opinions. European and Muslim, traditional and modern at the same time (Göle 2003), whose roots comprise multiple points of origin from a Saidian perspective (Said 1984), they constitute a part of this new, singular generation of European society. This double singularity, from both European and Muslim traditional structures, conjugates a unique mode of governance and is one of the many factors making them extremely attractive and cohesive.

Study sample: young, skilled and diverse

The volunteers studied in this work break from previously established sociological ideal-types and usual subjects. They are involved in small, local, not-for-profit organisations founded in the late 2000s or early 2010s and work at the scale of their neighbourhood, their university or their town, mostly in the area of large and diverse metropolitan cities such as Paris, London and Warsaw. For all of the participants, their work in the charity is not paid. While classical mainstream NGOs comprise a volunteer base on average above the age of 40 and who do not work (retired, unemployed, etc.) (Chanial 2011; Voyé 2004), the volunteers of these small Muslim charities are mostly young people between the ages of 18 and 35 and work or study alongside their charitable activities. They are legally registered as not-for-profit organisations under the rules of the Charity Commission in the UK or their local district council in France (at the *Préfecture* as '*associations loi 1901*'). Most of these groups do not ask for state grants or subsidies, but are largely funded by donations and contributions from members and well-wishers. These organisations are very limited in scale, with a core team not exceeding a dozen volunteers (but with networks comprising hundreds of sympathisers), and the atmosphere is more of a family exempted from bureaucratic procedures; this increases the attractiveness and efficiency of these charities compared to larger ones (see Chapters 4 and 5). Most started as informal, unregistered groups (in the UK, a charity's budget must exceed £5,000 to be registered). Also, while large-scale Muslim NGOs, such as Islamic Relief or Muslim Aid, receive state funds and money from the corporate sector, the charities selected in this work are financially independent and their funding comes mainly from private donations and member participation, and very rarely from state grants and subsidies. Whereas most British or French mainstream charities are known for their distance from religious and spiritual trends – except in a few cases – these Muslim charities take their inspiration from Islamic ethics to guide their governance and project ideas.

All of these charities were founded as a response to precise, local, social problems. Amatullah was founded by a female-only team to provide help to prisoners and, later, to homeless people in Bagnolet, in a similar fashion to Children of Adam in London. Averroès was founded to help deprived students at the University of Jussieu. *Jeunes Musulmans de France* (JMF, Young Muslims of France) in La Courneuve aimed to provide complementary education support to high school students in the deprived North *banlieue* of Paris. Foul Express has set up alternative media for the sake of providing objective information for people from a diasporic background, who are often misrepresented in French mainstream media.

The selection of the participant charities for this study responded to particular criteria. Regarding the functionality of faith within social capital building and social cohesion, Furbey (2007, 36) points out four fields to explore: use of faith buildings, creation of diversity spaces, involvement in local governance and engagement in wider civil society. I wanted to study organisations which provide social services to the wider society and not just Muslims. As a consequence, this work neither focuses on cultural organisations such as mosques, meat certification or religious studies, nor on sports, youth or art clubs. Sports clubs or cultural associations only focus on the activities of their members and have limited public outreach. Also, the charities studied in this work are not exclusively 'Muslim' charities: they do not define themselves as 'Muslim', their volunteers are not all Muslim and they do not provide services only to Muslims. Although founded by Muslims and attracting a network of sympathisers sharing Islam as a faith or ethics, they can better be described as charities based on 'Islamic ethics', a set of values and principles inspired by Islam which impact their governance, topics of interests and etiquette.

As a consequence, the fieldwork has been restricted to specific kinds of charities: those providing support for the general public in the form of soup kitchens for the homeless, books and exam papers for university students or private tuition for high school students. They work as an open system, operating with different stakeholders of various faiths, beliefs and cultures, but their governance, decision making processes and diet are inspired by principles and values of Islam (see Chapters 4 and 5). Also, they introduce an important element in the European context: visibility. Some of the female volunteers wear the *hijab* and are in contact with the public and the authorities. Thus, they are an ideal opportunity to observe and analyse the impact of this visibility on different levels: volunteers, public and authorities.

Increased access to information has enabled the average citizen to become aware of global social and environmental challenges. The rise of smartphones, which popularised mobile Internet usage, brought a spate of virtual social networks such as Facebook, Twitter, Instagram and Snapchat. The charities in this study are familiar with the latest communication technologies and use them as tools through which they convey their messages. Therefore, volunteers using social media pay a lot of attention to the consequences of globalisation and neoliberalism, the rise in social inequalities, gender issues, racism, poverty and other issues such as healthier food, local entrepreneurship and environmentally friendly behaviours (see also Chapters 6 and 7). Due to their work on universal issues such as poverty and education, the charities attract volunteers with no particular faith or belief (see Chapter 4).

The charity organisations studied in this research operate at the local level, in a single neighbourhood or a university campus and undertake, amongst other things, the following actions or services: food and psychological relief for homeless people (Amatullah, Islamic Relief, Rumi's Cave, Children of Adam; see Figure 2.2), private tuition for high school students or immigrants (JMF) and exam paper archives for university students (Averroès). These organisations also organise cultural and informative events like fun days and fairs, film nights, book clubs and debates on a range of subjects, including poverty alleviation, racism and the environment (Foul Express, MADE, Rumi's Cave). Some also publish online articles on dedicated blogs or websites (Foul Express), whilst others convene conferences and symposiums with academics, politicians and activists. Tables 2.1, 2.2 and 2.3 show the different organisations studied in this work. Table 2.3 gives details about three organisations which do not fit exactly the selection criteria (some are large humanitarian NGOs) but have been studied as a means for comparison with smaller structures.

Whereas Western faith-based organisations use little to no religious symbolism in their practices and discourses (Lichterman 2005), Muslim charities overtly display various religious references. This phenomenon is paralleled by a new relation to society, especially helped by higher education and better social insertion (Lamchichi 1999). Understanding active citizenship and contributing to positive social dynamics as part of Islam are distinctive of the 'positive Islam' (Babès

Figure 2.2 Outreach session of Amatullah in Paris

Table 2.1 Main characteristics of the charities sample 1/3

	Averroès	Amatullah	Alaykumki	Foul Express	JMF
Year of foundation	2002	2006	2010	2011	2006
Localisation	Jussieu University, Paris	Bagnolet, France	Warsaw, Poland	No offices	La Courneuve, France
Activities	Exam correction papers Food for deprived students Campaigns and fundraising Cultural events Arabic courses	Mobile soup kitchens Arabic courses	Public events Round tables Open days	Alternative media Talks and round tables	Events for deprived and homeless people
Target audience	University students	Homeless people	Muslim Polish women and wider Polish society	French public	Local high school students
Average size of the core team	5–7	5–7	5	10	10
Estimated number of sympathisers	>100	>200	>100	>3,000	>300
Estimated yearly budget	<3,000€	<3,000€	Little to no budget	Little to no budget	<20,000€
Funding sources	Private donations, university	Private donations	Members' contributions	Members' contributions	Private donations, state
Founding members	University students	Young women of Bagnolet	Young Polish Muslim women	Young French Muslims from the corporate sector	Young local French Muslims
Place of residence of volunteers	Paris and surroundings	Ile de France region	Warsaw and abroad	Paris and surroundings, some abroad	La Courneuve
Average age of volunteers	20–25	20–25	18–25	25–35	18–25

The data here is accurate for 2009–2012.

Table 2.2 Main characteristics of the charities sample 2/3

	FCR*	Children of Adam	MADE	Rumi's Cave
Year of foundation	2012	2011	2011	2011
Localisation	No Offices	London	London	London
Activities	Coaching and training sessions Workshops	Soup kitchens	Campaigns Trainings workshops	Talks Artistic workshops Open mics Prayers and *zikr* Soup kitchens
Target audience	Muslim executives	Homeless people	Young British Muslims	Any public
Average size of the core team	5	5–7	5–7	5
Estimated number of sympathisers	> 50	> 200	>5,000	> 1,000
Estimated yearly budget	No budget	<£1,000	> £200,000	<£5,000
Funding sources	Members' participation	Private donations	Private donations	Private donations, sister charity
Founding members	Muslim executives	Young Muslim Londoners	Saif Ahmad	Sheikh Ahmed Babikir
Place of residence of volunteers	Paris and surroundings	London and surroundings	London and surroundings	London
Average age of volunteers	25–30	18–35	18–35	18–40

The data here is accurate for 2009–2012.

*The name has been changed.

Table 2.3 Main characteristics of the charities sample 3/3

	CCIF	Muslim Hands France	Islamic Relief France
Year of foundation	2002	2007	2010
Localisation	Paris	Paris	Paris's *Banlieue*
Activities	Legal support for victims of islamophobia	International humanitarian aid	Local and international humanitarian aid
Target audience	French Muslims	(donations) French Muslims	(donations) French Muslims
Average size of the core team	5	5	10–15
Estimated number of sympathisers	> 1000	> 500	> 1000
Estimated yearly budget	< 100,000€	< 50,000€	+/- 30,000,000€
Funding sources	Private donations	Private donations	Private donations
Founding members	Young Muslim charity leaders	French Muslim charity executives	French Muslim charity executives
Place of residence of volunteers	France, nationwide	Ile de France region	Ile de France region
Average age of volunteers	35–40	25–45	25–45

The data here is accurate for 2009–2012. These are other charities that are part of the sample and do not fit the selection criteria, but have been selective for comparative purposes.

1997) that they practise. In Britain, Muslims are over-represented amongst health professionals and are represented by parliamentarians and councillors (Suleiman 2009). They exhibit high educational aspirations for their children (Chua and Rubenfeld 2014; Taylor and Krahn 2005; Kao and Tienda 2005), and polls depict Muslims as 'model citizens' (Coles 2008). In Poland, many Muslims belonged to the upper- and middle-class immigration during the socialist era, which comprised medical doctors, engineers and diplomats (Górak-Sosnowska 2011). Most of the volunteers interviewed for this study had access to higher education and seemed to be conscious of their complex identities and issues like colonialism, and were concerned about the current negative media and political fascination with Islam. They seek to reconnect their spiritual and cultural backgrounds, and share interests in alternative therapeutic movements (cupping, homeopathy, energy-based healing) as well as other spiritual traditions like yoga (Haenni 2005). In the fields of music and art, most of the young Muslims I interviewed were interested in the learning of traditional Islamic geometrical patterns and calligraphy, but also modern Islamic art. Some looked beyond the traditional style of *nasheed* (acapella songs about God or the prophet Muhammad) to musical styles inherited from their cultural backgrounds with modern or traditional instruments, often mixing it with blues or hip-hop (Billaud 2015; Khan 2015), as seen at Rumi's Cave. These views contrasted with other views expressed among European Muslims, which do not support the use of music or gender mixing.

When referring to volunteers in this research, I refer to volunteers who involve themselves in charities in order to do voluntary unpaid work. The French equivalent, '*bénévole*', comes from 'benevolence', meaning 'good will'.[4] Liliane Voyé (2004) has suggested different types of traditional volunteerism:

- Palliative volunteering (humanitarian aid, soup kitchens).
- Growth volunteering, which itself is subdivided in different categories:

    1 Cultural volunteering (coaching, training).
    2 Socio-political volunteering like lobbying/campaigning.
    3 Social volunteering, purely for socialising.

The volunteers in these faith-based charities break with these traditional categories and from the stereotype of volunteers doing basic 'admin works: filing, cut-outs, typewriting' and who were 'retired (. . .) or elderly people' (Chanial 2011, 38). Although participants in this study perform basic tasks too, they come with 'high added value': they are coaches, team leaders, graphic designers, photographers, communication experts and teachers, willing to add their professional expertise to the charity's service for free. Although sometimes working with no budget, these small-scale organisations are able to obtain for free costly products or services such as advertising videos, pictures, websites, posters, communication and marketing strategies and human resources advice and training. As a consequence, they gain intellectual capital and a power of communication equivalent to multimillion-pound NGOs or large companies. However, because small organisations can only have a limited proximity network, one of the key differences is that smaller charities have to count on a finite set of available talent, as opposed to larger NGOs, which are capable of outsourcing skills and expertise.

With highly-skilled members, these local organisations are at the same time cultural hubs with a high potential for creative stimulation. They are formative experiences for members seeking to harness their talents, find inspiration and partners or secure a solid following. Marwan Muhammad, chief executive of the *Collectif Contre l'Islamophobie en France* (CCIF, Collective Against Islamophobia in France), has triggered the interest of thousands through his book, blog and later charity Foul Express (*foul* is the French for 'ful', an Egyptian meal). Abbas Zahedi, artist and auto-entrepreneur, experienced a founding period as manager at Rumi's Cave in London. Shehroze Khan, who produced an award-winning short film and ventured into a career in filmmaking, was once one of the familiar faces of MADE in Europe. Mehdi Bouteghmes and Seyfeddine Cherraben were key figures of JMF before being elected and becoming part of the city council of their town.

Similarly to other Muslim charities, volunteers in this study did not share the same social conditions, age, levels of education, culture, family backgrounds, religious practice or understanding of Islam with each other. Their cultural roots hailed from India, North Africa, the Caribbean, Pakistan, Bangladesh, East and West Africa, the Middle East and the Far East, not to forget France, Britain and Poland. The latter countries comprised mostly volunteers who converted to Islam. They followed different Islamic schools of thought or philosophies. These charities attract a mix of people of various levels of orthopraxy and professional backgrounds, working together. Some are students at universities, others work as doctors, engineers, or in private security companies, postal services, public services or are unemployed. The volunteers present themselves not according to nationality, ethnicity, professional occupation or social status, but identify more generally as 'Muslims' and, in some cases, as 'human beings', 'souls' or 'persons'. The diversity of their past experiences, childhood and families mean that there are a variety of personalities and characters. Therefore, the aim of this study is not to classify charities or volunteers according to their religious orientation or level of orthopraxy (see Chapter 1). The next section will expand on the sampling and study methodology.

Methodology, phenomenology and ethics

This study takes descriptive phenomenology as its main research paradigm, with a strong ethnographic approach. It uses participant observation and face-to-face interviews, which have been conducted with eighty-three equally gendered Muslim and non-Muslim volunteers aged between 18 and 45 years old, between 2009 and 2016.

My aim as a researcher is twofold. My first objective is to explicate how the participants perceive the world and understand experiences through their own consciousness. Second, and consequently, this study aims to deliver a description and an analysis of the data unaltered by any presupposed theory or concept.

These methodological choices, within the frame of phenomenological sociology, have been oriented by several considerations. The actors and the world sustain a reciprocal relationship where both impact on each other; the actors attempt to construct their world and life and, at the same time, the life-world impacts on them (Morin 1977 and 1986; Schultz 1967). As a consequence – echoing Edmund Husserl's vision – consciousness, reality and appearance should not be compartmentalised; this suggests that research should take into account the meaning of experiences and phenomena to individuals and demonstrate how they interpret them and how these participate in the building of their existence (Amath 2015; Pędziwiatr 2010; Denscombe 2003, 99; Creswell 1998, 236). Therefore, this research describes phenomena with the subjects' own words, references and meanings, using these as a basis for analysis. When aiming at presenting concepts, experiences and phenomena through the lens of participants, Husserl suggests suspending any scientific, philosophical, cultural or historical presuppositions (Cop. 2003, 5). Recalling his own words (Husserl 1982 [1960], 2) in his *Cartesian Meditations*, Husserl noted that 'anyone who seriously intends to become a philosopher must "once in his life" withdraw into himself and attempt, within himself, to overthrow and build anew all the sciences that, up to then, he has been accepting'. Thus, no specific theories were developed or applied prior to the fieldwork, until they could be substantiated (see the methodology applied in Amath 2015; Englander 2012 and Giorgi 2008). The charities and the volunteers have not been labelled, categorised or simplified as ideal-types in order to keep the work faithful to the complexity and diversity of the identities and dynamics at play. However, because I had no previous experience of working with or studying my subjects, preliminary bibliographical research was conducted in order to familiarise myself with the political, historical and social context of Muslims in France, Poland and the UK.

No particular assumptions were made prior to the fieldwork except one, which I decided to use in selecting my sample of participants. As I wanted to analyse the influence of social bonds and psychological and biographical elements and beliefs, following an anti-utilitarian analysis (Caillé 2009), I selected charities led by unpaid volunteers and focused my efforts on unpaid volunteers under the assumption that monetary motives or career, among other utilitarian motives, would play a minor role in explaining the involvement process of volunteers (Chanial 2001 and 2008; 2011 Nyssens 2008, 46; Besley and Gathak 2005). To summarise, I looked for charities whose frame of reference revolves around Islam but which work in an open system within wider society and are driven mainly by anti-utilitarian motives. The charities have thus been selected upon three criteria. They should:

1 Provide services to everyone, and not be centred on Muslims; work with non-Muslim volunteers without any distinction between faiths and cultures.
2 Be managed exclusively by volunteers.
3 Share Islam as a system of references; although their services are not exclusive to Muslims, their ethics, principles and actions are inspired by Islam.

44 *Muslim grassroots charities and method*

Because there were no databases existing at the time, the French charities studied in this work were selected through personal acquaintances and during the yearly *Rencontres annuelles des Musulmans de France* (RAMF, Yearly Meeting of Muslims of France) in Le Bourget (France), the most important yearly gathering of Muslims in Europe. My personal networks in Poland and the UK helped me to connect with organisations in these countries, but most contacts were made on the ground by asking people frequenting the main mosque during Ramadan (Wiertnicza street mosque) or at public events (Islamophobia Awareness Month in London, talks at the East London Mosque, Islamic Societies gathering such as the FOSIS yearly meeting or one Turkish organisation which I stumbled upon while wandering at the Warsaw Christmas market where they had a stall).

The fieldwork started with a first stage of participant observation. This phase, lasting on average four to six months, allowed me to familiarise myself with the volunteers and build bonds of trust through a regular presence while I participated in activities (serving meals to the homeless, sorting folders, etc.). The second phase mixed formal, semi-directed, in-depth interviews and informal discussions, which allowed for the triangulation of the data with an array of different procedures (Pędziwiatr 2010; Denzin and Lincoln 2003, 5; Creswell 1998, 5). I wanted to focus on the biographical trajectories of the main characters to try to obtain an in-depth understanding of the individuality and agency of the subjects' experience (Amath 2015, Pędziwiatr 2010; Cefaï 2007; Gibson and Hanes 2003, 183–4; Hollway and Jefferson 2000, 167) and thus allow for the other to be made 'fully real' (Berger and Luckmann 1967, 43). As a result, the data comprised fully transcribed interviews, notes taken during multiple conversations, observations and documents, all spread over a period of time from some weeks to some years. The phase of reading, extracting and categorising emerging themes was done without the help of software, which at the expense of a certain amount of time allowed me to grasp an overall 'feeling' for each interviewee, keeping in mind the general context and the personal circumstances for each and helping me to structure and organise my findings.

I introduced myself in an open manner as a student in sociology working on a PhD on the topic of Islam in Europe. Prior to interviews, I personally asked the permission of the interviewees and mentioned that the interviews would be anonymised. All of the participants had full access to the data and the findings and were consulted prior to publication. As a Muslim born to Polish Catholic parents who had grown up in France, I was placed in both an outsider and insider position. Because of my faith, I was met with support, trust, sympathy and hospitality by all the Muslim respondents, but this was not an obstacle for interviewing non-Muslim respondents. My faith appeared to the respondents only in particular settings or circumstances (mosque, religious gathering, prayer). In most situations, I did not feel the need to explain my beliefs. Being from Polish parents and being able to speak Polish also helped me to feel comfortable in a Polish-speaking environment and to interview participants in Polish when necessary. This allowed me to conduct in-depth interviews in which participants were open about revealing intimate parts of their lives. However, at the very beginning, starting this research with a very superficial understanding of Islam and no prior experience in the Muslim community deprived me of the understanding of some phenomena which were 'new' to me (although they became more familiar with time). On the other hand, coming from outside of the community allowed me to distance myself from my observations and critically question the phenomena, which perhaps would have been more difficult if I had already been familiar with these. Also, being seemingly part of the dominant society because of my ethnic background and appearance encouraged non-Muslim civil servants and authorities to reveal their personal views about Islam, Muslims in general and the participant charities with which they were communicating. This enabled me to gather opinions from both sides regarding how Muslims perceive representatives of the states and how the latter perceive their Muslim respondents, findings which are included in Chapter 3.

Notes

1. According to the 2011 UK Census, www.ons.gov.uk/census/2011census [last accessed on 15 Jan. 2017].
2. The Guardian. Britain's top 1,000 charities ranked by donations. Who raises the most money? www.theguardian.com/news/datablog/2012/apr/24/top-1000-charities-donations-britain [last accessed on 15 Jan. 2017].
3. Dictionary from the French National Centre for Lexical Resources, www.cnrtl.fr/ [last accessed on 15 Jan. 2017].
4. Dictionary from the French National Centre for Lexical Resources, www.cnrtl.fr/ [last accessed on 15 Jan. 2017].

References

Amath, N. (2015). *The Phenomenology of Community Activism: Muslim Civil Society Organisations in Australia*. Melbourne: Melbourne University Press.
Babès, L. (1997). *L'islam positif: La religion des jeunes musulmans en France* [*Positive Islam: The Religion of the Young Muslims in France*]. Paris: L'Atelier.
Beaumont, J. (2010). Transcending the Particular in Postsecular Cities. In: Molendijk, A., Beaumont, J. and Jedan, C. (eds.) *Exploring the Postsecular: The Religious, the Political, and the Urban*. Leiden: Brill.
Berger, P. L. and Luckmann, T. (1967). *The Social Construction of Reality: A Treatise in the Sociology of Knowledge*. Garden City: Anchor Books.
Besley, T. and Ghatak, M. (2005). Competition and Incentives With Motivated Agents. *The American Economic Review*, 95(3), 616–36.
Billaud, J. (2015). Instantanés de l'islam britannique [Instants of British Islam]. In: Göle, N. (ed.) *En-quête de l'Islam Européen*. Paris: Halfa, pp. 75–97.
Blühdorn, I. (2006). Self-Experience in the Theme Park of Radical Action? Social Movements and Political Articulation in the Late-Modern Condition. *European Journal of Social Theory*, 9(1), 23–42.
Bobineau, O. and Seraïdari, K. (2010). *Les formes élémentaires de l'engagement: Une anthropologie du sens* [*The Elementary Forms of Engagement: An Anthropology of Meaning*]. Paris: Temps Présent.
Caillé, A. (2008). La société civile mondiale qui vient [The coming global civil society]. In; Chanial, P. (2008) *La société vue du don*. Paris: La Découverte, pp. 349–63.Caillé, A. (2009). *Théorie Anti-Utilitariste de l'Action et du Sujet* [*Anti-Utilitarian Theory of Action and Subject*]. Paris: La Découverte.

Cefaï, D. (2007). *Pourquoi se Mobilise-t-on? Les Théories de l'Action Collective* [*Why Do People Mobilise? The Theories of Collective Action*]. Paris: La Découverte.
Chanial, P. (2003). La culture primaire de la démocratie: Communautés locales, publics démocratiques et associations [The Primary Culture of Democracy: Local Communities, Democratic Audiences and Charities]. In: Cefaï, D. et Pasquier, D. (eds.) *Les Sens du public: Publics politiques, publics médiatiques*. Paris: Presses Universitaires de France, pp. 269–89.
Chanial, P. (2001). *Justice, Don, Association* [*Justice, Gift, Charity*]. Paris: La Découverte.
Chanial, P. (2008). *La société vue du don* [*Society From a Gift Perspective*]. Paris: La Découverte.
Chanial, P. (2011). *La sociologie comme philosophie politique et réciproquement* [*Sociology as a Political Philosophy and Reciprocally*]. Paris: La Découverte.
Coles, M. I. (2008). *Every Muslim Child Matters*. Stoke: Trentham Books.
Chua, A. and Rubenfeld, J. (2014). *The Triple Package: How Three Unlikely Traits Explain the Rise and Fall of Cultural Groups in America*. New York: Penguin Press.Cope, J. (2003). *Researching Entrepreneurship Through Phenomenological Inquiry: Philosophical and Methodological Issues*. Lancaster University Management School Working Paper 2003/052, http://eprints.lanc.ac.uk/48660/1/Document.pdf [accessed Jan. 2017].
Creswell, J. W. (1998). *Qualitative Inquiry and Research Design: Choosing Among Five Alternatives*. Thousand Oaks: Sage.
Denscombe, M. (2003). *The Good Research Guide: For Small-Scale Social Research Projects*. Buckingham: Open University Press.
Denzin, N. K. and Lincoln, Y. S. (2003). *Handbook for Qualitative Research*. Thousand Oaks: Sage.
Duclos, B. and Nicourd, S. (2005). *Pourquoi s'engager? Bénévoles et militants dans les associations de solidarité* [*Why Getting Involved? Volunteers and Activists in Charities*]. Paris: Payot.
Englander, M. (2012). The Interview: Data Collection in Descriptive Phenomenological Human Sciences Research. *Journal of Phenomenological Psychology*, 43(1), 13–35.
Etienne, B. (1989). *La France et l'islam* [*France and Islam*]. Paris: Hachette.
Etienne, B. ed. (1991). *L'islam en France: islam, état et société* [*Islam in France: Islam, State and Society*]. Paris: Editions du CNRS.
Feixa, C., Pereira, I. and Juris, J. S. (2009). Global Citizenship and the 'New, New' Social Movements Iberian Connections. *Young*, 17(4), 421–42.
Fitzgerald, G. (2015). Patterns of British Government Engagements With Muslim Faith-Based Organizations: The Second Image Reversed? In: Suleiman, Y. (ed.) *Muslims in the UK and Europe*. Cambridge: Centre of Islamic Studies, pp. 76–89.
Frégosi, F. (2008). *Penser l'islam dans la laïcité* [*Thinking Islam Within Secularism*]. Paris: Fayard.
Furbey, R. (2007). Faith, Social Capital and Social Cohesion. In: Jochum, V., Pratten, B. and Wilding, K. (eds.) *Faith and Voluntary Action*. London: National Council for Voluntary Organisations, pp. 34–8.
Gibson, S. and Hanes, L. A. (2003). The Contribution of Phenomenology to HRD Research. *Human Resource Development Review*, 2(2), 181–204.
Giorgi, A. (2008). Difficulties Encountered in the Application of the Phenomenological Method in the Social Sciences. *The Indo-Pacific Journal of Phenomenology*, 8(1), 1–9.
Göle, N. (2003). *Musulmanes et modernes: Voile et civilisation en Turquie* [*Muslim and Modern: Headscarf and Civilisation in Turkey*]. Paris: La Découverte.

Göle, N. (2005). *Interpénétrations: L'Islam et l'Europe* [*Interpenetrations: Islam and Europe*]. Paris: Galaade.
Górak-Sosnowska, K. (2011). *Muslims in Poland and Eastern Europe, Widening the European Discourse on Islam*. Warsaw: University of Warsaw Press.
Haenni, P. (2005). *L'islam de marché: l'autre révolution conservatrice* [*Market Islam, the Other Conservative Revolution*]. Paris: Seuil.
Hollway, W. and Jefferson, T. (2000). *Doing Qualitative Meditations Research Differently: Free Association, Narrative and the Interview Method*. London: Sage.
Husserl, E. (1982) [1960]. *Cartesian Mediations: An Introduction to Phenomenology*. London, The Hague, and Boston: Martinus Nijhoff.
Kao, G. and Tienda, M. (2005). Optimism and Achievement: The Educational Performance of Immigrant Youth. *Social Science Quarterly*, 76(1), 1–19.
Keck, M. E. and Sikkink, K. (2014). *Activists Beyond Borders: Advocacy Networks in International Politics*. Ithaca: Cornell University Press.
Kennelly, J. (2011). *Citizen Youth: Culture, Activism, and Agency in a Neoliberal Era*. Basingstoke: Palgrave Macmillan.
Khan, A. (2015). Black, Female, Muslim and a Hip-Hop Artist: A Case Study of 'Poetic Pilgrimage'. In: Suleiman, Y. (ed.) *Muslims in the UK and Europe*. Cambridge: Centre of Islamic Studies, pp. 130–9.
Lamchichi, A. (1999). *Islam et musulmans de France: pluralisme, laïcité et citoyenneté* [*Islam and Muslims in France: Pluralism, Secularism and Citizenship*]. Paris: L'Harmattan.
Langman, L. (2013). Occupy: A New New Social Movement. *Current Sociology*, 61(4), 510–24.
Lichterman, P. (2005). *Elusive Togetherness: Church Groups Trying to Bridge America's Divisions*. Princeton: Princeton University Press.
McDonald, K. (2006). *Global Movements: Action and Culture*. Hoboken: Wiley.
Meyer, D. S. and Tarrow, S. G. (1998). *The Social Movement Society: Contentious Politics for a New Century*. Lanham: Rowman & Littlefield.
Modood, T. (2012). *Post-Immigration 'Difference' and Integration: The Case of Muslims in Western Europe, New Paradigms in Public Policy*. London: British Academy Policy Centre.
Morin, E. (1977). *La Méthode: La nature de la Nature* [*Method: The Nature of Nature*]. Paris: Seuil.
Morin, E. (1986). *La Méthode: La vie de la Vie* [*Method: The Life of Life*]. Paris: Seuil.
Newton, K. (1999). Social Capital and Democracy in Modern Europe. In: Van Deth, J. W., Maraffi, M., Newton, K. and Whiteley, P. F. (eds.) *Social Capital and European Democracy*. London: Routledge, pp. 3–24.
Nyssens, M. (2008). Les analyses économiques des associations [The Economic Analysis of Charities]. In: Hoarau, C. and Laville, J-L. (eds.) *La gouvernance des associations*. Paris: Eres, pp. 27–51.
O'Toole, T. and Gale, R. (2010). Contemporary Grammars of Political Action Among Ethnic Minority Young Activists. *Ethnic and Racial Studies*, 33(1), 126.
Offe, C. (1985). New Social Movements: Challenging the Boundaries of Institutional Politics. *Social Research*, 52(4), 817–68.
Pędziwiatr, K. (2010). *The New Muslim Elites in European Cities: Religion and Active Social Citizenship Amongst Young Organized Muslims in Brussels and London*. Saarbrücken: VDM Verlag.

Pettinato, D. (2016). 'MADE a Difference?' – British Muslim Youth and Faith-Inspired Activism Between 'Post-Conventional Politics', 'Post-Secularity', and 'Post-Immigration Difference'. In: Suleiman, Y. and Anderson, P. (eds.) *Muslims in the UK and Europe II*. Cambridge: Centre of Islamic Studies, pp. 100–13.

Said, E. (1984). *The World, the Text and the Critic*. Cambridge: Harvard University Press.

Salvatore, A. (2004). Making Public Space: Opportunities and Limits of Collective Action Among Muslims in Europe. *Journal of Ethnic and Migration Studies*, 30(5), 1013–31.

Schultz, A. (1967). *The Phenomenology of the Social World*, trans. Walsh, G. and Lehnert, F. Evanston: Northwestern University Press.

Suleiman, Y. (2009). *Contextualising Islam in Britain: Exploratory Perspectives*. Cambridge: Centre of Islamic Studies.

Taylor, A. and Krahn, H. (2005). Aiming High: Educational Aspirations of Visible Minority Immigrant Youth. *Canadian Social Trends*, 79, catalogue no. 11–008, 8–12.

Voyé, L. (2004). Repenser le bénévolat [Rethinking Volunteering]. In: Soulet, M-H. (ed.) *Agir en société*. Fribourg: Academic Press Fribourg, pp. 83–118.

Wieviorka, M. (2005). After New Social Movements. *Social Movement Studies*, 4(1), 1–19.

3 Islamophobia: Countering alienation[1]

In the previous chapter, I examined the context of the foundation of these charities. Most of them started as informal, spontaneous initiatives set up in the area of a town, a neighbourhood or a university. Being of a small scale and with a focus on providing services to the local community, they would easily go unnoticed. However, since they are legally obliged to produce statuses and accounts, they come under the scrutiny of their local authority. These proceedings come with potential risks in countries such as France, where both securitarian and secular narratives push public services to consider any Muslim charity as a potential threat, thus alienating Muslims from mainstream society. This bias against Muslims falls under the label of islamophobia, as defined by the Runnymeade Trust (Conway 1997), and encompasses various forms of prejudice, abuse and hostility against Muslims emanating from individuals and institutions. Although debates are still ongoing about defining the term and even naming the phenomenon (like 'muslimophobia' or 'islamoparanoia' [Liogier 2015]), the aforementioned definition, which emerged first in early twentieth-century France, has been progressively adopted as the consensual one (Hajjat and Mohammed 2013). However, in a post-9/11 Europe, where the general public perception of Islam is at its lowest, these small organisations manage to restore a balanced image of Muslims to the public sphere, with much more efficiency than some large-scale national or European initiatives against islamophobia. In this chapter, I start by elaborating on the complex French context and the direct consequences of the political and media pressure on Muslims. I then draw a comparison with the situation in Poland, where history provided a completely different social and political environment for the Muslim charities in the capital city. I eventually analyse how, at a grassroots level, these local organisations build bonds of trust, smash prejudices and flip the mind-set of their audience and the authorities they depend on; they thus become agents of negotiation of their own image, boundaries and legitimacy, taking control over the dominant narratives and eventually creating a harmonious social environment.

Has Europe alienated its citizens?

Paris, 2012.
   Never has the CCIF been more powerful. After ten years of existence, a major grant from the Open Society Foundations has propelled this small consultative

member for the United Nations to the status of a major European player in the fight against discrimination at large and islamophobia specifically. In 2012, they launched a nationwide campaign with video spots on national TV channels and giant billboards across the country, with a simple motto advocating the acknowledgement of Muslims as French citizens equal to anyone else: 'We too, are the Nation'. They launched a cooperative programme at a European level with sister-organisations in eight countries through the Islamophobia Monitoring and Action Network (IMAN) project.[2] The CCIF file cases for most aggressions and crimes against Muslims in France. They mainly provide pro bono advice and attorneys, successfully settling hundreds of cases per year, and lobby the government, requesting equal rights for all citizens regardless of their religion and the rigorous application of the principle of *laïcité* (separation between church and state and freedom of religion for citizens). Their spokesperson, Marwan, later head of programmes at the Organization for Security and Co-operation in Europe (OSCE), boasts an eloquence and a command of statistics which leaves their opponents (usually defenders of a secularism of exclusion) at a loss for an argument.

Four years later, in 2016 – nearly thirty years after the first headscarf issue in France, when two female students were banned from entering a high school with their *hijab* – little seems to have changed. As the 2016 attempts to ban the 'burkini' on beaches failed (only women wearing the simple *hijab* were fined), controversies surrounding the visibility of practising Muslims do not seem to have decreased. NGOs and consultancy organisations such as Amnesty International,[3] CCIF or Open Society Foundations[4] point out the adverse policies of the French government against minorities and especially against Muslims. Indeed, for the past several years, French politicians have tended to have a more coercive interpretation of secularism (*laïcité*), whereas the concept, as stated in the 1958 constitution, implies only neutrality of the government and employees in public services. The European Human Rights Court has even pronounced a statement underlining France's infringement of the European Constitution because a Sikh citizen was not allowed to keep his *dastaar* (Sikh turban) on for identity pictures.[5] More precisely, the French government's strategy is more focused on developing a secular fundamentalist policy and actively trying to remove religion or spirituality from the public sphere (Baubérot 2006).

According to opinion polls published in mainstream media, 43% of the French population perceive Islam as a threat to society[6] and 84% are in favour of a ban of the *hijab* on the streets.[7] Although the objectivity of these quantitative studies has been questioned, they do not help to change a climate of rejection of Muslim citizens. 'Going out with the scarf on the streets in countries marked with secularism needs courage,' states Nilüfer Göle,[8] talking about the public pressure that practising Muslims face because of their visibility as the root of controversies around Islam (Göle 2005, 109). However, qualitative studies with deep fieldwork show an opposite trend when it comes to citizens meeting Muslim people in their daily life, which will be further discussed.

Past years have seen wide-scale initiatives, such as the 2012 joint campaigns in France and the UK (CCIF and Islamophobia Awareness Month)[9] and the

April 2013 petition in France[10] aiming to bring the topic of islamophobia onto the political agenda at a national level. Their effect was uneven, especially when viewed in light of the seriousness of the phenomenon, which seems to be the decade's challenge for Western European Muslims. Curtailing minorities' rights and individual liberties for the sake of national security has become a well-developed electoral strategy for both right- and left-wing parties. Populist discourses and methods are no longer monopolised by far-right organisations,[11] while simplistic or biased content floods mainstream media.[12] Tolerance towards racist speech has come to a point such that to declare oneself explicitly 'islamophobic' is no longer taboo. The surge in campaigns, conferences and meetings organised by Muslims since 9/11 and 7/7 has had little impact on governmental policies. Furthermore, after the 7 January 2015 Charlie Hebdo attacks in Paris, then following 13 November 2015 and eventually Nice in July 2016 (when respectively 130 people were shot in a concert venue and 86 were hit by a truck on a French national holiday), politicians have perceived increased security measures as the only possible response, while far-right activists continue to hold the average Muslim citizen responsible for these crimes. Thousands of houses, many with young children, have been raided in the early hours of the morning,[13][14] but fewer than a dozen individuals have been actually charged with terrorism. Fear and trauma among innocent citizens are by far the most tangible consequences of an out of control 'State of Emergency'. A strategy which produces resentment against the authorities becomes the foundation for more terrorist violence, plunging the country into a vicious circle, a maelstrom dragging France into the depths of the absurd, its government on the verge of becoming an authoritarian regime. Some volunteers I interviewed in the UK also complained about an oppressive climate. Nishat, a young woman studying at SOAS and a political activist in the UK and Pakistan, testified that:

> it's less visible than France but it's at the same level. Within my work, I see many abusive detentions, people being detained on political grounds, terrorism suspicions . . . on the streets, a few days ago, there was this woman who got her *hijab* pulled off, there was this guy in East London during the BBC interview. . .

Some others witnessed verbal abuse on a daily basis and confirmed Nishat's opinion that islamophobia, whether institutional or on the streets, is strong in the UK, but perhaps less visible than in France.

Regarding the charities in France, in the very early days following their foundation some charities were priority targets for French intelligence services.[15] The main concern of the government was their visibility (the *hijab*) or the explicit name of the group, as for example JMF or Amatullah. In practice, those charities faced no obstacles when working to organise public events until after the Charlie Hebdo attacks, when JMF was denied grants because the local authority decided that 'their name was hard to deal with'. However, the situation evolved for Amatullah, which was founded in 2006. The charity, which organised soup kitchens for the homeless, was under surveillance for months before the city council deemed their actions to be beneficial for the town. At the time of this research, they were granted offices and venues for their occasional events, such as open days, anniversaries or fundraising and publicity. The charity Averroès, based at one of the main universities in Paris, had aroused fears of proselytisation, but as the charity became more familiar to the administrative services, they were granted venues inside the university for their activities and events.

On the Eastern side of Europe, according to Konrad Pędziwiatr, neither Muslims nor other minorities were a major concern for politicians before the mid-2010s.[16] As late as 2012, never had a Muslim faced hate speech or been a victim of criminal deeds in Poland based on their faith.[17] Based on the interviews of organisations' leaders and believers conducted during my fieldwork,[18] Polish society was portrayed as open to cultural and/or religious differences. However, the media have traditionally depicted Muslims as both an external enemy (terrorism, extremism, human rights violations, etc.) and an internal enemy (the theory of Islamisation of Poland). The situation in mainstream society has dramatically changed since 2015: mosques have been attacked with pig heads, cemeteries have been desecrated and anti-Muslim mobilisations have been held in the wake of the parliamentary elections.[19] Górak-Sosnowska introduced the concept of 'platonic islamophobia'. Platonic islamophobia describes hatred against Muslims despite never having met them:[20] 'Muslims do not take the work of the others, even though we have no Muslim neighbourhoods, we do not like them.'

According to Górak-Sosnowska and Pędziwiatr, hatred against Muslims has no ideological roots and is not based on rational arguments.[21] However, far-right organisations and web-based discussion groups often import idioms from their Western European counterparts, such as the theory of 'invasion/Islamisation of Europe' or 'the loss of Europe's cultural legacy'. Those arguments fall flat, as a possible Islamisation of Poland is questionable with only 0.1 per cent of the population identifying as Muslim after more than six centuries of Muslim presence. Also, the citizenship debate arouses less tension in Poland than in France: most volunteers interviewed do not find any incompatibility between being Muslim and a Polish citizen at the same time.

The Polish charities studied in this work focus on the perception and understanding of Islam by the wider Polish society. They often organise and participate in open days at the mosque, conferences and roundtables with religious leaders and politicians and are active on social and mainstream media. Volunteers do not have any identity complexes, identifying both as Polish and Muslim. Although they may not have an official status, they nevertheless remain highly active. One remarkable example is the distribution of roses in the streets by the Alajkumki Muslim young women's association. In November 2012, they wrote a letter describing the prophet of Islam and summarised his life. This letter was attached to a red rose and then distributed on the streets of Warsaw by the girls, who were dressed in black and red. This operation, *Róże Miłości*[22] (roses of love), was successful, as the whole stock of roses was given to people; sometimes people just kept the letter rather than the flower. Also, two Polish Muslims, M. Kochanowicz and M. Marszewski, initiated a conversation between Polish 'Islamophobes' (later self-defined as 'Islamosceptics') and other Muslims. The project, started on a Facebook page, at first produced mixed results. However, people from this discussion group agreed to have a meeting in a café and met for half a day. As a result, many from both sides expressed satisfaction and the feeling of having had a 'positive experience' and having 'learnt something new'. Although this experience remains quite exceptional, in France the dynamics of dialogue I witnessed were much slower and not confrontational.

The media coverage, politicians' discourse, government policies and far-right activism offer an alienating narrative, in the sense of excluding Muslims from mainstream society. Moreover, they are commoditised as tools for political parties to gain the popular vote and thus seem to have no control over their image in the public sphere; public policies and debates on TV about Islam or Muslims rarely invite Muslims to take part in the discussion and rather depict Muslims as a problematic entity (Hajjat and Mohammed 2013; Meer et al. 2010; Baubérot 2006). Furthermore, this rejection from mainstream society triggers as a reaction apartist perceptions (Gest 2010, 12), leading individuals to disrupt or withdraw from democracy. The divide operated by politicians and the media and the pressure brought by the securitarian narrative for decades have had a strong impact on Muslims, with tangible mental health issues as a direct consequence (Mehmood 2015; Davids 2011; Amer 2005; Chakraborty and McKenzie 2002). The impression of being under constant threat makes a marginal part of Muslim citizens enter another vicious cycle: that of self-alienation. In my observation of social media activity, I noticed that many Muslims talked and shared on social media stories of attacks on Muslims, abuse, aggressions, biased media coverage, stigmatising political discourses and so on: the CCIF Facebook page in France, generally featuring these kind of stories in order to publicly expose them, is followed by more than 100,000 people as of 2016, and its posts gather on average several hundred 'likes', 'reactions' and 'shares'. Also, many expressed an adverse view of elements representing the established political system; consequently, they do not trust local authorities such as the city council, to the point that they refuse to engage in any form of dialogue with them or even to perceive themselves as citizens (see also Chapter 5). Further, many comments on Facebook groups and pages, commonly Anglophone, around decolonial studies expressed a form of pessimism, as their commonly expressed arguments were that Muslims, amongst other ethnicities and religious groups, have been wounded, still suffer from the remains of imperial, colonial and globalising trends and will continue to suffer from these as long as the dominant society is in place in France – this is the narrative of movements such as the PIR (*Parti des Indigènes de la République*). Many of these online groups use an antagonistic lexicon to divide society in a binary perspective between 'allies' and 'enemies'. On these pages, divergent opinions are often considered betrayals and any Facebook 'friend' or 'ally' who expresses divergent opinions becomes suspicious. Many participants defined themselves through an apophatic identity: by what they are not (I am not White, I am not Christian) or by what they are against (against the establishment, against the elites), thus building their cognitive space with items to be potentially rejected. The formation of the identity of such groups is passive and based on the filtering and selective rejection of political and media discourse. Their critique of the current system is deprived of any ideas or solution, and through the dehumanisation of their designated opponents, they perpetuate the cycle of domination by sustaining the dominator culture (Hooks 2003 and 1992). This passive and apophetic identity is opposed to the building of identity through action, as seen in charities (see Chapter 4). However, whether these alienating trends are external or internal, according to Gest (2010, 25–30), Muslims do not undergo a complete alienation (in the sense of Marx), as they do not completely disengage from their local political system; nor are they completely supportive of it: 'they simply exist'. Gest (2010, 25–30) supports the idea that Muslims in twenty-first-century Europe cannot be alienated in the era of blogs, NGOs and online social networks; they may be 'apart' but still use new means of mobilisation and participation within the system.

In a different dynamic, some Muslims adopt a more solution-based approach. Jennyfer embraced Islam a few years ago and lives in a small town in the south of Paris. She chooses to post on Facebook only positive stories: her conversations at work, how people are kind to her or others, how religiosity is discussed between colleagues, her efforts to smash prejudices with kind words or small attentions. She returned an USB stick she found in the street via mail with a small card where she wrote a quote from a *hadith*: 'Do to others what you want for yourself.' Her attempts to change mind-sets about Muslims go together with changing Muslims' mind-sets about politics and citizenship. Every week, she invites people from her local mosque to attend the city council meetings, which are open to the public, and encourages them to ask questions. Sana, living in England, shared a similar point of view with a different experience:

> I feel sick at generalisations, people who only criticise and share negative stories. It's the things you do when you're first year at SOAS. I mean, it's important, I needed to figure out what the problems were, but now we can't stay focused on our wounds, we need to move on, we need to think about our future. We need hope. I face discrimination on a daily basis, but if we start seeing everything as negative, then we would stop living.

Sana, 27, from a Pakistani background, got her Bachelor's in History at SOAS. Interested in decolonial studies, she explained her journey:

> Like a few years ago, I wouldn't even read a letter if it was written by a white man. But I've been struck by how bell hooks talks about ending the cycle of domination. It's also not what God wants from us. There is good and bad in everyone, we cannot generalise. We need to think about solutions.

Many others like Sana and Jennyfer believe that only dialogue will be able to make a difference; and my observations showed that they turned out to be right.

Dialogue as a key for contemporaneity

For analysing the impact of the sustained presence of Muslim charities in their local area, my aim was to gather opinions from the public and the authorities. I started to interview student beneficiaries of Averroès, the charity printing exam paper corrections in the university. I asked about their general impressions of Averroès, especially to non-Muslim beneficiaries. What were the keywords that first came to mind? For many, the first thought was about the setting of the premises: 'exam papers' or 'food supplies'. For many others, the first idea was about the atmosphere: 'relaxed'. Then came keywords such as 'youth', 'activities' and 'conviviality'. But still for a large number, there was 'nothing special'. These latter comments indicated a complete integration of the charity into the university: Averroès is a part of the social landscape, as are many other charities, and 'nothing special' struck the beneficiaries about the charity although Averroès is the only organisation on campus that has Arabic calligraphy on the walls and an overrepresentation of female volunteers wearing the *hijab*. Religion and its visibility had no importance for the beneficiaries. People sometimes come to the office to check on their friends who happen to volunteer often:

Is Said there?
- He was there a moment ago, but he couldn't stay at the reception.
- I'm asking because I like to have some news of people.

Conversely, when Muslim beneficiaries were interviewed about their impressions of Averroès, they first noticed the presence of 'Muslims' and 'girls wearing *hijab*'. My interviews made me realise that the religiosity of most volunteers seemed to be invisible to everyone in the sample of non-Muslim beneficiaries, which comprised two dozen people. *A contrario*, it was the first thing noticed by the half-dozen Muslim beneficiaries interviewed. Unexpectedly, whereas for non-Muslim students seeing young women in headscarves seemed to be something normal on the campus, for Muslims students seeing other Muslims working publicly seemed to be exceptional. Is being Muslim and visible in France something perceived as so exceptional that it surprises other Muslims?

Once a year, these different charities organise open days (see Figure 3.1). These are the opportunities to meet potential volunteers, donators and civil servants. Many non-Muslim families come during the open days organised by Amatullah or the 'education forum' organised by JMF. The latter is a yearly event where JMF invites people in higher education or professionals to talk about their studies or jobs to younger people, such as high school students, who come along with their parents. These families come for various reasons, but mainly because parents and children have the opportunity to find ideas about what to do in higher education or as a career. One mother testified that they came 'because I want my son to have ideas what to do in the future'. 'I wanted to go to the forum because I don't know what to do after my Bac [Baccalauréat – WB] and I like Maths,' said one young

56 *Islamophobia: countering alienation*

Figure 3.1 Open day of Amatullah in Bagnolet

boy, while a young woman recalled her conversations, saying 'I liked talking to professionals very much'. At Amatullah's open day, between the testimonies of volunteers or homeless people who benefit from their services, one could find food stalls, drawing workshops, a kid's corner and an inflatable castle (see Figure 3.2). One mother explained that she wanted 'to bring my children so they can have some fun'. Nobody mentioned a word about Islam or Muslims. The public perceives the events for what they offer: the forum offers tools for young people to consider future studies or career and the open day offers a moment of fun. People talked similarly about Averroès, thanking them for their work of collecting exam papers and printing their corrections. Also, these charities are the only ones providing these services in their local area. However, according to the charities' executives, things were not easy at the beginning, as Hassan from JMF said:

> At the beginning, it was difficult with the city council . . . at the beginning yes, they didn't know us but then, when they saw what we are doing, they trust us now. Mistrust is not that much a fear of Islam. It was a fear of political recuperation of the charity's work. (. . .) For the city council, it was scary to see young people initiating many activities while they were short of new ideas.

Shemseddine talked about the threatening city council:

> The city council doesn't like us because our projects are competing with theirs, as for the education forum. They once refused us a space at the last

Islamophobia: countering alienation 57

Figure 3.2 Inflatable sumos fight in Jussieu University, during Averroès's open day

minute, without explanations . . . We had to come with 40 people at the city council meeting asking for explanations and fortunately, they resigned from their decision.

The left-wing mayor at the time, Gilles Poux, paid a visit to JMF's yearly 'Education Forum'. The venue for the forum had been dedicated especially to JMF for the weekend by the city council. This kind of support, although legal, is often avoided by mayors as it sparks the ire of local far-right groups. When interviewed about the fact of supporting a visibly Muslim charity, Poux replied:

It's a charity very involved in the district, which provides tuition for high school students, homework support, which regularly wishes to make this initiative to help young people choosing their studies; in this frame, concerning the city council, we have a policy, it's every time we have charities or individuals wanting to undertake things, which have a meaning, which are for the general interest, well, we give them resources, this is why we offer them this gymnasium, this is why we offer them technical and material resources for them to build this initiative because there are lots of volunteers, many dynamics; and I believe that our society needs the participation of its citizens and when some charities get involved, well, we are here with our resources, completely available. (. . .) It's a charity which helps young people, I would say, not in a goal of religious obedience but, I would say has a goal to respond to a need of general interest. In France, there was and there are other charities, there is the Catholic Relief which we are helping, because these are works of general interest. Another thing is this or that charity developing cultural activities, for instance, but at this moment, it is in their own frame, but when there are suggestions which respond to the general interest, whatever are the charities undertaking these, we are available stakeholders. It seems logical to me and there is no need to forbid any activity as long as it answers needs.

For the mayor, this 'general interest' work legitimises the presence of the charity in the public sphere and the support of the city council. Interviews with elected city council members seemed to paint a portrait of a mayor's team which is open-minded on matters of culture and religions. Muslim workers are allowed to pray in their offices. Another member of the city council, François, who has known the young people involved in JMF for more than twenty years, recalled the debates at the beginning of JMF:

The president [chief executive] was hesitating keeping the term 'Muslim' in the name of the organisation. I told him: 'It's very good, keep it.' I don't want people to sacrifice their identity because people have opposite ideas. (. . .) It makes people worry because prejudices are hard to kill.

But François emphasised the positive dynamics it allows:

Walls fall when people meet each other. Some politicians came to attend to 'solidaricité' [a festive event for homeless people] and the Education Forum and realised that things are not as they thought. Everything is possible with meeting people, especially for those who are targets of those controversies. Among ten people, two will completely change their mind-set, three will say 'let's wait and see,' and five will remain completely against. But we need to focus on the two who change their mind.

When interviewing civil servants from Bagnolet, the home town of Amatullah, one could hear the same discourse regarding the charity. Mr. B., adjunct to the mayor, testified: 'The city council is on good terms with Muslims in Bagnolet. I personally supported the foundation and the beginning of Amatullah for this side of the Muslim religion which is about helping the poor.' He confessed that the beginning was not very easy:

There was lots of mistrust, suspicion and surveillance . . . by the intelligence services especially. Politicians and other charities were asking: 'Why are they here, what are they looking for, what do they want?' (. . .) During the charities forum [organised each year by the city council], seeing women wearing the veil was a problem, was creating tensions, they were not accepted by other charities (. . .) nowadays, the mayor supports their action, even though there are still reluctances and tensions towards Islam from politicians and civil servants, but this is because of the climate spread by the government.

Islamophobia: countering alienation 59

In the case of the students' charity Averroès, volunteers and public services are regularly in contact due to the relatively small size of the campus and the frequency of the initiatives. Fatima spoke about how the administration showed acts of administrative kindness: 'They gave us the room number ten, although they usually give it to no one. Mr. M1. pressured them for us to have the authorisations.'

Mr. M1., head of the events schedule at the university, testified:

> It's rather a good thing, it's positive, with projects like the funfair, the exam papers, the meals ... people are respectful ... but for the headscarf, some are annoyed, many, among my co-workers ... especially women [sic] ... But as long as it's not imposed, it doesn't bother me; there are girls without, girls with, it's an open-minded organisation.

He continued about the headscarf; he would have liked to have a conversation about it with the women, but his civil servant status seemed to create a limit. He pointed out the negative role of the government:

> I, myself, personally, I don't understand. People used to do it in the rural areas, but it's outdated ... I never asked them why do they wear it ... but it would be good to organise a discussion about it [sic]. But I work for the public services, I don't want to create tensions around these kind of questions ... Let's hope that the climate will change, it would need to blow up the current government.

Mr. M2., in his fifties and head of the students' life department, expressed the same open-mindedness. He appreciated the mobilisation of the organisation, but again, the headscarf raised questions:

> From an institutional point of view, I have nothing to say, nothing to complain about. First, when it comes to religion, there are Muslims and non-Muslims in Averroès. (...) Girls are a driving force for this organisation. I see more girls than men ... they organise their events, we help them once every term. There are charities we never see, there are around 80 organisations on the campus, 400 people and some lively organisations like Averroès. There is an involvement and a respect of the authority one never saw at my times (...) It's a charity which respects laws of the republic and the rules of the university. Averroès is part of the active charities at the university, which are involved in the relations with the administration. I like the little girls of Averroès very much. There are actions, such as those of the UNEF or the Students Forum, which are explicitly political, in a bad sense. But the goal of charities like Averroès is much more profound. Beyond that, I don't care about what motivates them.

Regarding the headscarf, he did not hesitate to speak his personal opinion:

> From a personal point of view, I'm shocked. I hope that when they grow up, they have a less rigorous religiosity. It's a bit like Christian extremists.

(...) However, saying this, I'm opposed to the law forbidding the headscarf. Otherwise, it's secluding a certain amount of people in their homes, in the *banlieue*, even if not everyone comes from there. At least, coming to the university, the policy is that they can have the opportunity of seeing the world. At the same time, they don't dress all in black with gloves. These are lively colours, it's nice. But it would be nicer with their hair in the wind [sic]. One can be Muslim and live their religion as they wish . . . but me personally, as some of my colleagues, I don't understand how a woman can put this on her head.

But when questioned about whether he would like to understand, he replied:

I would never dare to ask them [sic]. It would be inappropriate, she might get annoyed. But if one day there is an event about this issue, I would be interested. I would be happy to attend. Indeed, as we know each other very well, I believe they would invite me. But I could not make the first step [sic].

In continuing these testimonies, Ms. C. and Mr. L. – respectively managing the submissions for grants and resources for the students' organisations – emphasised the positive contribution of Averroès:

At the beginning, eight years ago, they were explicitly a confessional organisation with 'Muslim students' written in their statuses. They wanted an office and the university council allowed them to run for elections. But since then, the statuses have changed, there is no reference to Islam anymore and their description is ordinary. It's the only students' organisation which is independent from any political party.

Mr. L. pointed out the family spirit of the organisation: 'We often see members coming back several years after they left Averroès, whereas in other organisations (except for the Forum),[23] their presence is punctual, they go and never come back.' On the issue of the headscarf, he said:

Many colleagues are annoyed by the headscarf and comments are generally negative. But it was never an obstacle for the organisation's activities. (. . .) A debate on the matter would be difficult to set up, especially if civil servants attend.

Mr. L. was saddened that 'there is lots of ignorance among the staff'.
Listening to their reaction, Fatima said:

It's true we don't necessarily think about explaining this choice [of the headscarf]. For us, it's obvious. If someone asks the question, I would answer, but there, it's true I never thought about it [sic] [about the debate idea]. It has to be further thought.

Dialogue between Muslim volunteers and public services breaks boundaries. This is what N. Göle describes as experiencing 'contemporaneity': 'contemporaneity is not a mere chronological experience of present times, but an experience of recognition' (Göle 2005, 11). As an illustration, she compares it to the Mostar bridge in Bosnia: 'as in the reconstruction of the old Mostar bridge, it is necessary to find commonalities between ways of doing, among civilisational differences for the bridge, or the bridges, stand and link people, religions, regions and continents' (Göle 2005, 31; my translation). This encounter is a necessary condition for a plurality to exist: 'pluralism exists only from the moment when it is lived' (Amiraux 2006, 47). Interviews of the beneficiaries, public and authorities showed that perceptions of Islam and Muslims change through time and dialogue. In a few years' time, suspicious attitudes gave place to supportive ones. The main factors for this shift, found in the civil servants' interviews, were the personal and regular conversations with some key volunteers over the years. Although they might not understand religious practices fully, they saw people they knew personally getting involved for the whole community. They witnessed the support of local residents or students from all faiths and none, and all these factors combined lead to an eventual consequence: these charities became key stakeholders in their local area.

Agents of negotiation, agents of trust

The beginnings of these organisations triggered fears that they were proselytes or in the process of radicalisation. Interviews showed that after several years, the religious visibility and, generally, the religiosity of the volunteers became accepted by public services, even though it was not always understood on a personal level. Their situation evolved to the point where the city council or the authority they depended on would support them in their activities by offering resources or spaces. In the case of Averroès, there was a willingness to discuss the situation with the members in order to better understand their religiosity. However, this willingness is self-censored by nonverbal rules of *laïcité*, which tends to be interpreted as 'secularism', inducing a fear of talking about religion while a civil servant on duty. On the volunteers' end, knowing that there is a willingness for dialogue reassures them. But then, who will take the first step? The secularist policies of the government seem to carry weight in the process. These observations show the importance of face-to-face meetings and dialogue between volunteers as well as civil servants; they are able to change, even on a modest scale, their perceptions of each other about culture, differences, society or even the world. Beyond these tensions, the charities which do gather more than a few citizens have a tangible structural power (Barthélémy 2000), and this, because of their emergence in the public sphere, is in its sense an arena of conflicting meanings (Eley 1992) and a political community matrix (Laville 2010, 16). From being the 'others', Muslims slowly become part of the social landscape. The concept of Islam humanised as Islam is linked to familiar names and faces. Reciprocally for the volunteers, the State is not a vague and inaccessible concept anymore, represented only by high-level politicians or the parliament. Moreover, the charities' work is recognised as 'constructive' for the community, the town and the university by the authorities. As key stakeholders, they therefore become legitimate and build a cohesive network of supporters which serves the broader community and dampens hatred and misconceptions at a local level amidst a creeping Islamophobic climate.

As a consequence, they 'thicken' the trust between them and the authorities. Whereas formal organisations and authorities usually form weak ties with their respondents and hardly gain trust from them ('thin' or 'abstract' trust) (Misztal 1996, 72; Listhaug 1995; Dogan 1994, 306–7; Granovetter 1973), these volunteers shift the dynamic in the sense of a 'thicker trust'. Thick trust generates a mechanical solidarity which occurs in contexts of intensive and daily contacts between people (Newton 1999, 14; Williams 1988, 8). Usually observed in closed models, here the contact between volunteers and civil servants develops this form of trust in an open, but microscopic, system. Supported by the city council or other authorities, they have the power to make their voices heard and enable individuals to be part of the local political life. As a result, by negotiating their presence in the social landscape, they are negotiating on their own terms their visibility, their legitimacy and the image of Muslims in the eyes of the public. By reclaiming their own narrative and controlling the image of Muslims working for the common good, they make alienation impossible. Charities like Amatullah, JMF or Averroès are perceived by their beneficiaries and their surroundings (their neighbourhoods) as alternatives to politics which are unable to respond to the needs of deprived citizens. It was observed by Boddie and Cnaan (2006, 288) in their study around faith-based services in the United States that

> caregivers relying on faith happen to be often closer to their neighbourhood than public services (. . .) and their beneficiaries, independently from their true progress, prefer social workers relying on faith and see them as more helpful and concerned compared to public services.

The sustained presence of these initiatives and the dialogue of their members withers suspicion and fear through these three steps: de-alienation, reconnaissance and, eventually, empowerment.

One limitation of these findings is that the situation is different from one country to another. In France, for example, these dynamics are facilitated by the fact that most legal procedures require a face-to-face meeting with the authorities (requesting a venue at the university, organising public events in the town) which manage venues, approve communication and control security policies. Opportunities for dialogue therefore arise spontaneously, which might not be the case in London, where little-to-no face-to-face interactions with the authorities are required. On the other hand, even in France, this does not provide opportunities for different faith groups or organisations to meet. Also, these charities are not free of some obstacles; recent events and the change of administration in the city council can have an effect, as in the case of JMF, which was denied state funds in 2015 because of the fear awoken after the Charlie Hebdo attacks.

The action of French and Polish Muslim charities also raises the question of proselytisation. As the interviews above relate, one of the main suspicions of the

French government about local Muslim charities was that the organisations have a 'hidden agenda' and use their activities as a cover to secretly attract people to Islam. In Islam, the concept of *da'wa* (propagation of the values of Islam) has different interpretations. The charities studied here are not *da'wa* organisations and have no explicit goal of conveying the message of Islam or bringing new people to the faith. However, many volunteers are aware that their actions could be a form of implicit *da'wa*, in the sense that their visibility as Muslims might cause the public to build their perception of Islam and Muslims according to what they have seen while observing the charities' activities. One female volunteer said: 'I got involved because the perception of Muslim women in society wasn't right. Women are not shown enough'. Many are aware of the poor opinion of Islam in the media and the government. While changing mind-sets is not their primary goal, it provides more reasons for some volunteers to get involved. However, most of these grassroots charities do not invest massively in communication. At the time of this research, none of them had recently updated websites or Facebook pages or many followers on social media, although they showed huge numbers of supporters in 'real life'. They are the polar opposite of mainstream, explicit-*da'wa* organisations such as IERA[24] in the UK or others, for which communication is a priority. Relying mainly on word of mouth, Amatullah, Averroès and JMF focus on the quality of the services they provide within the limits of their local area.

The cohesive environment and sustained dialogue between charities and authorities enables a humanisation of Muslims and Islam, which are therefore seen as partners rather than as an abstract and threatening entity. By contributing to society at a local level on mainstream issues, grassroots Muslim charities remove lexical constructions based on binary distinctions between cultures, ethnicity or religion such as 'Muslims/non-Muslims' or 'Them/Us'; rather, these organisations help consider society as a wider 'Us'. Tackling poverty and lack of education in deprived areas in France made their presence a legitimate one for public services, rather than a threat to security, as observed in the first decade of the century. In Poland, their extreme minority situation causes Muslims to adopt extrovert behaviour and focus on a dialogue with wider Polish society. Also, a climate of respect is underpinned by a government that officially recognises Islam as part of the Polish culture and people who, on average, have an open-minded approach to cultural and religious differences. There is probably no straight answer as to how to curb hatred and islamophobia, but these charities provide a unique yet efficient way to install sustainable dialogue and understanding between Muslims, citizens of different generations, all faiths and none and the authorities, thus producing a harmonious and therefore attractive social environment, as will be demonstrated in Chapter 4.

Notes

1 This chapter contains sections adapted from a previously published work: Barylo, W. (2016). Muslim Charities in Europe: Redefining a Positive Image of Islam in the Public Sphere at a Grassroots Level. The Case of France and Poland. In: Suleiman, Y. and Anderson, P. (eds.) *Muslims in the UK and Europe II*. Cambridge: Centre of Islamic Studies, pp. 114–28.

2 IMAN: Islamophobia Monitoring and Action Network. http://iman-project.org/about-iman/background/ [last accessed on 15 Jan. 2017].
3 Amnesty International Report (2012). *Choice and Prejudice: Discrimination Against Muslims in Europe.* London: Amnesty International.
4 Open Society Foundations Report (2011). *Les Parisiens Musulmans. At Home in Europe project.* London: Open Society Foundations.
5 United Nations Centre for Civil and Political Rights. Session 102, Communication no 1876/2009 released on 27 September 2011. Pacte international relative aux droits civils et politiques.
6 IFOP Poll for LeFigaro (October 2012). *L'image de l'Islam en France.*
7 IFOP Poll (23 March 2013). Les Français et le port du voile ou du foulard islamique par des employées de lieux privés accueillant du public
8 Göle, N. (17 November 2013). *European Public Islam seminar*, EHESS, Paris.
9 For CCIF see: www.noussommeslanation.fr/. For the Islamophobia Awareness Month see: http://iamonth.org/ [last accessed on 15 Jan. 2017].
10 Multiple authors. Contre une loi stigmatisante, pour une commission sur l'islamophobie. www.change.org/fr/p%C3%A9titions/contre-une-loi-stigmatisante-pour-une-commission-sur-l-islamophobie [last accessed on 15 Jan. 2017]; Baubérot, J. (29 mars 2013). Ne stigmatisons pas les musulmans! *Le Monde*, n° 21210, 20.
11 Hammarberg, T. (28 October 2010). *Le discours populiste stigmatise les musulmans européens.* Commissioner for Human Rights, Council of Europe. http://commissioner.cws.coe.int/tiki-view_blog.php?blogId=2&bl=y&offset=30 [last accessed on 01 July 2013].
12 Gresh, A. (26 October 2012). *Cette lancinante 'menace islamique.'* Blogs le monde diplomatique.
13 Human Rights Watch. France : Abus commis dans le cadre de l'état d'urgence. www.hrw.org/fr/news/2016/02/03/france-abus-commis-dans-le-cadre-de-letat-durgence [last accessed on 15 Jan. 2017].
14 Amnesty International. Des vies bouleversées » L'impact disproportionné de l'état d'urgence en France. www.amnesty.fr/sites/default/files/eur2133642016french_final.pdf [last accessed on 15 Jan. 2017].
15 Author's interview (Mayor's assistants of Bagnolet and La Courneuve), La Courneuve, Bagnolet, 2012.
16 Author's interview (K. Pędziwiatr), Cracow, 6 December 2012.
17 Author's interview (K. Górak-Sosnowska), Warsaw, 5 December 2012.
18 Author's interviews (various people in 2012), *Polish Muslims: An Unexpected Meeting* 2013 film documentary, Paris: Light Inc.
19 K. Pędziwiatr, presentation on the 28 January 2017 at the East London Mosque.
20 Górak-Sosnowska, K. (23 January 2006). Platoniczna islamofobia? *Arabia.pl*, www.arabia.pl/content/view/282077/2/[last accessed on 01 July 2013].
21 Author interview (K. Pędziwiatr), Cracow, 6 December 2012.
22 Róże Miłości www.youtube.com/watch?v=Y56UOekhXDY [last accessed on 15 Jan. 2017].
23 Students' organisation with a Jewish background.
24 Islamic Education and Research Academy

References

Amer, M. (2005). *Arab American Mental Health in the Post September 11 Era: Acculturation, Stress, and Coping.* Theses and Dissertations No. 1403. Toledo: University of Toledo.

Amiraux, V. (2006). Speaking as a Muslim: Avoiding Religion in French Public Space. In: Jonker, G. and Amiraux, V. (eds.) *Politics of Visibility: Young Muslims in European Public Spaces.* Bielefeld: Transcript Verlag, pp. 21–52.

Barthélemy, M. (2000). *Associations: Un Nouvel Âge de la Participation?* [*Charities: A New Age of Participation?*]. Paris: Presses de Sciences Po.

Baubérot, J. (2006). *L'Intégrisme Républicain contre la Laïcité* [*The Republican Fundamentalism Against Secularism*]. Paris: L'Aube.

Boddie, S. C. and Cnaan, R. A. (2006). *Faith-Based Services*. New York: Howarth Pastoral Press.

Chakraborty, A. and McKenzie, K. (2002). Does Racial Discrimination Cause Mental Illness? *The British Journal of Psychiatry*, 180(6), 475–7.

Conway, G. (1997). *Islamophobia: A Challenge for Us All; Report of the Runnymede Trust Commission on British Muslims and Islamophobia*. London: The Runnymeade Trust.

Davids, M. F. (2011). *Internal Racism: A Psychoanalytic Approach to Race and Difference*. London: Palgrave Macmillan.

Dogan, M. (1994). The Pendulum Between Theory and Substance: Testing the Concepts of Legitimacy and Trust. In: Dogan, D. and Kazancigil, A. (eds.) *Comparing Nations: Concepts, Strategies, Substance*. Oxford: Blackwell, pp. 297–313.

Eley, G. (1992). Nations, Publics and Political Cultures: Placing Habermas in the Nineteenth Century. In: Calhoun, C. (ed.) *Habermas and the Public Sphere*. Cambridge and London: MIT Press, pp. 289–339.

Gest, J. (2010). *Apart: Alienated and Engaged Muslims in the West*. London: Hurst.

Göle, N. (2005). *Interpénétrations. L'Islam et l'Europe* [*Interpenetrations: Islam and Europe*]. Paris: Galaade.

Granovetter, M. S. (1973). The Strength of Weak Ties. *American Journal of Sociology*, 78(60), 1360–80.

Hajjat, A. and Mohammed, M. (2013). *Islamophobie: Comment les élites françaises fabriquent le "problème musulman"* [*Islamophobia: How French Elites Fabricate the 'Muslim Problem'*]. Paris: La Découverte.

hooks, b. (1992). Eating the Other: Desire and Resistance. *Black Looks: Race and Representation*. Boston: South End Press, pp. 21–39.

hooks, b. (2003). *Teaching Community: A Pedagogy of Hope*. Hove: Psychology Press.

Laville, J-L. (2010). *Politique de l'association* [*The Politics of Charities*]. Paris: Seuil.

Liogier, R. (2015). Interview by Marion Dautry and Pauline Verduzier. "Riposte laïque: 'On est dans du racisme culturel.'" *Journal Du Dimanche*, June 25. www.lejdd.fr/Politique/Riposte-laique-On-est-dans-du-racisme-culturel-739328 [last accessed on 15 Jan. 2017].

Listhaug, O. (1995). The Dynamics of Trust in Politicians. In: Klingemann, H-D. and Fuchs, D. (eds.) *Citizens and the State*. Oxford, Oxford University Press, pp. 261–97.

Meer, N., Dwyer, C. and Modood, T. (2010). Beyond "Angry Muslims"? Reporting Muslim Voices in the British Press. *Journal of Media and Religion*, 9(4), 216–31.

Mehmood, M. (2015). The Role of Self-Esteem in Understanding Anti-Semitic and Islamophobic Prejudice. In: Suleiman, Y. (ed.) *Muslims in the UK and Europe*. Cambridge: Centre of Islamic Studies, pp. 150–8.

Misztal, B. (1996). *Trust in Modern societies: The Search for the Bases of Social Order*. Oxford: Blackwell.

Newton, K. (1999). Social Capital and Democracy in Modern Europe. In: Van Deth, J. W., Maraffi, M., Newton, K. and Whiteley, P. F. (eds.) *Social Capital and European Democracy*. London: Routledge, pp. 3–24.

Williams, B. (1988). Formal Structures and Social Reality. In: Gambetta, D. (ed.) *Trust: Making and Breaking Cooperative Relations*. Oxford: Blackwell, pp. 3–13.

4   The attractive middle way

For a long time, Fatima A. was the only Muslim girl at school – until she reached 19. Her parents, from a Moroccan background, were the only Muslims in her home town, somewhere in the South of France. Her parents never imposed any practice of Islam on her and, according to her, they had a more 'cultural' than religious vision of Islam. When she went to Paris to prepare for her Bachelor's in Physics, she told me: 'I never lived with Islam, I learnt more during one year in Paris than during eighteen years in the South.' She joined Averroès because she wanted to join a charity managed by Muslims. She was amazed at seeing volunteers wearing the *hijab*; the year I interviewed her was also the year she decided to wear it. However, she was hesitant at first. The reason was that she felt uncomfortable working in an environment where men and women were working together:

> I asked myself if I should go because of the gender diversity, but in the end, it's not a problem for me. Sheikh Qaradawi's opinion states that from the moment there is a frame and hearts are sincere, there is no problem.

A similar experience occurred for Fatima C.:

> For me too, [gender] diversity was a problem in the beginning, but Wissam [chief executive at the time] explained to me the conditions, the different opinions and I agreed; what matters are the rules in the organisation, which I try to apply and sincerity of the heart.

Samia, another volunteer, tried to make sense of this:

> Men and women are mixed in the streets, in shopping malls, in the workplace. . . . So why all of a sudden should it be different within the charity? Even in Mecca around the Kaaba, men and women pray together. . . . So why not even in the mosque?

Although some cultural traditions have made it a norm to avoid gender mixing, these interviewees managed to change their minds and opinions after consulting friends or religious authorities.

Chapter 3 offered an analysis of how meeting face-to-face with the public and authorities can break down barriers, annihilate prejudices and eventually build a sustainable and harmonious social environment on the scale of a neighbourhood, town or university. First, Islam as a shared reference is a medium which helps to strengthen trust in a social network by mixing people from various religious opinions and different levels of orthopraxy. They are safe social spaces buzzing with different (and sometimes clashing) ideas, which eventually come to a middle way shared by everyone. Second, these organisations offer a major outcome which builds one's identity through action: doing works beneficial for the whole community, experiencing responsibility, accountability and travels and sometimes living life-changing experiences make volunteers reflect on their own lives. The last section of this chapter explains how and why these structures, due to their modes of governance, scale and work environment, are more attractive to young Muslim volunteers than other types of organisations. As a result, the informal governance and the family-like environment make a cohesive environment that appeals to volunteers of all faiths and none, enabling the building of remarkable social capital.

Charities as convivial social capital power plants

The study of these small charities cannot be separated from the analysis of the role of Islam as a social environment comprising shared symbols and references (see Chapter 1). Here Islam acts as a medium helping to build social capital. Islam is an attractive factor for potential Muslim volunteers who are looking to get involved in an environment which can contribute to their spiritual growth. These organisations are also attractive because these are safe spaces in which volunteers will not be judged for their appearance, clothing or beliefs and in which they are safe from the discrimination and abuse many experience in daily life. References to Islam are present in every aspect of the volunteer's life through time, space, discourse and action: it is a system that binds people, objects, ideas, time and space. A charity's name is often inspired from elements around the Muslim cultural universe: it might contain the name of a scholar or a philosopher (Averroès) or an Arabic name . . . or it might just contain the word 'Islam' or 'Muslim', as in *Jeunes Musulmans de France*. Foul Express chose the name of a common meal, 'ful' – a basic food easily available in Egypt – as both a symbol for an easily accessible content and an explicit link to the diasporic roots of its contributors.

On the premises of charities such as Averroès, Amatullah, Rumi's Cave and others, one can find elements such as the Qur'an, Islamic philosophy books, pictures of the Kaaba, poems, calligraphies, surates framed under glass and hanging on the walls and also some *hadith*: 'Please leave the premises clean and tidy, cleanliness is part of faith.' The premises are also the spaces where people gather to pray or to break fast during Ramadan. For some of the most dedicated volunteers, it is also the space where some spend their nights working, especially before exams (at Averroès) or important events. Most of the premises are close to a mosque, which becomes a hub where people gather and sometimes attend religious discussions or Arabic language courses (Averroès, Amatullah, Rumi's Cave, Muslim

Hands France, JMF, MADE). Islam is also present in discourse through expressions such as *inshaAllah, alhamdulillah, MashaAllah* ... Sometimes, the presence of these elements is such that some leaders insist on their use, like Shamsuddine: 'I have insisted for Islam to be more present at JMF, people should not be afraid to say *Salaam Alaykum.*' This is also the case for Stephane – part of the alternative media Foul Express – who would not imagine writing an article without writing '*inshaAllah*'. In addition, diverse clothing styles sometimes comprise *hijabs* and *qamises* (long robes worn by men) of various colours.

These spaces are intimately connected to common times: prayer times, breaking of the fast, common lunch breaks, common working sessions and team meetings. Sometimes, when the *adhan* (call to prayer) rings on the phone of a volunteer, a meeting can be interrupted or ended for prayer; sometimes the *adhan* is a rhetorical device used for urging the team to make a decision before the prayer time or to close a discussion. These interferences are not disturbances, but are part of daily life. At Amatullah's and Islamic Relief, volunteers gather in a circle before and after every outreach session. This moment is used to give and listen to feedback from everyone, without any sense of hierarchy, and to welcome newcomers. Whether volunteers are Muslim or not, the circle is used to convey spiritual reminders, especially when it is close to some religious event (*Hajj, Eid* . . .). As a result, these opportunities contribute towards building a solid social network and, furthermore, create bonds of trust between volunteers.

Connections are often made between terrestrial action and the afterlife: Julien titled his guidelines handbook for outreach volunteers 'Manual for the *Hassanate* collector' (*hassanates* meaning rewards for good deeds in the Islamic tradition). In Amatullah's rules for soup kitchens, volunteers are encouraged to smile because smiling is a *sadaqa*, an act of worship in Islam. People settle arguments by reminding each other that they are brothers and sisters in faith. Volunteers often participate in other charities with Islamic ethics working on social issues. People consult *shouyoukh* (Islamic scholars) when making important decisions, such as at Foul Express. Entertainment also breaks with usual trends: while other charities at the university use loud music and alcohol, Averroès, like most Muslim charities included in this work, prefers to organise open-air lunches (see Figure 4.1), video game challenges or quiz events. The symbolic capital of the charities contributes to an environment of familiarity where volunteers can express ideas or display behaviours without the fear of being judged (as opposed to the 'outside world'): these are 'safe spaces'. These spaces also stimulate the reflection of some on the way they express their Muslim identity and values, such as with the *hijab*.

For Fatima at Amatullah, the charity is a time and space for religious development: 'The charity strengthens my faith with the community. For the *hijab*, it was a turning point in the charity, one year ago. In fact, the charity is the continuity of the mosque.' In her journey, the charity environment led her to reflect about her own practice of Islam and eventually made her decide to wear the *hijab*. Seeing other volunteers comfortable with their outfits, many realise that it is possible to live,

Figure 4.1 Eid picnic in Regent's Park, London

work and socialise while wearing the *hijab*, although for most volunteers this decision is a long-term personal process independent from the charity environment.

In a certain way, joining a charity is also a way of rediscovering a personal balance, as for Fatima A., who, after two years of preparatory courses with 'psychological pressure, loneliness and the impossibility to wear the headscarf', was happy to find an environment in which she felt surrounded by a family and accepted with the headscarf. She was especially looking for a Muslim charity to reconnect herself with Islam, something she had been unable to do at a younger age: 'My family lives in a town where they are the only Muslims, they didn't want to draw attention; I had to learn everything by myself.' Joining a charity was, for her, 'coming back to the roots'. Her journey was similar to Wissam's:

> I was the only Muslim in my classroom and our only source of knowledge was my mother. (. . .) When I was studying at Centrale [an engineering school], my cousin told me about Averroès and their tuition services. What struck me was to see sisters wearing the *hijab* and when one comes in, people say '*Salaam Alaykum.*'

Both Fatima and Wissam found an environment they had not known before. For Jean Fateh too, environment was important: 'I like to find an atmosphere where Islam is present.' For Intissar, joining Foul Express was a first, for him 'to see something else than work, meet new like-minded people'. For Farida, working at Muslim Hands, she found in the charity a space safe from racism:

> When I came to France, I started studying at the Sorbonne University. It was in 1989, the same year as the first headscarf issue. Once, people insulted me and spat on me, in the middle of Paris. I was shocked.

For Marwan, as for many others, being in a charity is 'being in a family'; many at Foul Express are single, work for companies and live away from their parents. This is also the case in London for people around Rumi's Cave: many are students or workers from abroad, away from their families and in search of a hub where they can reconnect to a familiar atmosphere which gives them a sense of community.

Among volunteers, there is a huge diversity of religious schools of thought and orthopraxies. Volunteers detached from ritual practice easily meet some others with a more literal understanding of the texts. As many follow religious classes in training centres such as CERSI[1] or IESH,[2] people compare different religious arguments and interpretations or personally search on the Internet for talks, papers or books from religious scholars. They discuss with each other, for example, what they have seen in their parents' countries:

> In Morocco, when they slaughter a sheep, they put their hand in the blood and leave a mark on the house. Apparently it's a protection or for bringing good luck.
>
> • But that's disgusting [sic].
>
> I know, but is it permissible or not, in Islam?

These exchanges also become possible because of the trust shared between volunteers in the environment of a safe space. The charity becomes a hub buzzing with different, if not divergent, opinions and ideas, and volunteers need to pick a side and build their own understanding of Islam. As a result, after some months or years, many volunteers do adjust: those not practising may end up wearing the *hijab* and praying, whereas those with a more stringent understanding may gain some flexibility.

Because music has been a long-time taboo in some dominating interpretations, Sheikh Ahmed Babikir set up Rumi's Cave in London, a religious space that allows Muslim musicians to perform. Umar commented that 'it's impossible to practise at home because of family and the only places you had open mics were the pubs'. With the help of the opinions of renowned Muslim scholars such as Sheikh Hamza Yusuf, music (which can be a devotional practice) has eventually gained consensually some legitimacy in the Muslim sphere, to the point that Muslim charity fundraisers now often feature singers and musicians. Consensus also manages divergent opinions, as for Shamsuddine, chief executive of Amatullah, when a young woman came dressed in a sleeveless shirt:

> A brother came to me saying that it's unacceptable, that we should send her back home or do something. I decided not to do anything and wait. I told him: 'you will see, she will realise about the environment, she will adjust by herself.' Indeed, the next time she came, she was wearing a more respectful outfit. People say that I'm laxist or that I tolerate things too much . . . but I focus my pedagogy for me not to hurt people . . . it's very easy to break people down.

Shamsuddine said he had taken this example from the Prophet Muhammad and the way he reacted when a man urinated in the mosque.[3] His choice of letting the young woman wear her outfit and realise by herself the general trend shows an empathic approach aware of human feelings. This empathic approach is characteristic of what French sociologist Alain Caillé describes as a convivial society (Caillé 2011a and 2011b), in which 'people work together and take care of each other' (Humbert 2011, 129).

These elements help to build a network of volunteers with various levels of orthopraxy, but also appear to be attractive to non-Muslims. Antoine, 26 and atheist, was invited by a friend to meet and talk to homeless people for the first time during an outreach with Amatullah: 'I found reality difficult, it's hard to meet the people I was cleaning and sanitising the camps [Antoine works as manager for the city council's cleaning team.' He assessed his experience as 'positive': 'The volunteers are really nice, we talked about football, films, it was really pleasant.' Océane, 24, is not Muslim but has chosen to do an internship at Amatullah for her studies: 'There is no problem doing my internship in a Muslim charity. The atmosphere is more humane. I have lots of Muslim friends and the most important for me is that we gather around a common cause.' Béatrice, 23, wanted to pursue her studies with a master's degree in humanitarian action and work in the charity sector: 'I have chosen Muslim Hands because I didn't want an environment with pressure. Here we can talk about all sorts of things, and have deep conversations, it's different to other [non-Muslims] charities.' When the time comes for celebrations such as Eid or Ramadan, volunteers share not only scriptural points of view, but also explain the personal meaning they give to these rituals. In charities like Amatullah or Islamic Relief, where outreaches once gathered people in a circle for performing invocations, now these are explained to non-Muslims, who are also invited to participate. Julien, who was on one of the managing teams at Islamic Relief, explained each time to everyone:

> We will be performing *du'as*, which are invocations, this is something we do before every outreach; we usually ask God for forgiveness, for strength, for love . . . but even if you're not Muslim, you can say anything if you want, share a thought, make a wish or anything, in any language you want.

Julien, who embraced Islam a few years back, translated the concept of *du'a* in a way to which non-Muslims can relate: a prayer to God becomes a wish or sharing of thoughts, which are exactly the purpose of the *du'a*, but without the transcendental dimension of religious invocations.

Working with people of all faiths and none is quite common for these small scale organisations. One major example is the case of Alajkumki in Poland. Their starting point was the fact that many young Polish women embracing Islam were living alone in some remote cities far away from any physical Muslim community and with little knowledge of Islam, and were often rejected by their families. Aware of the hatred and abuse from the authorities in Western Europe, Alejkumki realised that their main challenge was, beyond supporting these women, to prevent discourses of hate and stereotypes in Poland, where the Polish Muslim community is still small and almost invisible. All year round, they organise round tables, conferences and open days, invite religious leaders, politicians and media and reach out to the public with events such as *Róże Miłości* (roses of love), where they offer red roses to people passing on the streets, along with a short biography of the prophet of Islam. This initiative inspired a group of French women to do the same in 2013 on the Champs Elysées in Paris. Rumi's Cave often invites artists such as poets, storytellers, spoken word artists and calligraphers from other faith backgrounds (Christian, Sikh, Jewish, Rastafari, etc.) to perform or share their knowledge. Faiz recalled the first time a group of Rastafari percussionists came to the Cave: 'At the beginning, they were looking strangely at us, they didn't know if they would fit, they were feeling uncomfortable, but when they started to play, they saw people were enjoying it and they went full on.'

These charities provide a solid social network, a 'new family', develop bonds of trusts and facilitate coordinated actions with tangible outcomes, three elements which contribute by definition to the building of a strong social capital (Newton 1999; Putnam 1993), as also observed by Amath (2015) and Pędziwiatr (2010). These micro-societies, by their emphasis on human relations, relations with the environment or wider society and wanton acts of kindness, are characteristic of convivial societies (Caillé 2011a and 2011b; Humbert 2011). This very conviviality, because of the logic of gratuity, is one of the main reasons – according to Alain Caillé (2011b, 151) – why they are so 'important' and 'socially efficient'. This environment is characterised by a 'thick' type of trust (Newton 1999, 14; Williams 1988). This enables a strong solidarity between subjects specific to social structures, with intensive and regular face-to-face contact and empathic behaviour, which French sociologists also describe as part of 'conviviality' (Caillé 2011a; Humbert 2011). This social capital contributes to the spiritual development of volunteers, the building of their identity (Vermeersch 2004; Canda and Furman 2010; Dubet 1994) and a longer lived engagement (Newton 1999, 4–5). Social capital becomes the functional equivalent of fraternity (Newton 1999, 5). As a result of this thick trust, the opinions of everyone are valued by each other and, thus, the mixing, confrontation or discussion of different or divergent opinions leads to the adoption of consensual religious interpretations and mind-sets in the sense of social harmony. Lichterman (2005, 256) observed, through Christian American charities, that 'the style of the group influences what people can believe, say and do together'. As this section showed how these Muslim charities build their social capital by providing a strong social network and trust, the following sections will focus on other components of social capital, especially outcomes and effectiveness, as reasons for their attractiveness.

Building identity, giving a meaning to life

Getting involved in a charity responds to volunteers' expectations in various ways which will be discussed in this section. First, charitable action gives these young people the opportunity to spend their time in a useful, meaningful way. Second, while offering activities different from the daily routine, they are means through which to find a balance in life. Third, volunteers realise that they can tackle social problems with their own hands; they feel a sense of responsibility and empowerment. Finally, meeting different people living in different conditions, or travelling abroad, happen to be life-changing experiences which have a strong potential to determine the volunteers' future decisions and ways of life.

The need for spending their time in a useful manner, like being helpful to others, is a sufficient reason for many to get involved, as for Mohamed, who was working as an engineer and studying at the same time. He was at the same time the vice–chief executive of Amatullah: 'I wanted to make my time useful for the others, but I didn't know how.' Amira did not have a precise idea: 'I don't have a set goal in my life, but I know that I want to help orphans'; joining Amatullah was for her a step in that sense. Fatima A. was looking for a charity as a way to pursue her spiritual journey, similarly to Najah, who says: 'I believe my faith led me to get involved, but also to reach out to others.' Fatima A. recalls how reading books pushed her to get involved: 'I read Iqbal and it made me want to live my life with faith as its matrix. It's the same idea I found with Tariq Ramadan.' The quest for action can also be fuelled by concerns on a wider scale, as said Abdullah or Samia, 'for showing a better image of Muslims'. For the volunteers who embraced Islam, joining a charity was a way to live their spirituality more intensely. Max, who embraced Islam a few weeks before joining Amatullah, 'wished to experience the charity sector'. This was also the case for Jennyfer, who had not been involved in any charity before embracing Islam but who since had 'gravitated around some charities' before finding Foul Express; she also got involved in a spoken word collective and in her local mosque. Ayoub presented a very rational decision: 'I wanted to join a humanitarian organisation because it was part of the list of things I wanted to do in my life. I was looking for meaning since high school thanks to philosophy lessons.' Some others joined to satisfy a personal need; Nooruldine spoke about his 'obsessional' commitment, the need to feel 'gratitude and love from others'; similarly, Samia A. wanted to 'feel alive and finally human, feel that others need me. It may seem selfish, but I know that it's part of who I am, that this need present since a long time, only starts to bloom.' For others, joining the charity sector responds to the quest for concrete, immediate action, delivering a tangible outcome.

74 *The attractive middle way*

Beyond any affinity for action, some are looking for results, or to make a tangible difference for themselves or others. This was Muntasser's journey; he had long wanted to be an 'actor and not [a] viewer'. He left the corporate sector to work as a freelancer and joined Muslim Hands as a volunteer. For many, as for Muntasser, the corporate sector does not fit their expectations or ethics. This was also the case for Marwan, who left his job as a trader. In addition to an absence of trust in politicians, the charity sector has a double function: it deals with problems the government does not solve, such as meals for homeless people (see Figure 4.2). This action is direct and concrete: people work with their hands and the outcome is immediate. As Sarfaraz from Amatullah said, 'this is real politics'. For Shemseddine, it was rather life experiences which led him to reflect upon getting involved: 'On my end, I grew up in the middle of people involved, drug problems, rivalries, mediation.' The social problems in his neighbourhood pushed him to get involved in JMF with the aim of changing young people's lives in his local area.

Social participation of Muslims does not fit a predetermined model or pattern (Barise 2005). The first weeks in a charity are an opportunity for new, various and rich life experiences: meeting new colleagues, living in a new environment, new activities and a new pace in life. These are times when volunteers are usually highly involved and motivated. This phase can range from a few weeks to a few months, during which volunteers regularly attend activities and actively participate. As Abdallah recalled, these are times when volunteers learn and receive a lot: 'We give, but truly speaking, it's us who receive. It's an incredible life lesson. (. . .) In fact, the meal is just an accessory.' The more action the charity has to

Figure 4.2 Young volunteers during a soup kitchen of Amatullah in Bagnolet

offer, the more the subject is motivated and able to manage multiple tasks. Musa, for example, was already working in two paid jobs, studying at the university and was chief executive of Averroès at the same time. Also, generally, the more volunteers are involved in the charity, the more they practise the rituals of Islam, such as supererogatory prayers or fasts. Encounters, dialogue and exchanges with colleagues and beneficiaries are new experiences that allow for some to explain their point of view to others, discussing ideas and confronting one's prejudices with reality. Abdullah from Averroès never participated to a soup kitchen, but then decided to try one at Amatullah. It was the first time he had met homeless people: 'I didn't know homeless people were nice and smiling people . . . I see the person smiling after I talked to him, I realise how important it is to help others.' Many volunteers, like Abdullah, realise the importance of religious concepts through social action. Therefore, social action as a religious practice makes religious knowledge less abstract.

However, often most experiences, like meeting the homeless, are disturbing or shocking, especially if it is the first time. It fuels a quasi-continuous process of questioning, as was the case for Samia: 'My questioning got intensified within the charity. I discover many things and then I ask myself even more questions, I need answers.' Through this phase of intense activity, experiences and questioning, they realise they are building their persona and identity, as was the case for Wissam: 'Everyday situations are illuminating and make me gain maturity.' Joining the charity is in itself a shock or an 'eye-opener'. In all cases, volunteers are on a journey in which they link values, education and memories (as seen above) to direct implementation. These psychologically impactful events leave a mark in the mind and are often turning points in one's life. The common key for all these experiences is the phase of personal, if not intimate, self-questioning about, as Marwan said, one's role in the world or one's aim in life. This phase of reflection allows the person to redefine one's priorities and to build or rebuild one's perception of self, life and society. In the aftermath of this process, the person can define volunteering as a way of life.

Mohamed recalled how charitable works allowed him to change his perspectives on life. Seeing deprived people who graduated once but lost everything from one day to another allowed him to redefine his priorities in life: 'I went through a phase of self-questioning, thanks to lessons, sermons and testimonies. I realised that diplomas guarantee nothing. (. . .) At the beginning, I was doing things for the others, no it's only for Allah.' Therefore, volunteers rebuild their perception of self, of society or the world. They make a compromise between 'inherited' and 'aimed' identities (Dubar 1998, 257). This phase of personal redefinitions is fundamental to the identity building of the volunteers, according to S. Vermeersch (2004, 682; my translation): 'They are more active towards their own experience, which they have to redefine on their own and more critical, in the sense that it is for them to make sense of this experience.' The charity environment gives volunteers the opportunity to build their own subjectivity and work on their own identity (Dubet 1994). Identity therefore 'emerges in the confrontation of the identification of self and the identification by the others, the latter allow[ed] to confront or adjust the identification of self' (Vermeersch 2004, 685; my translation). This building of identity through action is opposed to the apophatic identity which emerges when passive actors only filter the labels stuck to them by external factors (media, political discourses; see Chapter 3). Getting involved in a charity 'challenges the *status quo*' and triggers changes 'within the self, within relations and in social and structural conditions' (Canda and Furman 2010, 314–15), making it a 'transforming practice' (Canda and Furman 2010, 314–15). This same process allows the volunteers to build their own understanding of citizenship and their role in a society:

> according to their personal and familial trajectory, the future perspectives offered to them, their modes of insertion in the society and the perception of it, they fathom differently their role as citizens and create for themselves their own possibilities of belonging to a collective and practice citizenship differently.
>
> (Venel 2002, 274)

Most of these new experiences are multiple and intense and happen in a relatively short time. Getting involved in a charity allows an individual to some extent to renew, demolish and then rebuild relations with others and one's spirituality. Everything is questioned, analysed and redefined in a way such that a new 'self' and 'collective' identity emerge. In this sense, by reconstructing their identity through experience, they are building their identity through a quasi-phenomenological process, in Husserl's sense (1982 [1960], 2). All these experiences show the importance of experiencing the 'otherness' for social cohesion between structures and within them. The charity experience builds in the volunteers' mind parts of what Stéphanie Vermeersch defines as an 'array of values':

> it is in that direction that we have synthesised love, fraternity or humanity with the concept of humanism and the different figures getting involved in the life of the city, by the one of citizenship. Humanism and citizenship are two different arrays that the volunteers have in common, in which they will take, but in which everyone makes a choice according to what they believe is their personal conception of the meaning of their action.
>
> (Vermeersch 2004, 693)

Building their identity in relation to others as in charities, they thus realise the universe of possibilities and ways to act at their level and then become an 'actor of change' (Canda and Furman 2010, 314). Volunteers and their respective charities are in a relationship of inter-construction, the realisation of individuality (Chanial 2011, 124).

The outcome of bringing together people from different cultures, socio-economic conditions or ideas is a concept well understood by Issa, a civil servant in a small town. He used to bring youth from deprived areas to Senegal or Morocco for them to dig wells and build schools and libraries. He observed that making these young people responsible for a collective project had a huge impact on the young volunteers, allowed them to feel more self-confident and build their identity and their vision of the world, and acted as a vaccine against getting involved in crime. The charity allows individuals to find a balance when volunteers lack cultural references, look for a sense of family or community, try to answer questions about their identities, or simply spend their time doing good deeds rather than work for a corporation which seems sometimes nonsensical to them. The shared references to Islam, the informal governance and the family-like environment are attractive for many. These charities provide even more than a safe environment: they happen to be social spaces buzzing with ideas, which are unique opportunities to confront or discuss different points of view and eventually encourage balanced opinions to consensually emerge. Experience of otherness changes individuals and groups. From a wider perspective, it transforms the society and gives new meaning to the key concepts of citizenship, governance and democracy through a renewed experience of political participation. These changes also operate due to other particular characteristics of these charities, which will be discussed in the following section of this chapter.

Different, efficient and therefore attractive

Most initiatives in this study start from the observation that, at a local level, government institutions do not solve problems such as homelessness, students in financial difficulty or precarious school support for high schools. Most volunteers do not trust the government to solve these problems and appear to be rather critical towards politicians who generally view greater religiosity in a person as a more major problem than poverty (see Chapter 5). Because modern but 'immodest' governments and institutions are failing its citizens by not affording them space in which to manoeuvre (Crozier 1987), these charities seem to take over the baton from political parties that have turned into 'electoral agencies' and do 'not [represent] social movements anymore' (Touraine 1992, 483), that represent a democracy standing still. Cefaï (2007, 424) explains that one of the key factors of the attractiveness of charities comes from their simplicity and not being overly bureaucratic:

> There is a displacement of citizens' motivations and expectations towards new types of public participation. More flexible and less unmovable, they take place in charities and networks rather than in bureaucratic, centralised and hierarchised structures.

While traditional structures are characteristically large, slow and bureaucratic, these smaller charities can be fast, effective and informal. Assessing the impact of this flexibility on volunteers, the outreach of Amatullah has been compared to larger charities performing the same activities, such as Islamic Relief France. Samia, a 32-year-old woman working at an insurance company and part of the core team of Foul Express, wanted to volunteer at Amatullah to serve meals to the homeless: 'You know that they serve soup kitchens on this and this day. You just have to come, they give you gloves and a high-visibility jacket, tell you what to do and that's it. It's very simple.'

But when she wanted to try the same experience at Islamic Relief, she recalled a different experience:

> I went to see them during my lunch break from 11 A.M. to 2 P.M. I had to book an appointment, I came, I had to fill lots of forms, my ID card and even my CV, and then no answer for weeks. I tried to call them, but no answer. I couldn't believe I even had to hand them my CV [sic].

When one wishes to volunteer with Islamic Relief France, it is not rare to wait for several weeks or months before being brought on a 'test outreach', only to then wait up to several weeks between each outreach, depending on the schedule. Anna also compared her experience at Amatullah with Popular Relief, another major NGO (but not a faith-based one):

> We were receiving notices by email, that there was an event at this time and place and we were just going. People often look at the time, they are fond of procedures . . . I find Amatullah more humane: everyone knows each other, there is no need for authorisations, one can come spontaneously.

Zohra too worked for a large NGO, and recalled: 'I don't like the atmosphere, there is no humanity, people never take a break and have other things in mind. They come with another purpose.' Badr was a beneficiary of Amatullah and became a volunteer recently. He compared the experience with Amatullah with Islamic Relief and the French Red Cross:

> It's more humane, more natural, less industrial. They have their faults, like the schedule, but I prefer Amatullah to Islamic Relief. Amatullah is a charity on a humane level which responsibilises volunteers: everyone do the clean-up, everything is collective . . . contrary to Islamic Relief or the Red Cross . . . them, it's more like a factory.

Besides providing an alternative to government structures or larger NGOs and ways to concretely experience social work, these charities also appear more efficient. As the above examples show, no particular bureaucratic procedure is needed to volunteer for Amatullah; no interviews and no CV are required. As a consequence, the organisation is able to hire volunteers faster, 'on the spot' and in larger numbers: whereas Islamic Relief France's outreach is limited to groups of five people, sometimes up to thirty volunteers participate in Amatullah's outreaches. Also, as shown above, the less formal environment, bonds of trust and strong social cohesion enables them to keep volunteers more motivated and committed in the long run (this will be demonstrated in more detail in Chapter 5). These phenomena are direct results of the small number of volunteers. Juan (2008, 80) states that in organisations, the smaller the number of people led by passion, the more the functional character and engagement of members increases. This is because the function of these microcosms is not controlled by external elements; rather, they are developed on the basis of original modes of governance, which break away from the usual (Rival 2008, 225). Bernoux (2008, 55–9) also explains the difference in dynamics between the corporate and charity sector:

> Very large charities have a similar if not identical way of functioning to companies; whereas small charities live a more fusional reality where the emphasis is put on the informal and non-verbal communication holds an important of not central position. (. . .) Collective action is therefore linked to the representations the members make of what can be the common good, as opposed to the common interest.

Bernoux (2008, 67) states that when one joins a charity, he/she does so in accordance with one's identity. In the same way, a charity that changes its focus or work without consulting its workers or volunteers risks alienating volunteers because it fails to prioritise human relations (2008, 71). The small number of volunteers and the prioritisation of human relations also provide various specific characteristics in terms of hierarchy, conflict resolution and experience of democracy within these charities.

A strong sense of flexibility can be observed in the pseudo-familial hierarchy of these charities. Even if there are rules, each member has the same responsibility of ensuring that activities are run smoothly. Unlike in bigger charities, which are usually founded by a famous public figure (Islamic Relief was founded by the renowned Hany El-Banna; Penny Appeal was founded by Adeem Younis, CEO of SingleMuslim.com, the UK's largest Muslim matrimonial website), in these small organisations, there is no single charismatic authority or figure, even for religious opinions, and no formal hierarchy. A synergy develops between 'leading' members and 'followers', with the knowledge that these roles are flexible and can be swapped over time. The president (or chief executive) is only consulted in a formal way if the decision has already been made by *shura* consultation (see Chapter 5, 'Shura, the viable chimera of democracy'); he or she intervenes only if no one else expressed themselves prior to this, thus allowing each to act and take responsibility. Here there are no executives or leaders, but instead an informal dynamic between 'elders', or people who have been volunteering for months, and 'newcomers'. The 'elders' are more experienced and know the guidelines well, and guide the 'newcomers' rather than manage them. As a result, the charity is managed in a way similar to that of a family rather than a company. Abdullah stressed the vision of Averroès regarding managing positions:

> One day, someone came to the premises and said: 'I want to be CEO of Averroès.' We looked at him and said that it was not possible. We will never elect someone who wants to be CEO. All the caliphs chosen by the people after the Prophet first declined the role out of humility.

The absence of a central or charismatic authority in a primary social structure (Cooley 1909, 23–4) allows organisations to experience 'true pluralism' (Allenby and Sarewitz 2010, 163) and to respond quickly and effectively to unexpected situations. At Averroès or Amatullah, the person in charge of the reception or the outreach follows a rota, but volunteers do have last minute setbacks. When such a situation occurs, some among the 'elders' can take over spontaneously; a few times, there were not enough volunteers for the mobile outreaches and unexpected events occurred, such as the person in charge falling ill at the last minute. Immediately, some off-duty 'elders' were called to take over, which allowed the outreach to happen.

This family-like environment also plays a major role in conflict resolution. Differences between various opinions, a too-quick interpretation of a colleague's words or a lack of dialogue can all trigger conflicts between volunteers. Usually, they do not last more than a few days, but the outcome is often similar in each situation. One night, around 1 A.M., while Amine was driving the truck of Amatullah, Sarfaraz, who had stayed in the back, was shaken a bit too much. On that winter night, everyone was far from home and exhausted after the outreach. As Sarfaraz was shouting, Amine stopped the truck and soon an argument sparked. Tarek, who was staying in the back with Sarfaraz, tried to be rational to calm down the situation, but there was nothing he could do. However, after twenty minutes, Sarfaraz and Amine were able to calm themselves down and reconcile: 'It's late and we are tired, it happens, but we are brothers after all.' In a similar argument, the bluntness of Fatima A. hurt Samia. The two young women decided to put some distance between them. A few days later, they started talking to each other again. Samia confessed: 'I don't resent her, she's my sister before all.' The words 'brother' and 'sister' are often used. They refer to any Muslim according to gender and, by extension, are used by volunteers to refer to any member of the charity (Muslim or not); this shows that relations between volunteers are not relations between average colleagues. These elements, used to dampen tensions, have a strong cohesive power among the volunteers. Many volunteers help the charities even after they have left university or the neighbourhood because of the 'spirit of family'. The 'peaceful ambiance', the possibility of talking about 'things not related to work and studies' and the possibility of 'learn[ing] about a different culture' (quotes from interviews in both France and Poland) are also main factors expressed by non-Muslim volunteers as motivations to get involved.

The work of charities, based on volunteers, is focused around a common idea, giving everyone some power over the goal; this, according to Crozier (1963), could explain the involvement of the relations and regulations of power. However, Bernoux (2008, 62) argues that power induces a 'reciprocal relation'. Charities appear as true democratic structures: 'democracy is a fundamental of charities' (Bernoux 2008, 62). Unlike abstract structures, which create weak ties between their respondents and thus function through thin or abstract trust (Misztal 1996; Listhaug 1995; Granovetter 1973), these face-to-face, 'empathetic' or 'reflexive' communities (Gundelach and Torp. 1997) produce primary democracy (Newton 1999, 20) through conviviality (Caillé 2011a; Humbert 2011). French sociologist

Patrick Viveret (2011, 40) posits that the effectiveness of this 'radical' form of democracy is based on the quality of inter-human relations. Newton (1999, 21) argues that primary democracy tends to produce conservatism, claustrophobia, hierarchy, ascribed status, power and the suppression, rather than the resolution, of conflict; the absence of bureaucratic control and monitoring can indeed expose smaller charities to corruption and mismanagement. However, I never observed this for the small charities in my sample. A legal case for corruption, misappropriation of funds and abusive redundancy was, however, filed by members of one of the humanitarian NGOs I have studied, which had a large base of donators and a budget of thousands of Euros. I therefore assume that career or financial motives are not as strong in smaller charities, which work on little-to-no budget and show a small following.

Although charities are effective means of creating bonds, even between people of divergent opinions, they are not always successful: individual expectations sometimes do not match the charity's environment. Stéphane, who embraced Islam one year prior to joining Foul Express, started to disagree when the decision was made to not label the charity as a 'Muslim' organisation: 'I feel hurt when I don't see an article with expressions like "*InshaAllah*". I wish they were more Muslim.' He eventually left the charity, whereas paradoxically, some volunteers left because they found the charity 'too Muslim'. However, what would happen if a charity were overtaken by people of a more exclusive mind-set? This happened once in France. Lisa, a volunteer for Amatullah, related her experience in a similar charity, but one that has deviated to a more rigorous governance and that eventually excluded women from their activities: 'I left them, they are too much into islamisation. Last December, they started not accepting women anymore for the outreaches. Now, the atmosphere is dead, they learn a *hadith*, they do their work and nobody talks to each other.' The charity's popularity plummeted and faced backlash from such a decision by losing a certain amount of volunteers. John Bowen (2011) points out that these initiatives and the resulting teaching of Islam vaccinates against radical thinking. Although the issue of religious extremism is not the focus of this work, further research could be done on the role of grassroots community organisations in the prevention of extremism of various kinds, and how it compares to current methods of criminalisation and systematic suspicion of strategies such as PREVENT (Elshimi 2016; Peatfield 2016), or arrests and raids on houses such as those displayed during the French *État d'Urgence* (state of emergency). While most research (Borum 2011; Lyrge et al. 2011; Precht 2007; Wiktorowicz 2005) and insider accounts (Qadir 2016) point out the role of social frustration, resentment and vulnerability,[4] these small organisations demonstrate that a nurturing social environment builds a cohesive strength in communities subject to deprived social or economic conditions.

As a conclusion to this chapter, it has been demonstrated that by providing social environments, safe spaces and times and a network of members with shared references, these charities are able to build a social capital based on trust and beliefs. Referring to the theories of political participation (see Chapter 1), the volunteers here do not necessarily join NGOs for rational or calculated motives.

Although the previous sections show that self-interest due to psychological benefit is present (Op. 1990; Tullock 1971), non-utilitarian motives such as bonds of trust, friendship, love, familiarity and possibilities of growth and meaning, play a major role in the process. The dynamics of face-to-face democracy, mentoring, conflict resolution and family-like hierarchy plunge the volunteers into the middle of an emotional economy. The charity is a place for emotional transactions and experiences rather than utilitarian ones. The inclusiveness of a given organisation goes in hand with its ability to remain attractive in the long run and its work's ability to be effective and sustainable (Chanial 2011). If charities like Amatullah, Averroès or JMF are, at the time of this writing, celebrating or past their 10th anniversary, it is also because they give their volunteers, many of whom come from deprived urban areas, the opportunity to make their lives meaningful. These are spaces in which 'principles of democracy, liberty, equality and solidarity become less abstract' (Chanial 2011, 108) and educate individuals as to the 'virtues of debates, acknowledgement and respect of the others, of responsibility; which are virtues inherent to the exercise of citizenship' (Juan 2008, 81), as will be developed in Chapter 5.

Notes

1 *Centre d'Etudes et de Recherche sur l'Islam* (Centre for Studies and Research on Islam).
2 *Institut Européen des Sciences Humaines* (European Institute for Humanities).
3 'While we were in the mosque with Allah's Messenger, a desert Arab came and stood up and began to urinate in the mosque. The Companions of Allah's Messenger said: Stop, stop, but the Messenger of Allah said: Don't interrupt him; leave him alone. They left him alone, and when he finished urinating, Allah's Messenger called him and said to him: These mosques are not the places meant for urine and filth, but are only for the remembrance of Allah, prayer and the recitation of the Qur'an, or Allah's Messenger said something like that. He (the narrator) said that he (the Holy Prophet) then gave orders to one of the people who brought a bucket of water and poured It over.' USC-MSA web (English) reference: Book 2, Hadith 559
4 See also Olivier Roy and the concept of 'islamisation of radicalism' www.lemonde.fr/idees/article/2015/11/24/le-djihadisme-une-revolte-generationnelle-et-nihiliste_4815992_3232.html [last accessed on 15 Jan. 2017].

References

Allenby, B. R. and Sarewitz, D. (2010). *The Techno-Human Condition*. Cambridge: MIT Press.
Amath, N. (2015). *The Phenomenology of Community Activism: Muslim Civil Society Organisations in Australia*. Melbourne: Melbourne University Press.
Barise, A. (2005). Social Work With Muslims: Insights From the Teachings of Islam. *Critical Social Work*, 6(2). http://www1.uwindsor.ca/criticalsocialwork/social-work-with-muslims-insights-from-the-teachings-of-islam [last accessed on 15 Jan. 2017].
Bernoux, P. (2008). De la Sociologie des Organisations à la Sociologie des Associations [From the Sociology of Organisations to the Sociology of Charities]. In: Hoarau, C. and Laville, J-L. (eds.) *La gouvernance des associations*. Paris: Eres, pp. 55–9.

Borum, R. (2011). Radicalization Into Violent Extremism II: A Review of Conceptual Models and Empirical Research. *Journal of Strategic Security*, 4(4), 7–36.
Bowen, J. R. (2011). *Can Islam Be French?* Princeton: Princeton University Press.
Caillé, A. (2011a). Du Convivialisme vu comme un Socialisme Radicalisé et Universalisé (et Réciproquement) [On Convivialism as a Radicalised and Universalised Socialism and Reciprocally]. In: Caillé, A., Humbert, M., Latouche, S. and Viveret, P. (eds.) *De la convivialité, dialogues sur la société conviviale à venir*. Paris: La Découverte, pp. 73–98.
Caillé, A. (2011b). Les indicateurs de richesse alternatifs: une fausse bonne idée ? [Wealth Indicators: A Wrong Good Idea?]. In: Caillé, A., Humbert, M., Latouche, S. and Viveret, P. (eds.) *De la convivialité, dialogues sur la société conviviale à venir*. Paris: La Découverte, pp. 141–66.
Canda, E. R. and Furman, L. D. (2010). *Spiritual Diversity in Social Work Practice: The Heart of Helping*. Oxford: Oxford University Press.
Cefaï, D. (2007). *Pourquoi se Mobilise-t-on? Les Théories de l'Action Collective* [*Why Do People Mobilise? The Theories of Collective Action*]. Paris: La Découverte.
Chanial, P. (2011). *La sociologie comme philosophie politique et réciproquement* [*Sociology as a Political Philosophy and Reciprocally*]. Paris: La Découverte.
Cooley, C. H. (1909). *Social Organization: A Study of the Larger Mind*. New York: Charles Scribner's Sons.
Crozier, M. (1963). *La société bloquée* [*Blocked Society*]. Paris: Seuil.
Crozier, M. (1987). *Etat modeste, Etat moderne* [*Modest State, Modern State*]. Paris: Seuil.
Dubar, C. (1998). *La socialisation. Construction des identités sociales et professionnelles* [*Socialisation: Construction of Social and Professional Identities Meditations*]. Paris: Armand Colin.
Dubet, F. (1994). *Sociologie de l'expérience* [*Sociology of Experience*]. Paris: Seuil.
Elshimi, M. (2016). De-Radicalisation in the Prevent Strand of the UK Counter-Terrorism Strategy: Towards an Alternative Conceptual Framework. In: Suleiman, Y. and Anderson, P. (eds.) *Muslims in the UK and Europe II*. Cambridge: Centre of Islamic Studies, pp. 35–47.
Granovetter, M. S. (1973). The Strength of Weak Ties. *American Journal of Sociology*, 78(60), 1360–80.
Gundelach, P. and Torpe, L. (1997). *Voluntary Associations: New Types of Involvement and Democracy*, paper presented to the ECPR Joint Sessions of Workshops, Oslo 1996.
Humbert, M. (2011). Convivialisme, politique et économie. Ivan Illitch et le "bien vivre ensemble" [Convivialism, Politics and Economics: Ivan Illitch and the 'Well Living Together']. In: Caillé, A., Humbert, M., Latouche, S. and Viveret, P. eds. *De la convivialité, dialogues sur la société conviviale à venir*. Paris: La Découverte, pp. 99–130.
Husserl, E. (1982) [1960]. *Cartesian Meditations: An Introduction to Phenomenology*. London, The Hague, and Boston: Martinus Nijhoff.
Juan, S. (2008). La sociologie des associations: dimensions institutionnelle et organisationnelle [Sociology of Charities: Institutional and Organisational Dimensions]. In: Hoarau, C. and Laville, J-L. (eds.) *La gouvernance des associations*. Paris: Eres, pp. 73–94.
Lichterman, P. (2005). *Elusive Togetherness: Church Groups Trying to Bridge America's Divisions*. Princeton: Princeton University Press.
Listhaug, O. (1995). The Dynamics of Trust in Politicians. In: Klingemann, H-D. and Fuchs, D. (eds.) *Citizens and the State*. Oxford: Oxford University Press, pp. 261–97.
Lygre, R. B., Eid, J., Larsson, G. and Ranstorp, M. (2011). Terrorism as a Process: A Critical Review of Moghaddam's Staircase to Terrorism. *Scandinavian Journal of Psychology*, 52(6), 609–16.

Misztal, B. (1996). *Trust in Modern Societies: The Search for the Bases of Social Order*. Oxford: Blackwell.

Newton, K. (1999). Social Capital and Democracy in Modern Europe. In: Van Deth, J. W., Maraffi, M., Newton, K. and Whiteley, P. F. (eds.) *Social Capital and European Democracy*. London: Routledge, pp. 3–24.

Opp, K-D. (1990). Postmaterialism, Collective Action and Political Protest. *American Journal of Political Science*, 34(1), 212–35.

Peatfield, E-J. (2016). Making Vulnerable: The Effect on Minority Communities of the Identification of Vulnerability Within Prevent. In: Suleiman, Y. and Anderson, P. eds. *Muslims in the UK and Europe II*. Cambridge: Centre of Islamic Studies, pp. 48–53.

Pędziwiatr, K. (2010). *The New Muslim Elites in European Cities: Religion and Active Social Citizenship Amongst Young Organized Muslims in Brussels and London*. Saarbrücken: VDM Verlag.

Precht, T. (2007). *Home Grown Terrorism and Islamist Radicalisation in Europe: From Conversion to Terrorism. An Assessment of the Factors Influencing Violent Islamist Extremism and Suggestions for Counter Radicalisation Measures*. Copenhagen: Danish Ministry of Justice.

Putnam, R. (1993). *Making Democracy Work: Civic Traditions in Modern Italy*. Princeton: Princeton University Press.

Qadir, H. (2016). *Preventing and Countering Extremism and Terrorist Recruitment: A Best Practice Guide*. Woodbridge: John Catt Educational.

Rival, M. (2008). Associations et entrepreneuriat institutionnel [Charities and Institutional Entrepreneurship]. In: Hoarau, C. and Laville, J-L. (eds.) *La gouvernance des associations*. Paris: Eres, pp. 215–25.

Touraine, A. (1992). *Critique de la Modernité [Critique of Modernity]*. Paris: Fayard.

Tullock, G. (1971). The Paradox of Revolution. *Public Choice*, 11(1), 89–99.

Venel, N. (2002). *Musulmans et Citoyens [Muslims and Citizens]*. Paris: PUF.

Vermeersch, S. (2004). Entre individualisation et participation: l'engagement associatif bénévole [Between Individualisation and Participation: Voluntary Involvement in Charities]. *Revue Française de Sociologie*, 45(4), 681–710.

Viveret, P. (2011). Stratégies de transition vers le bien-vivre face aux démesures dominantes [Strategies of Transitions Towards Well-Living in Face of Dominant Excesses]. In: Caillé, A., Humbert, M., Latouche, S. and Viveret, P. eds. *De la convivialité, dialogues sur la société conviviale à venir*. Paris: La Découverte, pp. 25–42.

Wiktorowicz, Q. (2005). *Radical Islam Rising: Muslim Extremism in the West*. Lanham: Rowman & Littlefield.

Williams, B. (1988). Formal Structures and Social Reality. In: Gambetta, D. (ed.) *Trust: Making and Breaking Cooperative Relations*. Oxford: Blackwell, pp. 3–13.

5 Crafting an active citizenship

While I was trying to understand how volunteers understand and perceive their involvement in charities, I saw smiles, listened to testimonies full of hope and met people thinking about a better world . . . but one question remained on my mind: how is it possible to make a real difference, to change the world with palliative services such as soup kitchens or basic tasks such as printing exam paper corrections? Jennyfer from Foul Express illustrated her point of view with a short South American story she liked to recall:

> Once there was a huge forest fire in the jungle. While all the animals ran away from the forest, a small hummingbird saw the fire. It flew down to the river, took a few drops of water in its little beak and flew back to the forest to pour the drops on the fire. The other animals saw it and laughed at it. They told the hummingbird: 'Why are you trying to extinguish the fire? You will never make any difference.' Then, the hummingbird replied to the animals: 'I am only doing my part.'

I then understood that Jennyfer, like many others, does not necessarily work to make a difference, but to accomplish a duty, a task; not to change a situation, even on a microscopic scale, but to do her best. In Chapter 4, I explained how the family-like environment, small number of participants and diversity of new experiences make these charities attractive and at the same time build social capital. Now, what makes these charities remain attractive through time? How do they remain strongly cohesive throughout the years despite their small size and the basic services they provide? Analysing the dynamics of commitment, I found that this sense of duty was one of the most important factors for keeping volunteers involved, and that this feeling can take various shapes: sense of responsibility, social accountability, preserving social bonds or even just faith. This will be the subject of this first section, explaining how this sense of duty makes the volunteers stay, even after their careers or family life take different turns. The second section explores a key issue: how do these charities make politics and democracy attractive again? Far from the politics of parties, which they completely distrust, the volunteers take the opportunity to experiment with alternative forms of governance that are more equitable and balanced; one of these is through informal *shura*, a consultative and consensual decision making process inspired by the Islamic tradition (and very different from similarly named '*shura* councils' in other parts of the world). While bureaucratic governments and education present a passive and unattractive idea of citizenship limited to a legal status of belonging, a large number of volunteers tend to unexpectedly adhere to an active vision of the concept. This leads volunteers to adopt original ways of defining themselves (as citizens) and reverse the stigma to display in the public sphere that, contrary to the widespread idea that Muslims cannot embrace democracy, they are Europeans, Muslims and active citizens altogether.

Staying committed

Staying committed in a small local charity is a challenge in itself. Members face various obstacles: crisis, conflict or loss of motivation, which lead volunteers to question their commitment. Canda and Furman (2010, 314) observed that commitment, as faith, has its own 'peaks' and 'pits'. Demotivational factors are various; for Mohamed, dealing with a workload outside of the charity was not easy: 'There are hard times, it happens that I lose motivation because of the studies and the job, but I make time to come for the reward.' For Fatima from Muslim Hands, routine and lack of respect from some donators were the main obstacles: 'It's monotonous, repetitive, it's hard . . . donators are sometimes insulting.' For Fatima from Amatullah, sometimes the lack of gratitude was a problem, especially compared to the work she had to provide:

> I was very active, I was in charge for the stall at the Bourget 2010, but I decided to have a break because I'm currently demotivated. The organisation is hard to manage with the job at the same time and volunteers are not that grateful. People criticise my lack of subtlety. I sometimes ask myself why not go to another charity, but Amatullah is like a baby: there is a responsibility towards beneficiaries and volunteers. . . . I am in charge, I cannot leave just like that. And there is the intention . . . But since then, I decided to get less involved. I still prepare food on Wednesdays.

For Oumar, the lack of action and results at Foul Express made him think of leaving. The fact that the charity does not label itself as Muslim 'made [his] motivation drop down to zero'. For Corinne and Rémi, their first experience at their local mosque was not easy either: 'The organisation is chaotic and internal conflicts demotivated us a lot.' However, most of the volunteers overcome crisis and stay; one reason common to all is because they feel their presence and work is, first, a duty.

Managers and elders involve themselves intensively, which sometimes leads them to sacrifice in another part of their life. For instance, nothing, in theory, forbids Averroès's volunteers from returning home after class. Nothing, in theory, obliges Amatullah's volunteers to come from very distant cities to serve the soup kitchen. However, some people, like Said, were willing to compromise on their studies: 'I don't go to classes, it's not good [sic]. Yesterday I came home and I told myself that I will study my courses until midnight, as I usually do, but then, I felt asleep around 10'. It was a similar situation for Jean Fateh: 'It's not easy to deal with everything at the same time. Sometimes, I cancel tuitions or I miss lessons at the university'. Abdullah took a week off from his internship in order to prepare the set-up of a big charity event organised by Averroès. When he was notified at work of a sensitive situation happening during a soup kitchen at Amatullah, Shamsuddine did not hesitate to make his way to assess and solve the problem, even if it meant coming back home to join his wife and daughter very late at night. The premises are a place of living in which volunteers eat, pray, meet and sometimes sleep, as does Musa, who often spent nights on location to prepare events for Averroès. This sense of duty leads some of them to override family restrictions, such as Fatima A: 'It makes me feel bad when I have to stay late at night and I have to lie to my parents [sic].' Some others, like Fatima from Muslim Hands, simply state: 'I don't have any other project in life than the charity. It's my whole life.' Beyond this general feeling, their commitment seems to be sustained by to particular factors often recalled during interviews. These factors appear to be fundamental when volunteers reach a critical point in their involvement, allowing them to overcome the situation and resume their commitment. The three main factors are a sense of responsibility, the preservation of social bonds and faith.

Responsibility and accountability

For the core team, getting involved in the charity parallels a sense of accountability. Whether the volunteers are in executive positions or not, they feel they have a duty to ensure that everything works smoothly. When Abdullah was not yet chief executive, he referred to the exam papers corrections he printed for other students, observing that since 'studies and exams are all over the year, thus we have to be there all over the year too'. Shamsuddine explained that he is kept at Amatullah because

> we have an appointment with them [the beneficiaries] every Wednesday and Saturday evening, whether it's windy, raining or it's -10°C; if conditions allow us, we have to be there because they're waiting for us (. . .) If I'm not there, it will not work.

Abdelkarim, chief executive of Muslim Hands, put the emphasis on this contract, which makes him engaged with the public: 'People expect we use their money in a certain way, therefore we have to ensure our service is up to their expectations'. For Tarik, there was no border between time dedicated to the charity and the rest:

> I'm very involved, my work is seven days a week, twenty-four hours a day and I even dream of the charity at night, and that people give to us [sic] (. . .) my wife tells me that the charity is my second wife.

88 *Crafting an active citizenship*

His main motivation was his responsibility:

> Donators trust us blindly. Money has to help. And there's a bit of self-satisfaction. Receiving money for the charity is like receiving money for yourself. (. . .) I leave my mobile on all night long, just in case, because a Muslim has to be helpful.

Shamsuddine expressed his feelings, saying 'it's not easy, sometimes there are tiredness, job, health issues (. . .) but if I'm not here, it will not work'. It was the same for Sarfaraz, who, thinking of the beneficiaries explained that 'they are waiting for us and if we don't come, nobody will come'. For Fatima from Muslim Hands, what kept her involved were the orphans. She was responsible for the orphan sponsorship programme and confessed that her work was 'very repetitive', but without her, 'nobody will take care of them'. Kader felt responsible towards the donators: 'Donators trust us blindly. Their money has to have some use'. Others, like Daoud, expressly admit to not liking the atmosphere: 'If it was for the people, or for the money, I wouldn't be working here. I am here for the deprived.' The duty to ensure some service was also emphasised by Warda:

> We were two dozens, but then only five people remained for the project. We didn't want to work in these conditions, if we didn't join for the goal, we wouldn't have stayed. Two years ago, in 2008, the atmosphere was disturbing, but respect between us was stronger.

The same situation was experienced by Fatima, who said 'I didn't agree with the governance, the understanding of religion for some, giving blindly', but she stayed 'for the love of Allah and the sense of duty, the final goal one must attain'. Many among the core team questioned themselves when hardships happened, like Fatima:

> In crisis situations, I take a break and I come back later because I constantly question myself. What makes me stay is my commitment and my responsibility. If I leave, if I don't stay committed, my life has no meaning.

Samia did the same: 'Was I present enough? Was I involved enough?' For Fatima, 'the charity is like a baby: one is responsible of the beneficiaries and the volunteers . . . I am responsible, I cannot leave just like this'.

This feeling of responsibility is also found in the ethical codes and decision making processes; Khadija, for instance, wanted to terminate her contract, for refusing to misuse donators' money: 'We are at a point where my work is being here from 9 to 6. I don't want to use donations for this.' The same logic led Marwan to leave his job as a trader so he would not 'make injustices anymore'. When suggesting activities for Moroccan orphans for a forthcoming trip with Amatullah, Mohamed was more in favour of a day at the zoo than a funfair: 'Going out should not only entertain them, but we should not deprive them from knowledge.'

For Shemseddine, responsibility had to be spread and shared among young people attending JMF's activities: '[the charity's project] is young people's responsibility. Leading young people to succeed, to never give up.' At Amatullah, everyone is made to feel their work is essential by giving them precise tasks to accomplish, such as pouring water in plastic cups or handling the meal for the beneficiaries, without which the whole chain cannot work. Samia from Foul Express recalled a notable experience in a group of French Muslim expats in London:

> The group works with a revolving responsibility: each session, one person reads and analyses a *surah* (chapter) of the Qur'an, another looks for the answers for the next time and another one cooks the food. Of course, if it's your turn to cook, you will make efforts to do something good [sic].

Many refer to the responsibility of keeping the charity running or making good use of donations with the Arabic word '*amana*', meaning a deposit, bond or obligation. The volunteers are also aware they are part of a team and that, because of the small scale of the organisations, their presence and voice matters at a collective level; thus the preservation of social bonds is another *amana* in these dynamics of commitment.

Social bonds

For Abdullah, 'what motivates me, it's first to be with people who share a same perception of the world and the same values'. It was the same thing for Musa: 'During times of hardship, what motivates me, is the bond between trusted people which increase and reveal themselves during crisis.' For Akhtar, 'what helped me is that I was surrounded'. For Jennyfer: 'I had a moment when I didn't know if I was at the right place in the organisation, if I should not go somewhere else. . . . But what kept me in the charity was fraternity, the bond I felt I shared with other members.' Some others, like Sarfaraz, found their motivation in the solidarity people express during hard times: 'When it's cold and when one sees the other brothers resisting, then we resist too.' For Najah, who once disagreed with the CEO: 'I changed since then. I didn't leave the charity because I'm persevering and patient. I spoke to the president [CEO], especially regarding the orientation of some articles and I realised that I was heard.'

On another level, maintaining a social bond with beneficiaries is also one of those 'cables' which hold volunteers committed. This side happened to be an important part of Amatullah's work, which focuses on the proximity to the homeless and the gift of time and words. As Abdallah testified, 'sometimes, they wait for us just to talk, because they know that with us, they can talk'. For Sarfaraz, when managing the outreaches 'what motivates me are the beneficiaries and the bond which is built between us. Sometimes, there are some hitches, but it always re-dynamises me when I think about the volunteers.'

The group seems to weigh the process of commitment importantly, in the sense that it acts like an environment, a cloth or a cocoon strengthening one's involvement because of the mutual support people express for each other. They become responsible not only for the activities they have to run, but also for their colleagues with whom they make the organisation work. Socialisation creates pressure which pushes volunteers to be active and makes a long-term commitment more attractive (Van Tienes et al. 2011, 382). Finally, faith, as an intimate relationship with God, also plays a role in sustaining one's commitment.

Faith

Hardships are often interpreted in light of Islamic scriptural sources and the stories of the prophets. Abdullah recalled various events which happened in a short amount of time. The cash box was stolen and the printer raised his tariffs almost at the same time: 'Alhamdulillah. These are little tests. We only get better with them. We take things positively [sic]. If we compare this to what the Prophets lived, it's nothing [sic].' When he took one week off his job to help the setup of an event at Averroès, raising funds for a school in Madagascar, he commented: 'This is Jihad [sic].' For Samia, keeping one's faith was essential, as she recalled the moment when 'it clicked' when she was in London: 'Everything began with those *halaqa*[1] circles, therefore it's for God. I hold fast to this idea of the circles.' For Oumar, about to leave because of having lost any motivation, and who had already written his farewell letter, a '*qyiam*[2] remotivated me'. For Fatima from Muslim Hands, hardships were seen as a proof of the divine love: 'And there is Paradise as a reward. After all, Allah tests people he loves the most, right?' Wissam prepared himself to be tested: 'It's gonna be very, very hard, we will feel powerless, but it's God's pedagogy. It's the *baraka*[3] that the project receives which makes things move forward.' It was the same thing for Fatima – not agreeing on many principles at Amatullah – but for her, 'the charity is a tool for getting closer to Allah. It's all that matters'. For Abdelkarim from Muslim Hands, 'trust in Allah' allowed him 'not to be afraid' when hardships showed up. This allusion to trust was also found with Issa. He recalled a hard time after an event:

> Losing seven thousand euros, to be stabbed in the back, it's not that serious, because everything has a meaning. It is said that there is no raindrop which trajectory was not decided by Allah. When trust is absolute, there is no reason to worry. People are surprised by my reaction when I tell them I got seven thousand euros stolen. They tell me: 'what [sic]. That's terrible [sic].' I reply to them that not at all.

Evoking faith as a factor for commitment is often heard among people who feel like working 'alone among the rest of the world', feeling as though they have a particularly difficult task compared to others, which they achieve alone, and rely more on divine relief than the others. Spirituality implies giving a capital importance to commitment and fidelity. The sole idea that life events do not happen by accident gives duties, context, conditions and social relations a very profound meaning (Van Tienen et al. 2011, 383). If, sometimes, Islam is not expressly mentioned, references to it appear behind the layers. Times of crisis and conflict strengthen and build identity and attachment to Islam as a frame of reference, in the sense that Islam is present in the environment, space and time and is shared with the colleagues, with whom bonds of friendship and trust are reinforced over time (see Chapter 4). There is a mutual stimulation process between colleagues, which regularly refreshes motivations. In some cases, faith supports one's commitment; in other cases, one's commitment supports one's faith. Also, challenges and conflicts are seen as opportunities to strengthen one another. In most cases, volunteers go back to a phase of intense activity. These experiences build stronger bonds and a stronger sense of attachment to Islam; through overcoming hardships, theoretical religious principles are confirmed by experience and then remembered as tools for overcoming future potential future conflicts. The average process could be transcribed as it follows: 'I know I overcame this because I trusted God and because I can rely on my brothers and sisters, therefore I know that this is what I need to do next time.'

On the other hand, volunteers who occasionally come to the charity do not feel the same intense responsibility. These are volunteers, such as Ayoub or Muntasser, who got involved in order to find answers on their personal journey, or Said, who mainly participated only 'if the others need [him]'. For those, spiritual references are almost absent from their discourse; they are believers who generally do not develop the idea of a believer responsible for the creation. Their goals are more of a professional level; be able to work, earn a decent life or 'do something useful'. The worldly life is held as a main reference, and reasons for getting involved are more practical. They do not look to obtain Paradise but rather to make their time useful. They are not looking to increase their faith or be loved by God, but rather to '[do] something for other humans because [they] are human'. God is 'somewhere there,' said Ayoub, adding, 'He is important.' But if during the interviews questions about God are not asked, the topic never comes up.

Eventually, for the larger part of volunteers, their understanding of Islam through the concept of *amana* and their awareness of the amount of money given and the key role of social bonds in the group are reminders that one has a duty to face hardships. This understanding is more often found among the volunteers of the core team, often in charge of administrative and human responsibilities. These same volunteers often understand the role of the believer as responsible for the others in light of the teachings of Islam. If Islam is not quoted explicitly as a factor for sustaining commitment, it is still intimately linked to it. This particular understanding of Islam is not a necessary condition for triggering a feeling of responsibility, but comes tightly intertwined with it. There is not a predefined process or journey. For some, this feeling is a direct result of their understanding of the texts; for others, it comes before the reading of the texts; and for some others, both processes are closely entangled. The same goes for social bonds; they are not kept systematically as a consequence of the religion. If some volunteers maintain bonds for the sake of religious principles, others do not link bonds and Islamic teachings at all. As a result, Islam as a social environment and a matrix of symbols, values, beliefs and norms plays an active part in building social capital and bringing motivation as per the Civic Volunteerism Model (Verba et al. 1995). However, beyond personal feelings and reasons to stay involved, these charities offer to volunteers ways of making their voices heard. Through the concept of informal *shura*, they experiment with alternative forms of democracy which, paired with their social works, impact on their understanding of citizenship and, ultimately, how these young Muslims present themselves in the public sphere.

Shura, the viable chimera of democracy

With the notable exception of Jeremy Corbyn in the UK, Bernie Sanders in the US and, to a limited extent, Justin Trudeau in Canada, all politicians praised by young Muslims for their opinions about social justice and engagement with minorities, none among the volunteers I interviewed had any trust in any politician. Even the newly elected Labour mayor of London, Sadiq Khan, despite being from a Pakistani Muslim family, raised more concerns than praises. The ephemeral joy of seeing a Muslim elected as the mayor of a European capital was superseded by comments referring to Khan as a 'Tory [conservative] in disguise'. The term 'politics' itself has a negative connotation. Samia, for example, said: 'Politics in France, it's only hypocrisy. I really feel angry towards them.' Abdullah directly linked politics to the laws about religious signs:

> What happens in France is anti-politics. Since 2004 and the law against the veil, what disturbs me is the treatment of Islam by media and politicians. (...) I do not trust politicians, they do things out of personal interest, they 'buy' Muslim votes as in Mantes, especially with our parents' generation. I, for one, look for those who have principles and don't try to satisfy their personal interests. For me, politicians have to be at people's service, not the opposite. (...) I encourage young people to vote because we have the power. But I personally prefer opting for the less worse because all politicians are not in line with Muslim ethics when one listens their opinion about justice, equality ... or environment.

For Fatima from Muslim Hands, 'politics in France is unfair with poor people. No one, whether from the right or left-wing, has found a solution yet.' For Muntasser,

> it's difficult to live in France because culture is too different. I would be tempted to fly away from France. There are more rights in France than in Arab countries, but politics in France is not respectful, everyone is in their comfort zone, it's difficult to feel as a citizen in France, one cannot make their voice heard, one needs to assimilate for having rights whereas one should not fight for this. It is revolting.

Fatima explained 'politics, it's only games of power and personal interest. (...) it's against the French motto'. For Yandé: 'Politicians? They're all liars, they only want power and money.' Nooruldine said that 'politics is going backwards, it does not fit anymore'. For Fatima from Amatullah: 'What happens is serious, Sarkozy [president at the time] is shifting to the far-right.' For Mohamed: 'It's all fake, it's a big scam.' Opinions are bitter, in line with the observations of Michel Crozier (1987), who writes about how the French administration, in order to avoid situations of conflict, is favouring a blocking bureaucracy. Alain Caillé (2011, 87) argues that this feeling of collective political powerlessness resides in the fragmentation of thought and action, resulting in an 'inverted totalitarianism'. Those volunteers are shocked and concerned by a wide range of injustices. If many are protesting against the 'islamophobic' climate in France, against murders of Palestinian civilians, the massacre of the Rohingya in Burma, or Black teenagers shot by the police in the US, they mobilise themselves for the Roma being marginalised and expelled from their houses or campaigning against the use of fossil fuels and over-consumption (see Figure 5.1). It is not a rare thing to find on social media posts facts such as 'the 35 wealthiest people on the planet own as much as the 3.5 billion poorest ones'. Injustices are revolting, whatever the skin colour or the religion of the victims; each conflict is able to make them concerned. The realisation that governments are unable to solve major social and economic problems is the point of origin for their involvement in charities. When the government is seen as unable to provide employment prospects for young people, JMF organises its yearly Orientation Forum (see Figure 5.2). Recalling Sarfaraz's words, in a charity like Amatullah, 'this is real politics'.

'Politics' comes from the Greek *polis*, meaning 'city'. The *polis* refers to what is common to every free citizen (Habermas 1962 [1978], 15). It is an open universe

Figure 5.1 Volunteers of MADE in a protest for divestment from fossil fuels in London

94 *Crafting an active citizenship*

Figure 5.2 At JMF's Orientation Forum in La Courneuve.

in which political action takes place (Emden and Midgley 2012, 3). The *polis* is the theatre of the citizens (Pocock 1998; Clarke 1994, 4–6). Habermas states that the *bios politikos*, the 'public life', is the one which used to take place on the *agora*, the market (Habermas 1962 [1978], 15). However, the *bios politikos* is not limited to a physical place; the public sphere refers to the whole of a connected group of people, gathered as a public (Habermas 1962 [1978], 38). It is easy to imagine the extent of such a sphere in the era of communication technologies and virtual networks that are able to gather a public of millions. The public sphere is a 'theatre of the world', 'a stage on which a spectacular drama unfolds,' (Göle 2005, 23), 'a scenic performance' (Amiraux 2006, 47). This is a space in which social actors play a public role and perform in front of others. In a sense, 'there is a sensorial and perceptive dimension to the public space, which gives to each of its participants the opportunity to face alterity and to be confronted to it in a physical space' (Amiraux 2006, 47). When it comes to collective action, Cooley gives to public opinion a fundamental importance: it constitutes the facilitator figure, ensuring communication between primary groups and their ideals on the one hand and social and political institutions on the other (Chanial 2011, 110). The subjects of this research are therefore actors who, in the name of their beliefs and/or various references and elements, are performing on the stage of the public sphere. Modern governments seem to forget that throughout history, the concepts of religion and politics have always been imbricated (Asad 2003). Through observations and interviews, it appears that Islam, as a spirituality, ethic and practice, is perceived as a key motivating factor for social action. Because the performance of

Islam happens in the public domain, in the *polis*, the actions and the Islam of these volunteers are political, in the sense of an element participating in the public life. However, this poses a problem for many European politicians.

The visibility of Muslims in the public sphere is considered, especially in France, as a threat to the principle of *laïcité*, interpreted by politicians as a duty of religious neutrality of the citizen (Baubérot 2006). According to Göle (2005, 109), 'the question of Islam in the public sphere is first, the question of its visibility'. Far-right groups or even 'left-wing' politicians such as French Prime Minister Manuel Valls do not consider the *hijab*, for example, in its intimate and individual dimension, but interpret it as a provocative political statement.[4] This is one of the explanations as to why seeing a women wearing *hijab* on the streets stirs controversy: her action is interpreted as crossing a forbidden border. Therefore, in France's aggressively secular and colonial tradition, while Muslims should remain invisible and ideally absent from the public sphere, the idea of Muslims acting as model citizens is a transgression. The particular situation in which these young Muslim volunteers operate is a disruption in the conservative-dreamed (and illusionary) European timeline: while for mainstream right-wing politicians Europe should remain Christian and White (as expressed by French MP and Minister Nadine Morano)[5] and Muslims should stay outside Europe, there are now European Muslims, religious and participating in the public sphere, who are visible in debates, on TV or at demonstrations. Especially when Muslims invest in mainstream fields of debates such as environment, social justice or feminism, they become chimeras, entities which should not exist according to far-right scenari. Being Muslim, they trigger fears (such as the phantasmagoric Islamisation of Europe). Being vocal, skilled and visible, they provoke, at the same time, wonder. They become monsters in the literal meaning. 'Monster' comes from the ancient Latin *monstrum*, which means to 'warn, enlighten, inspire'. The *monstrum* in Latin mythology refers to 'a miracle', an 'expression of the will of the gods'.[6] They incarnate the face of Europe that conservative minds do not want to look at, perhaps because they are their mirror at the same time.

The volunteers are aware they are visible as Muslims and that this visibility makes them responsible for changing the public's perception of Muslims, as Samia did: 'I got involved because the opinion on Muslims and especially Muslim women wasn't right. People and women are not on seen on the scene, thus I wanted to be an actor myself.' Abdullah spoke about the same will to challenge the narrative: 'It's for giving a better image of Islam, which is not good because of the media. And it's being helpful too.' In a society where Muslims are dehumanised (Chouder et al. 2008), this commitment is sometimes a reaction to the increased stigmatisation or an attempt to claim a 'true' Islam or emancipate themselves through religion (Göle 2003; Venel 2002). They are reversing the stigma and presenting themselves as citizens, religious and active at the same time. On the other hand, this visibility is not only the expression of a particular understanding of citizenship, but at the same time a matter of development and building of the subject (Fadil 2006; Göle 1995). When it comes to understanding the term 'citizenship', opinions are, however, mixed.

96 *Crafting an active citizenship*

Most understand citizenship from the perspective of implication. Through interviews volunteers drew two major trends when asked about citizenship: those who perceived it as passive and belonging to a country, and those who believed it implied an active participation in society. While preparing a stage play at JMF, a discussion started about defining citizenship. Hassan spoke: 'It's a real Jihad [sic]. It's about responsibility first [sic].' Marwa answered: 'But it's also about rights [sic].' Mariam agreed with both opinions and Shemseddine spoke: 'It's a moral responsibility towards others.' As Mamadou said: 'It's being an actor for the society', to which Saber replied, 'it's a journey towards good having all the tools provided by the State'. Being a citizen is 'being responsible', 'act[ing]', 'mak[ing] a difference' and 'contribut[ing] to fraternity', as Samia said – although it is 'having rights' and also 'duties', in the context of a state serving and listening to society. For Tarik, these duties are not limited to voting or paying taxes, but rather are focused on society: 'Citizens move the society forward, curb injustices.' For Abdullah, to get involved in politics was to put a burden on one's shoulders: 'Sarkozy goes on holiday to Morocco while people are starving in his country. I for one, I would be scared to run for mayor in my own city with such a responsibility.' He thought about an anecdote from the Islamic tradition, saying 'at the time of the first caliphs, no one wanted to be caliph', fearing the responsibilities they had to take on. In a larger perspective, citizenship goes beyond belonging; Yandé, Zeineb and Fatima, who felt they were 'citizen[s] of the world because citizenship is universal and the Earth is for everyone.' Fatima felt sad that 'for 90% of Muslims, Islam is more of a cultural heritage'. For Jean Fateh, 'citizenship is harmony within diversity'. Finally, for Imen and René, 'a good believer is a good citizen' or 'citizenship [has] values which are those of Islam', linking the concepts of believer and citizen through their roles and duties, which are perceived as similar. For Farida from Muslim Hands, 'citizenship is respecting values of the Republic. (. . .) I am infinitely grateful to France for what it gave us in terms of rights.' Furthermore, Mohamed links citizenship to gratitude towards God: 'Citizenship is belonging and duties towards people who surround us. It's also a kind of gratitude for what Allah gives us.'

For a minority, citizenship is rather a constraint and a compulsion to obey laws with which one does not necessarily agree. For some, it is even exclusively a French or European concept, 'something invented by the French'. They perceive citizenship as not compatible with Islam: 'Being a citizen means to obey politicians, therefore it's impossible to be a citizen and a Muslim at the same time,' said Akif from Muslim Hands. For Fatima from Averroès:

> I don't feel concerned by politics. . . . I want to go far away because respecting laws does not permit me to practise the religion. I don't feel I'm a citizen. For me, being a citizen is first belonging to a country and I find in France that citizenship is not compatible with religion.

Some even think about flying away to countries deemed to be more open to cultural or religious differences because, as Zeineb said, the 'situation in France doesn't allow [us] to practise Islam'. Soumia thought about leaving for London, 'except if the situation improves'. Identifying as a citizen is linked to the idea of the resident country a safe space, at which France visibly fails for these few French interviewees. It shows that the idea of citizenship has been damaged, perhaps due to the assimilationist political agenda in France. With laws targeting Muslims' visibility and recursive debates around the meaning of 'French identity' or the 'compatibility of Islam within the Republic', Muslims have been repeatedly othered; the idea of being a French citizen has been disconnected from cultural or religious particularisms.

However, those who adhere to the idea of citizenship and understand it as needing an active contribution to the society show a rather unexpected trend. Historically, with the centralisation of national debates in the parliaments and through the official curriculum, citizenship has been reduced to the state of belonging to a country, a fact which is materialised by the symbolic identity card. Citizenship is subdivided into 'rights for liberties' (e.g., freedom of belief), 'rights for participation' (e.g., to vote) and 'debtor rights' (taxes), which together respectively protect the citizens' rights, allow them to take part in the political process and allow the welfare state to be sustained economically (Cefaï 2007, 717). Sometimes, as in civic education classes for 12-year-olds, citizenship is a binary divided between 'rights' and 'duties', with the latter category referring to voting in a Marshallian definition of the concept (Marshall 1992 [1950]). As a consequence, from the Greek *polis*, modern citizenship has evolved to a form of passive societal belonging (Mann 1987). Delanty would even argue that a modern 'good' citizen is nowadays a good consumer (Delanty 2000). There is no emphasis on individual responsibility as the common assumption is that other structures and means such as politicians or technology will take responsibility (Styrdom 1999; Apel 1993). The third term of the French motto, fraternity, seems to have been forgotten in times far from war and famine, in an individualistic society of consumerism, where helping each other and DIY have become obsolete. The status of citizenship has become closer to the Ancient Roman conception, in which citizens were members of a state who benefited from civil and political rights guaranteed by this same State, rather than the Ancient Greek model, in which citizens were those who, benefiting from the rights granted by the City, participated in the political and religious life of the City.

Social organisations, however, challenge the narrowness of the judicial definition which results from combined nationalism and political modernisation (Pędziwiatr 2010), and some researchers argue these should be considered as the expression of a social form of citizenship (McKinnon and Hampsher-Monk 2001) or even a cultural citizenship (Rizman 2005; Rosaldo 1994), as Muslim ethics definitely play a role in young Muslims' understanding of civic obligations (Pędziwiatr 2010). As demonstrated in the interview data above, volunteers challenge and, at the same time, conform to traditional forms of citizenship, which is a trend one can extend to Muslims in Europe generally (Pędziwiatr 2010). The social participation of these young Muslims results in a citizenship learned in informal contexts, 'from the bottom' (Delanty 2002). Volunteers such as Yandé,

Zeineb and Fatima, who define themselves as 'citizens of the world', evoke trends related to the denationalisation of citizenship (Sassen 2002) and global citizenship (Heater 1999; Falk 1994), unwilling to identify with a nation and are in tune with a transnational idea of *Ummah* (global Muslim community) (Mandaville 2001). However, by embodying an active, participatory form of citizenship, which Daniel Cefaï (2007) calls 'concrete citizenship', they break from the current passive acceptation of the concept and refresh it as it was initially thought. Michael Walzer (1989) defines citizenship as the appropriation of universal attributes by a State and consequent ethical rules.

Official and historical texts such as the Declaration of Human Rights and Citizens of 1789 (article 2), the 1948 Universal Declaration of Human Rights (article 2) imply a duty to togetherness (Madec and Murard 1995). Therefore, the answer to why society has slowly accepted citizenship as a passive concept is unclear. Some researchers would define this category of positive, proactive civic engagement at different levels of politics and society as 'Active Citizenship' (Peucker and Ceylan 2016; Peucker and Akbarzadeh 2014, 4; Hoskins and Mascherini 2009, 462; Adler and Goggin 2005, 241; Mouffe 1992, 4). As such, active citizenship contrasts with the (neo)liberal 'non-participatory, interest-based politics of *homo economicus*, which traditionally served both as an empirical generalization and as an implicit norm of citizenship' (Crowley 1998, 167). These Muslim volunteers link the religious perspective to an active understanding of citizenship 'in order to improve conditions for others or to help shape the community's future' (Adler and Goggin's 2005, 241).

However, charities go even further in their practical implementations of democracy when they use alternative, more equitable modes of governance through tools such as *shura* (consultation and consensus) rather than universal suffrage, or there is an absence of pyramidal hierarchy. This consultation is informal and very different from '*shura* councils' in Middle Eastern countries. In Amatullah or Averroès, hierarchy only exists on paper, as it is a legal requirement for charities to have a CEO and a treasurer. Decisions are made in a consultative manner: every present member voices their opinion; the decisions are discussed and compared one by one before one is chosen unanimously. For example, when making decisions such as new policies, guidelines for the charity or deciding the next year's project, every member present at a meeting at Amatullah is asked to suggest ideas, as a sort of brainstorming, and then choose the favourite one. Then, in order to decide which option will be adopted, a discussion begins in which everyone offers arguments and pros and cons. The discussion does not end until everyone agrees on an idea. Most of the *shura* processes need a few hours, an evening or an afternoon, but some may last for days with phone or Skype discussions and one-to-one conversations between different members and the CEO. Eventually, a second meeting is held to validate the whole process., Although the CEO has the final word and is under no obligation to ask everyone, for some guideline decisions *shura* is a tool for him to use to consult the volunteers and take into account suggestions from other members, ensuring that the new rules benefit everyone and do not create any disagreement. Whereas the result of a vote can appear as a definitive sanction to the opposition, the result of a consultation is always flexible and evolutive. Tocqueville (1835) warned against universal suffrage and its risks of 'tyranny of the majority': nothing holds a society back from making a decision opposed to the general interest if the majority wins – as evidenced by the rise of far-right parties in Europe. Decisions undergo a bureaucratic process where the opinion of everyone is fixed and dehumanised through a voting bulletin.

Tocqueville soon realised the importance of associations in the realisation of an egalitarian democracy. In the twenty-first century, organisations producing thick trust and strong ties (see Chapters 3 and 4) were a response to a society characterised by individualism, atomisation, fragmentation and becoming more 'self-seeking, calculating, greedy, with weaker social ties and loyalties and a diminishing sense of trust and social solidarity' (Elshain 1995, 5–27). These elements are characteristic of a hyper-modern society. I define here 'hyper-modernity' as a culture of division and rationalisation (Touraine 1992) pushed to an exponential, hyperbolic development. This is in line with the concept of 'high modernity' as an unfaltering confidence in science and technology as a means to reorder the social and natural world (Scott 1998; Giddens 1991). Also called 'late modernity', or 'liquid modernity' (Bauman 2000), it is a form of developed, radicalised, chaotic modernity, the characteristic of which is the increasing feeling of uncertainty (Beck 1992), where people can change places, jobs, spouses or values, excluding themselves from traditional structures. In this volatile environment where individual responsibility disappears (Styrdom 1999; Apel 1993), these charities realised that politics are not the sole attribute of the State; and that the strengthening of democracy and its humanisation can only be achieved by them through a project 'made from collective actions initiated by free and equal citizens acting for a common good' (Laville 2010, 7).

Their thought is in the lineage of John Dewey (1927), underlining the importance of starting democracy 'at home' and in their neighbourhood, as writes Laville (2010, 4; my translation): 'the decisive importance for democracy of the preservation and the widening of a public sphere conditioned by the voluntary participation of the citizens'. In a risk society characterised by its extreme volatility, (Beck 1992), the volunteers experience co-responsibility and a primary form of democracy (Newton 1999; see also Chapter 4) or a 'primary culture of democracy' (Cooley 1909). The concept of fraternity is not dead, as social capital becomes the functional equivalent of fraternity (Newton 1999, 5) and enables one to fathom a society offering hope for individual and collective emancipation (Laville 2010, 11).

The orientation that these 'schools for democracy and solidarity' (Chanial 2003, 278–81) transmit through their customs and feelings has the potential to end later in the state institutions. The example of these Muslim charities can clearly be conceived as a birthplace, or the cradle (Chanial 2001 and 2008), of an innovative way of practising democracy enriched with traditional concepts and inspired by Islamic ethics. Muslim volunteers involved in charities adopt along their journey an understanding of the role of citizenship (and the role of the believer) as someone responsible and accountable. They substitute a formal, passive citizenship for a more active meaning, of participation and fraternity, reinventing a 'social' citizenship, if not 'concrete' (Cefaï 2007), 'renewed' (Madec and Murard 1995) or simply 'active' (Peucker and Ceylan 2016; Peucker and Akbarzadeh 2014, 4; Hoskins and Mascherini 2009, 462; Adler and Goggin 2005, 241; Mouffe 1992, 4). These young Muslims redraw the figure of the citizen, giving substance to juridical status (Cefaï 2007): if the citizen is not necessarily a believer, any believer is necessarily a citizen. Not only are Islam and citizenship seen as compatible, but they operate subjectively a fusion in common set of values. As per the findings of Pędziwiatr (2010), more than serving as a powerful unifying force and giving public life a philosophical and spiritual depth, Islam induces social and political participation. Through their small scale and their focus on human relations, these small charities are refreshing fundamental concepts of modern societies such as citizenship and democracy due to a governance based on trust, constructive conflict and compromises. Furthermore, these are true alternatives to institutions based on hierarchy, bureaucracy or procedures, through traditional tools such as *shura*. Far from seeking a stringent respect of the rules and limiting risks through the building of barriers and formal divisions, they develop remarkable flexibility and adaptability, allowing exchanges and mutual construction. Will one see larger institutions or structures inspired from these small-scale charities? Is it possible to adapt the governance of these small structures to larger organisations? Maybe see consultation being used at the scale of a neighbourhood or a town? These are points to be further explored. However, although inspired by traditional alternatives, these charities equally embrace the modern culture in which they are immersed. Whether it is in the fields of arts, new technologies or others, they are modern in many perspectives. It happens that even in terms of governance, they borrow techniques from the extremes of productivism and managerialism that they try to justify through Islam, having as a consequence mixed results.

Notes

1. Meeting and informal discussion about a religious topic.
2. Night of prayers and discussions similar to Halaqa.
3. Blessings.
4. Manuel Valls : "La question du voile relève d'un combat sur la condition des femmes". www.lepoint.fr/politique/manuel-valls-la-question-du-voile-releve-d-un-combat-sur-la-condition-des-femmes-10-04-2013-1652945_20.php [last accessed on 15 Jan. 2017].
5. Nabil Touati. "ONPC": Nadine Morano parle de "race blanche" (mais aurait dû consulter un dictionnaire). www.huffingtonpost.fr/2015/09/27/oncp-nadine-morano-race-blanche-dictionnaire-laurent-ruquier_n_8202250.html?utm_hp_ref=nadine-morano [last accessed on 15 Jan. 2017].
6. Dictionary from the French National Centre for Lexical Resources, www.cnrtl.fr/ [last accessed on 15 Jan. 2017].

References

Adler, R. and Goggin, J. (2005). What Do We Mean By 'Civic Engagement'? *Journal of Transformative Education*, 3(3), 236–53.

Amiraux, V. (2006). Speaking as a Muslim: Avoiding Religion in French Public Space. In: Jonker, G. and Amiraux, V. (eds.) *Politics of Visibility: Young Muslims in European Public Spaces*. Bielefeld: Transcript Verlag, pp. 21–52.
Apel, K-O. (1993). How to Ground a Universalist Ethics of Co-Responsibility for the Effects of Collective Actions and Activities. *Philosophica*, 52(2), 9–29.
Asad, T. (2003). *Formations of the Secular: Christianity, Islam, Modernity*. Stanford: Stanford University Press.
Baubérot, J. (2006). *L'Intégrisme Républicain contre la Laïcité [The Republican Fundamentalism Against Secularism]*. Paris: L'Aube.
Bauman, Z. (2000). *Liquid Modernity*. Cambridge: Polity Press.
Beck, U. (1992). *Risk Society: Towards a New Modernity*. London: Sage.
Caillé, A. (2011). Les indicateurs de richesse alternatifs: une fausse bonne idée ? [Wealth Indicators: A Wrong Good Idea?]. In: Caillé, A., Humbert, M., Latouche, S. and Viveret, P. (eds.) *De la convivialité, dialogues sur la société conviviale à venir*. Paris: La Découverte, pp. 141–66.
Canda, E. R. and Furman, L. D. (2010). *Spiritual Diversity in Social Work Practice: The Heart of Helping*. Oxford: Oxford University Press.
Cefaï, D. (2007). *Pourquoi se Mobilise-t-on? Les Théories de l'Action Collective [Why Do People Mobilise? The Theories of Collective Action]*. Paris: La Découverte.
Chanial, P. (2003). La culture primaire de la démocratie: Communautés locales, publics démocratiques et associations [The Primary Culture of Democracy: Local Communities, Democratic Audiences and Charities]. In: Cefaï, D. et Pasquier, D. (eds.) *Les Sens du public: Publics politiques, publics médiatiques*. Paris: Presses Universitaires de France, pp. 269–89.
Chanial, P. (2001). *Justice, Don, Association [Justice, Gift, Charity]*. Paris: La Découverte.
Chanial, P. (2008). *La société vue du don [Society From a Gift Perspective]*. Paris: La Découverte.
Chanial, P. (2011). *La sociologie comme philosophie politique et réciproquement [Sociology as a Political Philosophy and Reciprocally]*. Paris: La Découverte.
Chouder, I., Latrèche, M. and Tevanian, P. (2008). *Les filles voilées parlent [Women in Headscarves Are Speaking]*. Paris: La Fabrique.
Clarke, P. A. B. (1994). *Citizenship: A Reader*. London: Pluto Press.
Cooley, C. H. (1909). *Social Organization: A Study of the Larger Mind*. New York: Charles Scribner's Sons.
Crowley, J. (1998). The National Dimension of Citizenship in T. H. Marshall. *Citizenship Studies*, 2(2), 165–78.
Crozier, M. (1987). *Etat modeste, Etat moderne [Modest State, Modern State]*. Paris: Seuil.
Delanty, G. (2000). *Citizenship in a Global Age: Society, Culture, Politics*. Buckingham/Philadelphia: Open University Press.
Delanty, G. (2002). Two Conceptions of Cultural Citizenship: A Review of Recent Literature on Culture and Citizenship. *The Global Review of Ethnopolitics*, 1(1), 60–6.
Dewey, J. (1927). *The Public and Its Problems*. University Park: Penn State University Press.
Elshtain, J. B. (1995). *Democracy on Trial*. New York: Basic Books.
Emden, C. J. and Midgley, D. eds. (2012). *Changing Perceptions of the Public Sphere*. New York: Berghahn Books.
Fadil, N. (2006). We Should Be Walking Qurans: The Making of an Islamic Political Subject. In: Jonker, G. and Amiraux, V. (eds.) *Politics of Visibility: Young Muslims in European Public Spaces*. Bielefeld: Transcript Verlag, pp. 53–78.

Falk, R. (1994). The Making of Global Citizenship. In: Van Steenberg, B. (ed.) *The Conditions of Citizenship*. London: Sage, pp. 127–39.

Giddens, A. (1991). *The Consequences of Modernity*. Stanford: Stanford University Press.

Göle, N. (1995). *L'émergence du sujet islamique, in Penser le sujet* [*The Emergence of the Islamic Subject*]. Autour d'Alain Touraine, Colloque de Cerisy. Paris: Fayard.

Göle, N. (2003). The Voluntary Adoption of Islamic Stigma Symbols. *Social Research*, 70(3), 809–28.

Göle, N. (2005). *Interpénétrations: L'Islam et l'Europe* [*Interpenetrations: Islam and Europe*]. Paris: Galaade.

Habermas, J. (1978) [1962]. *L'espace public: archéologie de la publicité comme dimension constitutive de la société bourgeoise* [*The Structural Transformation of the Public Sphere*], trans. De Launay, J. B. Paris: Payot.

Heater, D. (1999). *What Is Citizenship?* Cambridge: Polity Press.

Hoskins, B. and Mascherini, M. (2009). Measuring Active Citizenship Through the Development of a Composite Indicator. *Social Indicators Research*, 90(3), 459–88.

Laville, J-L. (2010). *Politique de l'association* [*The Politics of Charities*]. Paris: Seuil.

McKinnon, C. and Hampsher-Monk, I. eds. (2001). *The Demands of Citizenship*. London: Continuum.

Madec, A. and Murard, N. (1995). *Citoyenneté et politiques sociales: un exposé pour comprendre, un essai pour réfléchir* [*Citizenship and Social Policies: A Presentation to Understand, an Essay to Reflect*]. Paris: Flammarion.

Mandaville, P. (2001). *Transnational Muslim Politics: Reimagining the Umma*. London: Routledge.

Mann, M. (1987). The Ruling Class Strategy and Citizenship. *Sociology*, 21(3), 339–54.

Marshall, T. H. (1992) [1950]. *Citizenship and Social Class*. Cambridge: Cambridge University Press.

Mouffe, C. (1992). *Dimensions of Radical Democracy: Pluralism, Citizenship, Community*. London: Verso.

Newton, K. (1999). Social Capital and Democracy in Modern Europe. In: Van Deth, J. W., Maraffi, M., Newton, K. and Whiteley, P. F. (eds.) *Social Capital and European Democracy*. London: Routledge, pp. 3–24.

Pędziwiatr, K. (2010). *The New Muslim Elites in European Cities: Religion and Active Social Citizenship Amongst Young Organized Muslims in Brussels and London*. Saarbrücken: VDM Verlag.

Peucker, M. and Akbarzadeh, S. (2014). *Muslim Active Citizenship in the West*. Oxon and New York: Routledge.

Peucker, M. and Ceylan, R. (2016). Muslim Community Organizations: Sites of Active Citizenship or Self-Segregation? *Ethnic and Racial Studies*, doi: 10.1080/01419870.2016.1247975

Pocock, J. G. A. (1998). The Ideal of Citizenship Since Classical Times. *Queen's Quarterly*, 99(1), 33–55.

Rizman, R. M. (2005). Nationalisme et citoyenneté démocratique. In: Conseil de l'Europe (ed.) *Concepts de la citoyenneté démocratique*. Strasbourg: Editions du Conseil de l'Europe, pp. 111–24.

Rosaldo, R. (1994). Cultural Citizenship and Educational Democracy. *Cultural Anthropology*, 9(3), 402–11.

Sassen, S. (2002). The Repositioning of Citizenship: Emergent Subjects and Spaces for Politics. *Berkeley Journal of Sociology*, 46, 4–25.

Scott, J. C. (1998). *Seeing Like a State: How Certain Schemes to Improve the Human Condition Have Failed*. New Haven: Yale University Press.
Styrdom, P. (1999). The Challenge of Collective Responsibility for Sociology. *Current Sociology*, 47(3), 65–82.
Tocqueville, A. de (1998) [1835]. *De la démocratie en Amérique [Democracy in America]*. Paris: Flammarion.
Touraine, A. (1992). *Critique de la Modernité [Critique of Modernity]*. Paris: Fayard.
Van Tienen, M., Scheepers, P., Reitsma, J. and Schilderman, H. (2011). The Role of Religiosity for Formal and Informal Volunteering in the Netherlands. *Voluntas*, 22(3), 365–89.
Venel, N. (2002). *Musulmans et Citoyens [Muslims and Citizens]*. Paris: PUF.
Verba, S., Schlozman, K. and Brady, H. eds. (1995). *Voice and Equality: Civic Voluntarism in American Politics*. Cambridge: Harvard University Press.
Walzer, M. (1989). Citizenship. In: Ball, T., Farr, J. and Hanson, R., (eds.) *Political Innovation and Conceptual Change*. Cambridge: Cambridge University Press.

6   Neoliberal metacolonisation

In the months preceding my move to the UK, I had the chance to attend one singular event at the Global Peace and Unity (GPU) fair in London. The GPU is probably the British equivalent to the French RAMF (*Rencontres Annuelle des Musulmans de France*), a yearly meeting of French Muslims in Le Bourget. Between food and charity stalls and speeches given by British Muslim superstars, I stumbled upon an intriguing open space inside of the prayer room. From the outside, I saw men and women walking around, carefully examining sheets of paper on the wall. The sheets were anonymous profiles reading as follows: 'ID number, Age, City, Ethnicity, Qualifications, Occupations/Hobbies'. It did not take me long to realise that the space inside of the prayer hall was nothing but a speed-dating event (see Figure 6.1). People were selecting the profiles which appealed the most to them, writing the IDs down on a list and eventually meeting and talking with their potential partners. People roamed around as if they were shopping in a supermarket, hesitating between a box of Twinings and PG Tips. I could imagine them saying 'the C29 looks nice, oh wait, the B14 seems interesting too'. Later in the day, in the GPU alleyways, I happened to pass by some couples, both wearing badges like C29 and D23. I could only think, 'I know where you both got these'. First, for anyone who knows the traditional way of finding a spouse according to Islam (and I do not mention traditions exclusive to some cultures), seeing Muslims involved in a speed-dating session appears to break a number of rules. If traditionally men and women do not meet alone for the purpose of marriage, making these meetings happen in a public space is one of the techniques the organisers have found to make it '*halal*' or '*sharia*-friendly'. But what struck me the most were the CV-like profiles, a mere matter of numbers and professional data. How were people supposed to select their potential partners solely according to their job and qualifications? With all these CVs, it seemed that the quest for a spouse had become a consumerist issue, as have many others. Even Muslims seemed to have succumbed to the sirens of rationalisation of the daily life. Trading complex human lives for CVs with figures and facts, people want problems to be solved faster, solutions to be more efficient. Potential spouses were products people selected, tried, bought and, perhaps, later replaced. Where had the human dimension gone? But, considering this event for what it was, a speed-dating session, what I saw was a mere copy-paste from the mainstream modern

Figure 6.1 Muslim 'marriage event' event at the GPU in London.

speed-dating principle, with a tweak to make it appeal to a Muslim audience. However, this event was only the tip of a much larger iceberg; I was only at the beginning of my realisations.

These young Muslims are able to refresh key modern concepts in light of their religion and ethics (such as citizenship; see Chapter 5), but they are also able to appropriate modern mind-sets and make them fit in the mould of *halal* requirements. In an attempt to build an identity that would simultaneously be faithful to traditions and the modern (Göle 2003), some highly skilled volunteers, working as executives for large, 'competitive', multinational companies embracing neoliberal standards, have implemented the methods that they have been taught in their corporate trainings in these small charities. Reshaping the traditional family-like environment and informal modes of governance in a workframe tinted with spirituality, they create an original form of result-driven Islam. Harvey (2005, 1) defines neoliberalism as 'the doctrine that market exchange is an ethic in itself, capable of acting as a guide for all human action'. However, Islam offers an anti-individualistic and anti-materialistic vision of life (Panjwani 2012a and 2012b). Volunteers are attracted by grassroots charities because of their flexibility and their ability to deliver concrete results quickly (see Chapter 4). They are seen as a more attractive form of politics than slow bureaucratic NGOs or the government (Panjwani 2012a and 2012b). The environment that grassroots charities offer focuses on friendship or family-like bonds and conviviality (Caillé 2011a; Humbert 2011). Rejecting any form of materialism, consumerism and a utilitarian vision of human resources, they appear to many as a social space safe from races

106 *Neoliberal metacolonisation*

for money, power and ego. Therefore, how do these charities manage the coexistence of two opposed reference systems? How do neoliberalism and corporate culture impact and reshape not-for-profit European Muslim charities? What are the outlines, characteristics and specificities of the charities resulting from this influence? What does this phenomenon translate into?

With the help of comparative elements taken in the wider context of different European Muslim communities in France and the United Kingdom, I here explore how different charities crystallise the fusion, if not the struggle, of growing as a Muslim charity in a modern, secular context. This chapter offers an overview of the working environment and how it contrasts with more traditional ones, especially through the virtualisation of exchanges and the dematerialisation of the working environment. Finally, I discuss how the influence of neoliberalism and elements of corporate culture have reshaped these Muslim charities, their volunteers and, on a larger scale, European Muslim communities.

Muslims, consumerism and neoliberalism

Traditionally, initiatives have been established to respond to religious prescriptions in the sectors of *halal* foods, ethical finance (Corbet 2015; Kammarti 2015) and funeral services (Balkan 2015; Ural 2015). The second decade of the twenty-first century saw mainstream clothing brands such as H&M and Dolce & Gabbana developing a range of products aimed at Muslim consumers. These products, such as *hijabs* or outfits derived from *abayas* (a loose robe-like dress), stirred controversy, as these brands also used Muslim fashion models such as Mariah Idrissi donning the *hijab*.[1] However, these clothing lines, belonging to the realm of 'modest fashion', are only the tip of a bigger iceberg of a wide range of products targeted at the Muslim demographic which was developed considerably earlier, with interest-free products in the banking sector since the 2000s (Kammarti 2015) and *halal* food (developed since the 1960s and 1970s). The emergence of fashion trends such as 'Islamic wear' and '*hijab* chic' are not only niche markets trying to render modesty as a consumption product (Kammarti 2015), but in a wider perspective, these are also attempts to show a 'cool' image of Islam.

While the 2000s and early 2010s saw a tidal wave of Muslim televangelism (like Amr Khaled) and Islamic hotlines coming to the West (Guidi 2015), these were superseded in the mid-2010s by YouTube preachers and renowned Islamic scholars setting up their YouTube channels (Nouman Ali Khan, Suhaib Webb, Yasir Qadhi, etc.). This atomisation of discourses and channels of knowledge has put an end to the religious monopoly by traditional authorities. Various bloggers and vloggers present various angles of their own vision of 'Islamic' lifestyle. Besides *halal* cosmetics, numerous blogs exist around the topic of 'modest fashion'. It is easy to find *hijab* or makeup tutorials for Muslims on YouTube, and their channels attract millions of followers. Visual content–oriented platforms such as Facebook, YouTube, Instagram and Snapchat allow for the experimentation of new forms of identity through clothing, arts and food. Mass access to social media and the consequent monetisation of YouTube 'views', Facebook pages and

Instagram 'likes' reduces the space between private content and advertisement; both are sometimes amalgamated in a form of marketing strategy. As a result, images conveyed by fashion brands and top-subscribed figures are emulated. Devotion becomes fashionable and fashion becomes a form of devotion like in 'Salafi-chic' trends, where traditionally strict outfits are displayed alongside Louis Vuitton accessories. Social media becomes, therefore, a way to build an apparent identity based on what people buy and wear and who they follow.

However, how original are these trends which fuse modern culture and traditional Islamic elements? Bands such as Deen Squad are copycats of American non-Muslim rap and hip-hop bands; their videos depict them dancing in *qamises* (long robes worn by men) in front of a mosque with moves and lyrics rooted in the same sources of inspiration and similarly depicting women as decorative elements: 'She's my halal diva / A painting on the wall / She's my Muslim Mona Lisa.'[2] In the UK, Harris J. (one million followers at the end of 2016) bears striking resemblances in his look, attire, musical style and lyrics to Canadian superstar Justin Bieber. Modern Muslims are no strangers to fandom phenomena in which singers and YouTubers mobilise crowds in a way historically seen for American pop stars. When 21-year-old Adam Saleh, who became famous for his prank videos on YouTube, advertised his presence in London in August 2014 through a single tweet, it resulted in a crowd of hundreds of young women, many wearing the *hijab*, shouting and running towards Saleh in Marble Arch.[3] The way people meet and marry has also been redefined by services such as Muslim dating websites and Muslim speed dating (Hadjab 2015), which merely copy modern matchmaking methods, with some jurisprudence tweaks to label it as '*halal*'. These phenomena of mass culture and emulation of mainstream 'Western' products are sometimes analysed as a 'Westernisation' or 'Americanisation' of diasporic minorities (Ali et al. 2006; Dwyer 2000; Gillespie 1995). However, these are more consequences of the modern global market economy, which is not exclusive to the 'West' (Mandaville 2001). In *l'Islam de marché* (Market Islam), Patrick Haenni (2005) posits that there is a phenomenon of individualisation of religion whereby more people prioritise their personal goals, such as individual wellbeing and seeking answers on the Internet rather than in books or meetings with local scholars, that results in knowledge of Islamic jurisprudence being reduced to a click-and-consume product. Will one see in a near future *halal* websites for 'hiring' *mahrams* (husband or unmarriageable kin)? Will one see Muslim Hipsters setting-up bars serving ZamZam water, which can be delivered at home by Deliveroo? Will some companies develop Über-like services for *Hajj* for superseding expensive travel agencies, or perhaps *Hajj* through virtual reality? Will one see *fatwa*-approved and *sharia*-friendly pornography? Everything seems possible.

For some Muslims who have been looking for solutions to curb prejudices and discrimination, consumerism can appear as a possible way to acquire legitimacy in the public sphere. Money has no ethnicity or religion, therefore consuming can work as a statement of conformation: Muslims are consumers like any others. In an interview given to the *Guardian*, the author of *Generation M* (Janmohammed 2016) summarises the motto of these young Muslims trying to fit in through consumerism and become legitimate in a society hostile to Muslims:

'Hello, we've got lots of money to spend, we're young, we're cool, please can you deal with us the same way you deal with everyone else?'[4] Experimentations mixing religious symbols such as the *hijab* with modern trends gave birth to the term 'Mipster',[5] coined as a hybrid between 'Muslim' and 'Hipster.' This trend has been embodied by the brand BENI [all capitals], among others, issuing in 2015 stickers for Mac laptops. Gaining a worldwide coverage after the release in 2014 of the 'Happy British Muslims' video',[6] BENI started to sell stickers with geometric shapes reminiscent of traditional North African or Andalusian Islamic patterns. The product (the descriptions of which did not bear any mention to Islam) encountered remarkable worldwide success and have been sold in Europe, the Emirates, Saudi Arabia, Malaysia, Singapore, the US and Canada as of the end of 2016 – not to mention that the widely famous American Muslim scholar Hamza Yusuf displayed one on his MacBook at a conference. How does some student in Indonesia relates to traditional North African patterns by sticking it on his/her MacBook? It is known that Muslims, especially from the South Asian diaspora worldwide, have been consuming South Asian culture as the expression of melancholia, a longing for a loved and romanticised past rooted in the Indian subcontinent (Lallmahomed-Aumeerally 2014); now the younger generation of Muslims is able to produce cultural content through arts and business that expresses the nostalgia for the imagined, idealised and romanticised pasts or roots of its community. Eisenlohr (2006) posits that there is a trend among Muslims seeking to relocate the *Ummah* (worldwide Muslim community) within a Middle Eastern and Arabic imaginary, having appropriated Arabic as their ancestral language; this can be illustrated by South Asians abandoning the Bangla/Hindi/Urdu '*bhai*' for the Arabic '*akhi*' (brother) when speaking to each other. In a different attempt than the book *Generation M*, in an interview for Buzzfeed the founder of BENI expressed his aim, of wanting to create a 'life brand' associated with a specific culture and content, arguing that brands 'don't understand the demographic' and therefore are 'exploiting' the Muslims as a niche market.[7] BENI and *Generation M* express the will for Muslims to produce their own narrative and be normalised as an active part of the economy (not just as consumers), presenting fashionable trend-setters, affluent entrepreneurs and resourceful creatives.

The sample of people featured in BENI, or shown and written about in similar blogs, videos, articles and other media are not any Muslims: they share certain characteristics. They are all entrepreneurs, artists or other creatives, often less than 30 years old and with a considerable following on social media. They may also own sports cars, wear designer clothes, travel to tropical destinations in the summer and spend their winter holidays skiing in the Alps.[8] Whereas BENI products and videos are overall well-received on social media, not everyone shares the same opinion, which has little to do with religion but rather representation. A discussion illustrates some of the main criticism of this perspective. Munazza, a graphics designer working in advertisement, discusses with her friends the various BENI videos and the 'Generation M' narrative:

Munazza: We're just exploited. Personal worth is set: it's flashy cars, success, glamourising things. . . . I'm so frustrated because it's becoming the narrative [sic]. Where is the love? We need stories for healing with love.

Friend 1: We had only two options: either the Islamophobic narrative served by mainstream media, or the religious *da'wa* salafi narrative. Now we have the Mipsters and this Generation M thing. How about all the people who do not fit the Mipster narrative, who are not tall slim and fair-skinned, rich, famous and creative?

Friend 2: How does that affect someone with depression and low self-esteem? I hate that Muslims are becoming a marketable brand.

However, in the same Buzzfeed interview and in conversations, the founder of BENI acknowledged various existing criticisms, including that the project might not be for 'everybody'. Many questions await answers. Will one see a counter-narrative emerging on social media? Will these trends become critical of themselves? If not, how will Muslims become accepted when Nike issues a *hijab* line? What pushes these Muslims to tap into various cultural realms to which they have no connection? Sayyid (2010) argues that Muslim identity is homeless as it has no overarching political structure to house it. In a Saidian (1984) perspective of travel, the transnational *Ummah* (worldwide Muslim community) has both religious points of origins (Mecca, Madina) and cultural ones (Africa, South Asia, the Middle East, etc.), and one precise point of destination (the place of settling). Muslims born in Europe, sometimes from parents of mixed cultural or religious backgrounds, have more points of origins to connect, and at the same time, multiple options for their aimed destinations. Moreover, the relationship within the European homeland is complex. Sana drew a comparison between her and parents' generation:

> They knew they had to live and participate in the society: be kind to their neighbours, get jobs, learn English, seek advice from English people, but they didn't have this emotional craving for acceptance like our generation. Living here it's like being in abusive relationship with parents: the state is a care giver and an abuser at the same time. The state takes care of you: you have the benefit system, the NHS, but at the same time, it tells you 'I don't want you here' with some politicians, the structural inequalities etc. It's confusing.

BENI's motto is 'if you don't define yourself, someone else will'. However, BENI and *Generation M* define Muslims as producers and consumers – preferably young, affluent and relatively wealthy. Key actors of this 'Generation M' are performing a metaphoric *hijra* (migration to more auspicious lands for religious practice) to an aimed and hoped-for space of acceptance. However, in sailing on the ocean of possibilities to reach this space of acceptance, the ship they choose to embark on for this journey is the volatile and uncertain neoliberal market. The question is whether this journey will actually reach its aim or if the ship will become the Raft of the Medusa. Paradoxically, this longing for a familiar heritage even produces the self-orientalisation of the subjects through a romanticised, idealised imaginary of the past (Aly 2015). These phenomena are characteristic of a process of de-diasporisation (Eisenlohr 2006), which is also indicative of a subtle but strong form of cultural, social, political and economic colonisation.

Metacolonialism and radical monopoly

Hussein Bulhan (2015) describes how market trends, international regulations, business methods, processes and generally culture worldwide are insistently suggested by or forced to adopt Western standards. In his article *Stages of Colonialism in Africa* (2015), he introduces the concept of metacolonialism. According to Bulhan, metacolonialism refers to 'a socio-political, economic, cultural and psychological system that comes after, along with, or among the earlier stages of colonialism' (2015, 244), or a 'colonial system that goes beyond in scope or behind in depth what classical colonialism and neocolonialism had achieved'.

Classical colonialism, which started with the invasion, occupation and exploitation of the Americas (Quijano 2000), was from the beginning economic, political, cultural and psychological. What started with the geographical occupation and control of land and then control of populations, resulted in a sustained 'occupation of being' (Bulhan 2015) which left behind enduring political, economic, cultural, intellectual and social legacies that kept alive European hegemony. The development and expansion of colonialism affected the thought, behaviour and generally the life of colonised peoples as well as the way formerly colonised peoples acquired knowledge, understood their history, comprehended their world and defined themselves. This was operated through the dissemination of Eurocentric epistemology, ontology and ideology, which emanated from, supported and validated the European monopoly of power, hegemonic knowledge, distorted truth, and deformed being of the colonised (Quijano 2000; Mignolo 2000a, 2000b and 2003; Dussel 1985 and 1996), while at the same time invalidating, marginalising and eroding the knowledge, experience and rights of colonised peoples (Alcoff 2007; Maldonado-Torres 2007). The erosion of social bonding, indigenous beliefs, values, identities and indigenous knowledge was achieved by the coloniser through different agents, such as missionaries, anthropologists, physicians and journalists, and the education of local agents through colonial schools to carry out the colonial mission. Neocolonialism (Amin 1973; Nkrumah 1965), on the other hand, started when so-called local colonial elites inherited the colonial state whose function was not to serve the colonised but to exploit them. Bulhan suggests that many African states turned after independence into a 'neocolonial machine that not only oppressed the people, but also worked to the advantage of former colonial powers and their allies' (Bulhan 2008).

Metacolonialism operates with a similar change of agents. Emanating from the same centres of power during the Atlantic slave trade, it has become global and subtle; it penetrates deeper in the collective mind and 'blurs the previous distinctions of social class, ethnicity and race' (Bulhan 2015, 244). While writers like Fanon (1967 and 1968) have operated with clear distinctions between colonisers and colonised, Bulhan argues that such distinctions are no longer adequate.

Anyone can adopt a colonial mind-set. Metacolonialism dictates European standards for conduct in national and international relations through economics and self-evaluation. This has tangible consequences in areas such as beauty standards (the global obsession with fair skin), international trade or Eurocentric theories and methods in science (see Chapter 1).

I would add, to complement Bulhan's definition, that metacolonialism is a form of colonisation which is not forced upon people, but is instead a set of economic, social, political and cultural conventions which:

1   People have to adopt in order to be perceived as legitimate in a given society;
2   Leave no space for local, individual, economic, social and cultural identities or uniqueness. It is a culture of conformation which makes identities redundant.

The most obvious form of metacolonisation is the case of hyper-modern[9] neoliberalism:[10] anything which cannot be quantified has no value, including elements such as emotions, feelings, spirituality, friendship, forgiveness, patience and compassion . . . unless it can be merchandised. As an example, Facebook, through monitoring and selling users' data to companies for the display of targeted adverts, is the epitome of the merchandisation of social bonds. All these aforementioned non-quantifiable elements are depreciated and seen as contrary to the idea of progress (patience is not competitive, kindness is for the weak, religion is retrograde). As a result, cultural legacies, history or spirituality have no relevance, except if they can be turned into profitable products. Added to secularism and embedded white domination, this environment creates such a social pressure that people who do not belong to European perceived standards (White, Christian/secular, neoliberal) are led either to abandon their identities (as in the French assimilationist model), or be labelled as deviants. Thus, one of the expressions of metacolonialism is a form of ethnonormativity (Aly 2015) by the dominant society. Consequently, because Islam has no market value *per se*, its spiritual and ritual dimension are rejected, demonised as 'retrograde', 'foreign' or abandoned for the sake of a hegemonious secularism; or exploited as a niche market through fashion, food and other consumables. As per religion is opposed to modernity, metacolonisation acts by boasting the superiority of certain concepts and processes, invoking technical or material arguments, a process which Ivan Illitch calls 'radical monopoly' (Clerc 2011, 133). When technical means are, or seem, too effective, it creates a monopoly which prohibits access to other means deemed less effective: highways, for example, do not accept pedestrians and bicycles; modern trade does not accept barter. By defining and promoting through education what should create 'success' or 'happiness' – such as a quest for grades, results, material possessions and career –society defines a norm which people are not forced, but enjoined, to embrace. Modern society in big metropolises such as Paris and London offer a very limited range of action: for living, one has to pay bills and rent; for paying the bills, one has to work for a company; for continuing to work, one has to show results. Contemporary society and managerial culture are creating dependence through radical monopoly, turning the human being into a mere tool – into a machine serving these very same elites who will eventually subjugate him (Clerc 2011, 135). When this culture penetrates traditional communities and either makes them abandon their identities and traditions or enjoins them to adapt utilitarian methods to exist and justify those identities and traditions by distorting religious scriptures, which is anti-utilitarian by essence, it is a form of colonisation. The concept of radical monopoly can be applied to how social media has reshaped the gain of wealth and affluence.

In the age of social media, online presence has become a synonym of power. Individuals who do not work in traditional spheres but who obtain high media coverage (politics, cinema, music, sports) are able to earn a living from their media and Internet presence (Kim Kardashian is probably the best example). Major brands have realised that any individuals enjoying a certain number of followers on social media are powerful marketing and advertising tools. As a consequence, by featuring products and brands in seemingly ordinary posts (posing in the bedroom with a certain shampoo and talking about its merits on Instagram, writing a thank-you line for a hotel in post relating to travel abroad), seemingly ordinary individuals are able to earn a living from of their social media presence. What was initially a virtual social space for staying in touch with friends has become a gigantic shopping mall. And because consumerism in the age of the Internet has become related to identity, the intentions of some public figures under the spotlight has become harder to decipher for many. Muslim millennials (those usually born after 1980) who have been experimenting with new forms of engagement with a wider audience as a means to curb prejudices have triggered heated debates. A major example is the controversy surrounding Noor Tagouri's appearance in *Playboy Magazine* in September 2016.[11]

> I did it (. . .) for people who come after me to reclaim their power to kick down closed doors and break through glass ceilings. I did it (. . .) to demonstrate that there is nothing more powerful than a woman being unapologetically herself.[12]

Noor Tagouri posed in covering clothes with her *hijab*; the issue is therefore definitely not linked to religious norms, but to the ethics of choosing to pose for *Playboy* – a magazine traditionally known for objectifying women – as a woman not wanting to be objectified. But beyond the question of whether or not Noor Tagouri posing in *hijab* helps the discussion or adds one more costume to a wardrobe of fetishes,[13] the debate drifted to the very question of the purpose of her online presence:

> She represents that new generation M type – the extremely affluent, extremely privileged Muslims who reproduce the capitalist machine, whilst claiming to break stereotypes when the real work being done by hundreds of dedicated Muslims, the grass-roots, community-work, who never get a fraction of the publicity she gets.[14]

Many online commenters compared the *Playboy* interview to other Muslim women posing in *hijab* for other magazines, which were conversely celebrated but drew much less attention: American runner Rahaf Khatib's appearance on the cover of US magazine *Women's Running*[15] the same week went almost unnoticed. Contrary to Muslim female public figures in sports, for example, for which online fame is a consequence of their offline achievements, Noor Tagouri's aim of becoming the first television anchor to wear the *hijab* in the US is dependent on her online presence. Ibtihaj Muhammad and Asma Elbadawi gained major followings because one is a national fencing champion and the other is a professional basketball player and a talented poet; their careers would not be affected if they decided to close their online accounts. Conversely, Noor Tagouri's existence revolves around and is dependent on her online presence, which focuses exclusively on herself as an individual. However, in the age of social media, a massive online following means privilege, and this is perhaps the underlying issue that triggered controversy.

Social media has become a well-established marketing machine: anyone with an Instagram, Facebook or YouTube account with around 100,000 followers or above is able to not only get paid for views and product placement, but is also able to get free hotel nights, meals at renowned restaurants and travel discounts, in addition to being able to create links easily with people in top industries. Therefore, the controversy does not target Noor Tagouri as much as it targets this 'Generation M' club of privileged Muslims. As Fatima Ahdash pointed out in her comment, Noor Tagouri may be a Muslim woman wearing the *hijab* (thus initially a potential figurehead of the fight of Muslim women for legitimacy in the public sphere), but her growing popularity made her become part of an inaccessible elite, and the *Playboy* interview epitomises her journey. Many Muslim women could relate to figures such as Ibtihaj Muhammad and Asma Elbadawi, whose careers have been paved with hardships but who have kept faithful to their values in hostile environments: they are disrupters of modern secular, neoliberal conventions. Noor Tagouri has written that she agreed to the interview on 'her own terms'. But then, what are her own terms? Because not every Muslim woman is able to have Noor Tagouri's online following, to travel or to attend prestigious galas and be selected by famous mainstream magazines such as *Playboy* (and not everyone would be willing to the latter). Many Muslims felt suddenly disconnected from a woman to whom they could no longer relate. Noor Tagouri's fame is rooted in issues of race, colour, class and skin privilege, which illustrate a form of ethnonormativity (Aly 2015) from within. This ethnonormativity orients behavioural choices like the selection of spouses (Grewal 2009): American Muslim have better chances of getting married if they are Arab or White, or at least fair-skinned, slim and come from a rich family. However, not every American Muslim woman can be the light-skinned, Arab, middle-class lady that Noor Tagouri is. In the age of social media, the domination of images reflecting current beauty and material preferences (which become standards) has adverse effects on mental health (Kross et al. 2013; Anderson et al. 2012). As a consequence, young Muslims find themselves caught

114 *Neoliberal metacolonisation*

between two ethnonormativities, coming from both the dominant society and from within. However, when did the standards of being fair-skinned and slim became global standards? Although research shows that these standards are often residue from colonisation and white supremacy policies (Blay 2011), they are not solely the result of Western colonisation *per se*, which is an opportunity to highlight the nuance between colonisation and metacolonisation. While current global beauty standards emanate from Europe and America (with Paris, London and New York considered as the world's capitals of fashion), Balogun and Hoang (2013) show that some instances predate colonialism, and in the current globalised world, other factors are taken into consideration, such as multinational cosmetic companies or global media consumption. In her study of Miss India, Dewey (2008) shows how economic liberalisation policies in India shape pageants' conformation to international standards. As seen above, although the presence of colonial authority has taken different routes, the subtle embedding of Western beauty standards and their transfer into local norms shows how the globalised world acts as the echo chamber of colonial times through media, industry and economy. Metacolonisation as conceptualised by Bulhan is the residual echo of classical forms of colonisation. A further question would be to determine how different structures, contexts and initiatives dampen or amplify this echo.

In Noor Tagouri's own words, the interview was indeed a demonstration of power; however, what power is this? Is this the power of a person who has struggled and challenged conventions to reach her aim against all odds, offering a hopeful story to the unprivileged? Or is it the power of a person who accessed her status by conforming to dominant conventions, according to modern neoliberal standards of consumerism and individual fame? Is she actually reversing the stigma, or going along with the idea that she has been accepted by the dominant system? Amalia Ulman's artistic project and social experiment *Excellence and Perfections*[16] has demonstrated that the more online personalities perform according to conventional behaviours, the more people will engage with them and the more popular they will become. As a consequence, the means of personal expression of individuality offered by social media, overruled by dominant normative standards, happen to be illusory. This also explains why social media figures who perform this ethnonormativity in the shape of the replication of cultural (skin shade, fashion), social (wealth, status) or gender norms (hyper-feminisation/masculinisation) are often the most popular. As a conclusion, these social media personalities, although controversial, are not the 'problem' pointed by their critics; they are only symptomatic of greater structural forces. Even the critics of Noor Tagouri are probably caught in the same normative pitfalls. In general, social media is such that whether critiques are positive or negative, they all lead to the same result: they provide more media coverage for their subject. The critiques of Noor Tagouri have no effect but to add more fuel to a powerful advertising machine. However, in a smaller context, how does the 'active individualism' (Routledge 2003; Gill 1995) of neoliberalism affect the anti-individualistic, anti-materialistic message of Islam (Panjwani 2012a and 2012b)? The next section attempts a micro-sociological study of discourses and performances in the context of small charities.

The paradox of Muslim managerialism[17]

FCR[18] is an organisation that trains 'Muslim executives' using other Muslim executives and offers coaching sessions and seminars around personal development or project management in light of 'Islamic values'. FCR's aim is to create a network of all Muslim student unions in French engineering schools, copying the existing French engineering school student networks. This network would allow participants to demolish the obstacles of classical recruiting systems (which discriminate against people who have beards, wear *hijab*, or do not allow employees to pray at work).

The executive bureau comprises students who have completed the prestigious curriculum of French Engineering Schools and work in aeronautical, automobile and nuclear engineering. They market their image as 'successful' education and financial achievement, which legitimise their role as 'experts' and 'trainers'. Inspired by coaching manuals, they offer training sessions copied from the corporate sector: brunch is served at the beginning; the trainer is on stage with a PowerPoint presentation filled with graphics, amongst which are verses of the Qur'an and *hadiths*. At each meeting, everyone receives a file with a notebook, documents and pens with the organisation's logo (see Figure 6.2). Trainers wear three-piece suits with ties and use a vocabulary mixing corporate Anglo-Saxon terms and Islamic references in Arabic.

At FCR, most of the members have achieved the 'prestigious' *Classes Préparatoires* (preparatory courses for competitive entry exams), high-level 'prestigious' engineering schools (Polytechnique, HEC, Centrale), are working for

Figure 6.2 Seminar for coaching young Muslim executives.

highly-specialised 'prestigious' companies such as the CEA (Committee for Atomic Energy) or Aeronautics and are proud to exhibit themselves as examples of 'successful' individuals because of their 'prestigious' studies and careers. This picture legitimates their role as trainers, or 'experts', appointed by the board for designing the programme.

The lexicon used by members of FCR is punctuated by terms and idioms such as 'group dynamic', 'leadership', 'to boost', 'performance', 'excellence', 'role model', 'team building', 'buy in' and 'people developer', all used in English, while everyone in the audience was from the non-profit sector. People are being categorised in binary divisions between the 'motivated' and the 'skilled' and are developing a utilitarian vision of human resources: 'tooling the partners'. In order to understand the responsibility of the human being on Earth as a 'manager' serving God, the latter is compared to the 'CEO' of humanity. They use the language of competitive corporate management and life is described as a wide 'project planning', a 'scheduler' wrapped in Islam. Qur'anic verses and *hadiths* are selected to encourage those 'who will lead the Muslim community' by 'aiming at success, enhancement, perfection'. They often depict the Prophet Muhammad as 'an example of leadership'. Seminars and workshops are organised following the same rules as corporate training sessions: brunch, formal display (speaker at the front, trainees at the back), projector, PowerPoint presentation filled with diagrams, etc. Before the session begins, everyone receives a folder with a notebook and pen branded with the charity's logo, and trainers all wear finely-tailored suits. FCR offers the 'art' of 'managing' the *Ummah* (worldwide Muslim community) and, to a greater extent, FCR teaches how to manage the managers. Management is defined as the 'art or the manner to lead an organisation, to direct it, to plan its development and to control it' (Thiétart 2003) and, moreover, it is 'placing the concept of performance at the heart of the organisations' functioning' (Avare and Sponem 2008, 116). When one aims at 'managing the management' (Avare and Sponem 2008, 116), it is called 'managerialism'; it is more of a system which induces a whole process of quantification and extreme rationalisation, 'turning qualities in quantities (. . .), making exist in a numeral form what was expressed only with words' (Avare and Sponem 2008, 117). This performativity culture (Grace and O'Donoghue 2004, iv) diminishes the place of the humane dimension as 'it does not allow to conceive the meaning of actions' (Avare and Sponem 2008, 123) and leads individuals to perceive themselves as 'calculated beings' (Miller 2001). However, this trend of inspiration from managerialism is not without its share of paradoxes.

Attending FCR's seminars, emphasis is put on words like 'success' and 'performance', which are recursively repeated, and the workshops use scenari like one comparing God to the CEO of a company and the audience to His employees: the Qur'an and *hadith* seem to have been turned into management handbooks. This managerial vision is found with greater amplification in the UK, where large-scale charities function like businesses. For some British Muslim NGOs, in private documents, the donators are called 'clients' and 'customers'. The collection of funds depends on the rate of engagement, which is obtained through entertainment;

fundraising dinners often host guests that include the most famous imams, scholars, singers or celebrities, to the point where charities become a substitute for artistic production companies. Tommy Evans, a well-known artist, illustrates this: 'is there any record label for Muslim artists? Tell me, what are the main record labels for Muslim artists in the UK? Charities'.[19] Corporate culture, consumerism and mass culture therefore become intimately interwoven.

Financially successful models from the corporate sector appear attractive to Muslims in need of methods of growth, organisation, management, leadership and governance. The growth of initially small initiatives leads to a process of bureaucratisation, which impacts on the effectiveness and attractiveness of the charities. Aware of the donation power of Muslim households, many charities design activities through marketing methods directly inspired by neoliberalism, increasing 'consumer choice' (Brenner and Theodore 2005; Jessop 2002; George 1999) and monetising each possible detail with tailored user fees (Brenner and Theodore 2005; Routledge 2003; Jessop 2002; George 1999). Meticulous procedures are designed and calculated, and each process is rationalised. Every possible element is quantified and every action is monitored – if not the monitoring processes themselves. The infinite possibilities of social media and virtual networks also unleash a race for 'likes' on Facebook, retweets on Twitter and 'views' on YouTube, all tinted with verses from the Qur'an, *hadiths* and other quotes from the scriptures, masking aggressive marketing methods. This reconciliation with mass consumption translates into a mind-set where corporate values of 'success' and 'achievement' dominate; new individual ideals become popularity, presence and wealth. In visual attempts to legitimate donations, young activists exhibit their selfies with Syrian orphans, Nasheed singers or famous scholars such as Tariq Ramadan. The need to show is amalgamated with the need to be seen. Charities organise, support or take part in events (like the Muslim Lifestyle Show, Living Islam), or are paired with media channels like the couple formed by Penny Appeal and its sister company British Muslim TV. Charities need to perform their social actions, and therefore they need to be shown. In their terms, their visibility, measured by 'likes', becomes a shortcut for their efficiency and their legitimacy; they become brands. The amount they collect from the *zakat* and other *sadaqa* is subject to their performance and presence on the stage of the theatre that is social media. Their ritual performance of Islam is subject to that of their ego.

Conferences and seminars in France, the UK and the US are held to encourage young Muslims to become 'leaders'. A quick analysis of semantics allows them to frame the paradox when Muslim charities are using the concept of 'leader'. FCR extensively uses the term 'leader', like another French Muslim organisation anonymised as RNE, aiming at creating 'Muslim elites' and training students to enter competitive, prestigious engineering schools. Conversely, charities such as Amatullah or Averroès do not have leaders, in the sense that they have not a single authority or body deciding or enforcing rules; everybody is responsible for the charity and the senior members are only present in order to supervise, guide or make suggestions (see Chapter 4 and 5). The adoption of codes and methods of competitive corporate management shows the emergence of a Muslim 'prosperity theology' in which material success is deemed as a sign of divine approval (Hunt 2000, 332); this is fitted paradoxically into a religious narrative advocating detachment from worldly possessions. These phenomena are not recent; one could see many similarities with Christian American Evangelism. What one observes in the Muslim charity sector are often copied and adapted versions of dynamics seen in more mainstream cultures. John Bowen (2011) explains this by Muslims being pragmatic: if such things work for others, why shouldn't Muslims do it too? The Instagram generation is a producer of content but has sacrificed the production of meaning. Also, these phenomena are indicative of the access of younger generations of Muslims to higher socio-economic positions. They are also indicators of a greater will to fit into mainstream society by pursuing the widespread goals of 'success' and 'happiness' and implementing materialist philosophy in a non-materialist matrix of reference. In that sense, implementing corporate methods in the voluntary sector seems to be an experimentation of a hybrid form of spirituality. The hybrid they become raises a paradox: by embracing a culture of performativity (Grace and O'Donoghue 2004) and result-driven methods inherited from the corporate sector such as managerialism, they compromise on the humane dimension they initially offered (Caillé 2011a and 2009; Laville 2010). The paradox raised by the use of result-driven corporate methods in the realm of charitable works shows that and or religion do not necessarily create a barrier between tradition and modern influence. When organisations place emphasis on informality and start to implement methods designed for companies, their members usually have little will to cooperate and work for their individual interests (Bernoux 2008, 55–9). According to Alain Caillé (2011b), cultures and identities can be threatened when modernity is combined with the over-rationalisation of processes and systematic quantification. These have resulted in the dehumanisation of the human being through the utopian desire of controlling the environment, turning the human being into a *homo oeconomicus* – who earns, possesses and consumes (Humbert 2011, 121).

The 'colonisation' of religious groups or initiatives by corporate management (Grace and O'Donoghue 2004, iv) and its culture of individualism (Routledge 2003; Gill 1995) subdues the anti-materialistic and anti-individualistic message of Islam (Panjwani 2012a and 2012b) for the sake of conforming to a hegemonic culture (Mandaville 2001). However, it is still hard to determine to what extent this phenomenon is a sole experimentation, or an attempt to conform to specific practices to fit the wider society. However, not every volunteer in this research adopts this mind-set; some are reluctant to accept it, and many have become aware of the normative policies of large multinational companies. They have probably realised that all the semantics of 'prestigious' schools, studies and career are elements needed for the sole replication of the elites. As more volunteers do not feel attracted by top careers, perhaps they have understood that 'prestigious' comes from the Latin *praestigium* and means 'illusion'. The construction – or the reconstruction – of faith-based environments by modernity (and *vice-versa*) is an indicator of the conception of a new, original identity, which young European Muslims are still forming. The dialogue between the supporters of the idea of

'Muslim elites' or 'leaders' and those working for a more authentic and humane approach will perhaps give rise to alternative mind-sets and modes of governance already existing at the grassroots level. Rather than transforming the human being into a machine that serves the elites, who will eventually subjugate said human being (Clerc 2011, 135), perhaps it could be the result of a fusion of modern models for efficiency and more traditional models of human relations.

Notes

1 Caroline Mortimer. Mariah Idrissi: H&M's first hijab-wearing model says her work 'isn't immodest'. www.independent.co.uk/news/uk/home-news/mariah-idrissi-hms-first-hijab-wearing-model-says-her-work-isnt-immodest-a6673901.html [last accessed on 15 Jan. 2017].
2 Genius.com. Muslim Queen Lyrics. http://genius.com/Deen-squad-muslim-queen-lyrics [last accessed on 15 Jan. 2017].
3 "YouTube Stars TruestoryASA Bring Marble Arch to Standstill", *5Pillars*, http://5pillarsuk.com/video/youtube-stars-truestoryasa-bring-marble-arch-to-standstill [last accessed on 15 Jan. 2017].
4 Interview with Shelina Janmohammed, author of Generation M, IB Taurus, 3 September 2016 – The Guardian Online. www.theguardian.com/world/2016/sep/03/meet-generation-m-the-young-affluent-muslims-changing-the-world [last accessed on 15 Jan. 2017].
5 "Somewhere in America #MIPSTERZ," www.youtube.com/watch?v=68sMkDKMias [last accessed on 15 Jan. 2017].
6 Pharrell - Happy British Muslims! #HAPPYDAY. www.youtube.com/watch?v=MvlmXhcRLMY [last accessed on 15 Jan. 2017].
7 Interview of Nadir Nahdi on Buzzfeed on the 26 November 2016 www.buzzfeed.com/aishagani/beni-global-millennial-creative-space [last accessed on 15 Jan. 2017].
8 Brown Man Skiing in a White Man's World // 008. www.youtube.com/watch?v=6tZR_uMUO_I [accessed on 20 Jan. 2017].
9 See 5.2.
10 As per Harvey's (2005, 1) definition of neo-liberalism as 'the doctrine that market exchange is an ethic in itself, capable of acting as a guide for all human action'.
11 News.com.au. American journalist and hijabi Muslim Noor Tagouri photographed for Playboy magazine. www.news.com.au/lifestyle/real-life/true-stories/american-journalist-and-hijabi-muslim-noor-tagouri-photographed-for-playboy-magazine/news-story/aeeb7d802d47551eec530324c43b84be [last accessed on 15 Jan. 2017].
12 Salam . . . I know, right? http://noortagouri.com from her response to online criticism, on 30 September 2016. [last accessed on 15 Jan. 2017].
13 Uddin, A. T. and Younis, I. (28 September 2016). Playboy's Interview With a Muslim Woman Mocks Modesty and Offends Women. *The Washington Post*, www.washingtonpost.com/news/acts-of-faith/wp/2016/09/28/playboys-interview-with-a-muslim-woman-mocks-modesty-and-offends-women/ [last accessed on 15 Jan. 2017].
14 Fatima Ahdash 25 September 2016, posted publicly on Facebook.
15 Women's Running. Our Cover Shoot With "Run Like A Hijabi" Rahaf Khatib. http://womensrunning.competitor.com/2016/09/inspiration/cover-shoot-hijabi-runner-rahaf-khatib_65031 [last accessed on 15 Jan. 2017].
16 Cadence Kinsey. The Instagram artist who fooled thousands. www.bbc.com/culture/story/20160307-the-instagram-artist-who-fooled-thousands?ocid=fbcul [last accessed on 15 Jan. 2017].
17 This section contains elements adapted from a previously published work: Barylo, W. (2016). Neo-Liberal Not-for-Profits: The Embracing of Corporate Culture in European Muslim Charities. *Journal of Muslim Minority Affairs*, 36(3), 383–8.

18 The name has been changed.
19 Tommy Evans, at a meeting of British Muslim artists at Film Pill studios, 27 February 2016.

References

Alcoff, L. M. (2007). Mignolo's Epistemology of Coloniality. *CR: The New Centennial Review*, 7(3), 79–101.
Ali, N., Sayyid, S. and Kalra, V. S. eds. (2006). *A Postcolonial People: South Asians in Britain*. London: Hurst.
Aly, R. M. K. (2015). *Becoming Arab in London: Performativity and the Undoing of Identity*. London: Pluto Press.
Amin, S. (1973). *Neocolonialism in West Africa*. New York: Penguin Press.
Anderson, B., Fagan, P., Woodnutt, T. and Chamorro-Premuzic, T. (2012). Facebook Psychology: Popular Questions Answered by Research. *Psychology of Popular Media Culture*, 1(1), 23–37.
Avare, P. and Sponem, S. (2008). Le managérialisme et les associations [Managerialism and Charities]. In Hoarau, C. and Laville, J-L. (eds.) *La gouvernance des associations*. Paris: Eres, pp. 111–29.
Balkan, O. (2015). Till Death Do Us Depart: Repatriation, Burial, and the Necropolitical Work of Turkish Funeral Funds in Germany. In: Suleiman, Y. (ed.) *Muslims in the UK and Europe*. Cambridge: Centre of Islamic Studies, pp. 19–28.
Balogun, O., M., Hoang, K. K. (2013). Refashioning Global Bodies: Cosmopolitan Femininities in Nigerian Beauty Pageants and the Vietnamese Sex Industry. In: Jafar, A. and Casanova, E. (eds.) *Global Beauty, Local Bodies*. London: Palgrave, pp. 1–21.Bernoux, P. (2008). De la Sociologie des Organisations à la Sociologie des Associations [From the Sociology of Organisations to the Sociology of Charities]. In: Hoarau, C. and Laville, J-L. (eds.) *La gouvernance des associations*. Paris: Eres, pp. 55–9.
Blay, A. Y. (2011). Skin bleaching and global white supremacy: By way of introduction. Journal Of Pan African Studies, 4(4), 4–46.
Bowen, J. R. (2011). *Can Islam Be French?* Princeton: Princeton University Press.Brenner, N. and Theodore, N. (2005). Neoliberalism and the Urban Condition. *City*, 9(1), 101–7.
Bulhan, H. A. (2008). *Politics of Cain – One Hundred Years of Crises in Somali Politics and Society*. Bethesda: Tayosan International Publishing.
Bulhan, H. A. (2015). Stages of Colonialism in Africa: From Occupation of Land to Occupation of Being, *Journal of Social and Political Psychology*, 3(1), 239–56.
Caillé, A. (2009). *Théorie Anti-Utilitariste de l'Action et du Sujet [Anti-Utilitarian Theory of Action and Subject]*. Paris: La Découverte.
Caillé, A. (2011a). Du Convivialisme vu comme un Socialisme Radicalisé et Universalisé (et Réciproquement) [On Convivialism as a Radicalised and Universalised Socialism and Reciprocally]. In: Caillé, A., Humbert, M., Latouche, S. and Viveret, P. (eds.) *De la convivialité, dialogues sur la société conviviale à venir*. Paris: La Découverte, pp. 73–98.
Caillé, A. (2011b). Les indicateurs de richesse alternatifs: une fausse bonne idée? [Wealth Indicators: A Wrong Good Idea?]. In: Caillé, A., Humbert, M., Latouche, S. and Viveret, P. (eds.) *De la convivialité, dialogues sur la société conviviale à venir*. Paris: La Découverte, pp. 141–66.
Clerc, D. (2011). Ivan Illitch, une figure importante de la critique de la société industrielle [Ivan Illitch, an Important Figure of the Critique of Industrial Society]. In: Caillé, A.,

Humbert, M., Latouche, S. and Viveret, P. (eds.) *De la convivialité, dialogues sur la société conviviale à venir*. Paris: La Découverte, pp. 131–8.

Corbet, R. H. (2015). Tayyib: British Muslim Piety and the Welfare of Animals for Food. In: Suleiman, Y. (ed.) *Muslims in the UK and Europe*. Cambridge: Centre of Islamic Studies, pp. 67–75.

Dewey, S. (2008). *Making Miss India Miss World: Constructing Gender, Power, and the Nation in Postliberalization India*. New York: Syracuse University Press.Dussel, E. (1985). *Philosophy of Liberation*. New York: Orbis Books.

Dussel, E. (1996). Modernity, Eurocentrism, and Trans-modernity: In Dialogue With Charles Taylor. In: Mendieta, E. (ed.) *The Underside of Modernity: Apel, Ricoeur, Rorty, Taylor, and the Philosophy of Liberation*. Atlantic Highlands: Humanities Press, pp. 129–59.

Dwyer, R. (2000). *All You Want Is Money, All You Need Is Love: Sexuality and Romance in Modern India*. London: Cassell.

Eisenlohr, P. (2006). The Politics of Diaspora and the Morality of Secularism: Muslim Identities and Islamic Authority in Mauritius. *Journal of Royal Anthropological Society*, 12(2), 395–412.

Fanon, F. (1967). *Black Skin, White Masks*. New York: Grove Press.

Fanon, F. (1968). *The Wretched of the Earth*. New York: Grove Press.

George, S. (1999). *A Short History of Neo-Liberalism: Twenty Years of Elite Economics and Emerging Opportunities for Structural Change*. Conference on Economic Sovereignty in a Globalising World, Bangkok, pp. 24–6.

Gill, S. (1995). Globalisation, Market Civilisation and Disciplinary Neo-liberalism. *Millennium*, 24(3), 399–423.

Gillespie, M. (1995). *Television, Ethnicity and Change*. London: Routledge.

Göle, N. (2003). *Musulmanes et modernes Voile et civilisation en Turquie* [*Muslim and Modern: Headscarf and Civilisation in Turkey*]. Paris: La Découverte.

Grace, G. R. and O'Donoghue, P. (2004). *Spiritual and Moral Development Across the Curriculum in Catholic Schools*. UCL CRDCE's: Professional Focus Series: Resources for Staff Development. London: UCL.

Grewal, Z. A. (2009). Marriage in Colour, Race, Religion and Spouse Selection in Four American Mosques. *Ethnic and Racial Studies*, 32(2), 323–45.

Guidi, D. (2015). Les réactions artistiques aux controversies: L'espace artistique comme lieu de dédramatisation des grands débats de société liés à l'islam [Artistic Reactions to Controversies: The Artistic Space as a Space for Dedramatisation of Big Social Debates Related to Islam]. In: Göle, N. (ed.) *En-quête de l'Islam Européen*. Paris: Halfa, pp. 345–67.

Hadjab, W. (2015). Scénographie de l'amour halal en France [Scenography of Halal Love in France]. In: Göle, N. (ed.) *En-quête de l'Islam Européen*. Paris: Halfa, pp. 292–319.

Haenni, P. (2005). *L'islam de marché: l'autre révolution conservatrice* [*Market Islam, the Other Conservative Revolution*]. Paris: Seuil.

Harvey, D. (2005). *A Brief History of Neoliberalism*. Oxford: Oxford University Press.

Humbert, M. (2011). Convivialisme, politique et économie: Ivan Illitch et le "bien vivre ensemble" [Convivialism, Politics and Economics: Ivan Illitch and the 'Well Living Together']. In: Caillé, A., Humbert, M., Latouche, S. and Viveret, P. eds. *De la convivialité, dialogues sur la société conviviale à venir*. Paris: La Découverte, pp. 99–130.

Hunt, S. (2000). Winning Ways: Globalisation and the Impact of the Health and Wealth Gospel. *Journal of Contemporary Religion*, 15(3), 331–47.

Janmohammed, S. (2016). *Generation M*. London: IB Tauris.

Jessop, B. (2002). Liberalism, Neoliberalism, and Urban Governance: A State-Theoretical Perspective. *Antipode*, 34(3), 452–72.

Kammarti, B. (2015). L'interpénétration européenne de la Finance Islamique [European Interpenetration of Islamic Finance]. In: Göle, N. (ed.) *En-quête de l'Islam Européen*. Paris: Halfa, pp. 172–95.

Kross, E., Verduyn, P., Demiralp, E., Park, J., Lee, D. S., Lin, N., Shablack, H., Jonides, J., Ybarra, O. (2013). Facebook Use Predicts Declines in Subjective Well-Being in Young Adults. *PLoS ONE*, 8(8), e69841, doi: 10.1371/journal.pone.0069841

Lallmahomed-Aumeerally, N. (2014). A reading of Bollywood Cinema as a Site of Melancholia for Indo-Mauritian Muslim Female Youth. *South Asian Popular Culture*, 12(3), 149–62.

Laville, J-L. (2010). *Politique de l'association* [*The Politics of Charities*]. Paris: Seuil.

Maldonado-Torres, N. (2007). On the Coloniality of Being: Contributions to the Development of a Concept. *Cultural Studies*, 21(2–3), 240–70.

Mandaville, P. (2001). *Transnational Muslim Politics: Reimagining the Umma*. London: Routledge.

Mignolo, W. (2000a). *Local Histories/Global Designs: Coloniality, Subaltern Knowledges, and Border Thinking*. Princeton: Princeton University Press.

Mignolo, W. (2000b). The Many Faces of Cosmo-Polis: Border Thinking and Critical Cosmopolitanism. *Public Culture*, 12(3), 721–48.

Mignolo, W. (2003). *The Darker Side of the Renaissance: Literacy, Territoriality, and Colonization* (2nd ed.). Ann Arbor: The University of Michigan Press.

Miller, P. (2001). Governing by Numbers: Why Calculative Practices Matter. *Social Research*, 68(2), 379–96.

Nkrumah, K. (1965). *Neocolonialism: The Latest Stage of Colonialism*. New York: Routledge.

Panjwani, F. (2012a). Fazlur Rahman and the Search for Authentic Islamic Education: A Critical Appreciation. *Curriculum Inquiry*, 42(1), 33–55.

Panjwani, F. (2012b). Why Did You Not Tell Me About This? Religion as a Challenge to Faith Schools. In: Alexander, H. and Agbaria, A. (eds.) *Commitment, Character, and Citizenship: Religious Education in Liberal Democracy*. New York: Routledge, pp. 116–28.

Quijano, A. (2000). Coloniality of Power, Eurocentrism, and Latin America. *Nepantla: Views From South*, 1(3), 533–80.

Routledge, P. (2003). Convergence Space: Process Geographies of Grassroots Globalization Networks. *Transactions of the Institute of British Geographers*, 28(3), 333–49.

Said, E. (1984). *The World, the Text and the Critic*. Cambridge: Harvard University Press.

Sayyid, S. (2010). The Homelessness of Muslimness: The Muslim Umma as a Diaspora. *Human Architecture: Journal of the Sociology of Self-Knowledge*, 8(2), 129–46.

Thiétart, R-A. (2003). *Le Management* [*Management*]. Paris: Presses Universitaires de France.

Ural, N. Y. (2015). La place des défunts musulmans dans les cimetières français et allemands [The Place of Deceased Muslims in French and German Cemeteries]. In: Göle, N. (ed.) *En-quête de l'Islam Européen*. Paris: Halfa, pp. 320–44.

7 From resistance to self-determination

I recall this cold and rainy day of November 2013. Having recently moved to the UK, I found myself feeling desperately alone while surrounded by work colleagues and acquaintances. By alone, I mean with no people to rely on, find support from or share time with. I had just experienced the symptoms of the business of society and people having no time because of career and studies; but I still had my fieldwork to pursue and whatever my mood, I needed to carry on. Unexpectedly, on this rainy November day I found that I was not the only one who felt this way. That evening was my first at Rumi's Cave. The place was small, even smaller than a shop. Turquoise wooden frames around the windows revealed the name, barely visible in the rain. The scent of buhoor flooded the barely lit space; the walls were covered with traditional Indian miniatures; rugs lay on the floor alongside pillows, populating the room. The place was packed and hosted a colourful, bubbling crowd of men and women from many various origins, who drank tea and coffee and ate biscuits. The night's talk followed the screening of Charlie Chaplin's movie *Modern Times*. Late as usual, I had not attended the screening, although I had seen the film ages ago. I could still recall how the character had pointed out, in 1936, the paradoxes of industrial modernity. A Malaysian scholar had been invited for a vivid discussion with the audience. Soon, the conversation deviated to the topic of Muslim charities. Echoing the facts and observations I have transcribed in Chapter 6, they criticised how the Muslim charity sector has become 'industrial' and 'deprived of Islam'. Talking about the overtaking of corporate culture and the 'disease of being busy',[1] a warm voice spoke: 'Look, I was working for Goldman and Sachs. I couldn't stand what was happening, I realised I had no life.' Faiz told his story about how he left Goldman and Sachs, moving away from work he deemed not ethical, to eventually dedicate his life to music. After the talk, in a private conversation, he expressed to me that he had gone through the very same things I was going through at that very moment. Then, before we left, he just told me: 'Come over whenever, let's chat, have some tea, play some music, you're welcome'. These were Faiz's words, but I did not know at the time that he had summed up the entire philosophy of Rumi's Cave – probably the most popular and vibrant faith-based community hub in all of London.

In previous chapters, I wrote about how, since the early twenty-first century, young European Muslims have become aware that the planet is undergoing a major, global and total crisis: economic, political, ideological, environmental, spiritual, social . . . As a consequence, many have set up, through charities, initiatives aimed at bringing alternatives to systems perceived as not sustainable. These initiatives have taken the shape of safe spaces and platforms which, inspired by Islamic traditions, put more emphasis on feelings, emotions, bonds of friendship, gift, conviviality and faith, keeping a sense of humanity in a society seen as more and more inhumane. They have tried to move away from the race for results and figures inherited from neoliberalism and corporate culture, where the human being, quantified, rationalised and monitored, becomes more of a machine which produces and consumes. In the era of mobile Internet and social networks, the volunteers in this study – reaching wider networks, more educated than previous generations and more skilled and highly qualified – have also become much more audible and visible in the public sphere. Beyond the fight against islamophobia and for minorities' rights, they think globally; beyond the usual Muslim social circles, they share the thought that the main dangers come from the excesses of unregulated neoliberalism, managerialism and the overwhelming of mass media, which encourage society, through a race for power, wealth and ego, to achieve a form of 'success' defined by material achievement (Caillé 2011a and 2011b). In line with Ivan Illitch's (1973) reflections, they feel the need for a warmer, more humane, more convivial society. They just want 'a better world' (see Figure 7.1). Inspired by their own diasporic cultures and spirituality within a more secular society, redefining identity and citizenship by their active dimension, experimenting with original modes of governance inspired from Islam (see Chapter 5, 'Shura,

Figure 7.1 Open canvas at the RAMF in Le Bourget: 'actions for a better world'

the viable chimera of democracy') and familiar with contemporary modes of communication, social spaces and virtual tools, they bridge the gap in a society seeing faith and belief opposed to its modern ethics. In a modern environment which tries to differentiate, name, label and quantify cultures, they are comfortable with their complex identity. However, because Western modern, secular societies tend to be adverse towards religious and ethnic minorities (Chapter 3), they have to resist the pressure of a white-dominated, sexist, colonial, imperial and neoliberal environment. This chapter offers an overview of these Muslim charities, first as spaces for resistance to a still hostile environment which operates a form of colonialism I refer as metacolonialism (see Chapter 6). In a society obsessed by rationalisation, their topics of interest are universal: organic food, fairtrade products, ethical finance, representative media, social inequalities, etc. In places like Rumi's Cave or Foul Express, they set up workshops, discussions and events around non-quantifiable elements: feelings, emotions, forgiveness, love, generosity and faith. This is often expressed in religious discourses by putting the emphasis on emotions and feelings as an important element of spirituality, which I refer to as an emotional theology. Holding firmly to their beliefs, they revive Islamic traditions by designing their own models: organic *halal* farming, finance without usury and minority-focused media. They also decolonise their environment, their options for consumption and their lifestyle. Contrary to their parents' generation, their aim is not career, studies, housing or income but rather reaching a level of spiritual well-being and living a life in line with ethics of social justice. They seek independence in all its forms: in finance, housing, food and independence from the media and the welfare state . . . Healing the wounds of rejection, these charities become spaces for growth. This is the main point of the chapter in its last section, regarding how these charities eventually become spaces for the emergence of self-determination.

Coping mechanisms[2]

Founded in 2011, Foul Express (*foul* is French for the Egyptian meal 'ful') was supposed to become a think tank. The idea to establish the charity came when its CEO-to-be published a book about his journey. Many young Muslim executives, lawyers and teachers could relate to his childhood memories: the issues of discrimination and criticism of the current political and financial system. The crowd that gathered around the book expressed a potential willingness to make a concrete difference, which led to the foundation of the charity.

Beginning its journey with a blog, then a website, Foul Express offers informative and opinion-based articles on various topics, including the environment, consumption, social representations, fashion, religion, visibility, politics (islamophobia, racism, conflicts) and education. The volunteers have various cultural backgrounds and religious orientations; many of them were not originally Muslims. During meetings, it is easy to spot people wearing the traditional *qamis*, sitting side-by-side with others wearing jeans and t-shirts or corporate outfits. As volunteers are based all over France, most of the activities and exchanges happen on the mailing list. The rare meetings happen at the CEO's flat or in a Muslim cultural centre. Meetings always conclude with a short *du'a* (invocation prayer) in French and Arabic. Many volunteers are executives in multinational companies or self-employed (in financial expertise, graphic design, filmmaking, media, gourmet cuisine, illustration and writing), and some are not graduates. The organisation struggled at the beginning to decide if it should define itself as Muslim or non-Muslim. Some volunteers left, either because they found that Foul Express was 'not Muslim enough' or because they found it was 'too centred around Muslims'. They consult scholars from the French island of La Réunion, as a reference; they give their opinion on projects and the content of some articles. However, the CEO always has the last word after consulting with the other members. The emergence of mobile Internet and virtual spaces of socialisation, such as Facebook, allow friends, communities and organisations to meet, organise and work without the need for in-person meetings. Documents common to the whole team can be shared via the cloud and meetings can be held on Skype. The world is thus becoming more of a village, whereby information, content and skills can be reached anytime and anywhere. There is no more centrality, and Foul Express uses such technology to gather members from all over France and Europe, targeting an international audience with quality content articles. Attracting members from various spiritual and cultural backgrounds, Foul Express showcases its identity as a European Muslim organisation with highly-skilled members. The workforce of the organisation appears similar to that of a professional media company, except that everyone works voluntarily for a charitable cause: to offer alternative media from a diasporic perspective.

The members' professional skills are used extensively: some graphic designers offer graphic data visualisations to illustrate the exclusion of minorities across Europe by turning abstract figures and numbers into colourful designs.[3] Foul Express also places emphasis upon humour as a counterweight to the unilateral narrative of mass media through the help of Bdouin, a comic designer who points at some of the paradoxes experienced by some Muslims in modern countries. The organisation makes room for testimonies and eye-opening experiences; one may find novellas written by members or simply their own thoughts on the realities of a consumerist society. On the mailing list, it is not rare to share artwork linked to activism found on the Internet (such as Banksy) or to invite others to art exhibitions. Members may attend protests in support of the Syrian people as well as piano concertos. When one observes the members issuing a remake of a classical eighteenth-century French painting for its campaign,[4] or some Foul Express members contemplating opening a *halal* restaurant serving traditional French cuisine, these initiatives appear as a mix of European identity and Islamic references. However, Foul Express's members had to find the delicate balance between the convenience of working from a distance and the deterioration of human relationships.

Foul Express does not have a physical office. For other classical charities (such as Amatullah or Averroès, providing food for deprived students and homeless people), the premises of the charity usually play a major role as a space for socialisation, prayer, breaks and rests, especially when it serves as a daily meeting point for the charity's members. At Foul Express, although there are no material premises, the Google Groups mailing list may play the role of virtual premises. However, having only online meetings and general communication may be disturbing for some new members, and emails are prone to generating regular misunderstandings, sometimes even triggering conflicts due to the lack of non-verbal communication. During some rare meetings (sometimes at a member's flat or in a restaurant), one would find food, times for prayer and informal conversations. Then, the question is: what is found between meetings? Except these occasional meetings, members rarely meet each other face-to-face. When structures do not have physical offices, do not belong to a certain geographical context and are neither strongly connected to a particular neighbourhood nor able to consistently bond members together, they are at risk of losing their attractiveness and the dedication of their members (see Chapters 4 and 5). However, in 2016, more than ten years after Foul Express was founded, the organisation still produces content and organises workshops. How have they coped with their situation to remain attractive and keep their members involved and committed?

Members may meet rarely but communication is nonetheless sustained through technology, especially by email lists and Facebook. These tools enable the rapid sharing of multimedia content, such as documents, videos, data and pictures, as well as allow everyone to share and archive content accessible from anywhere. Conversations, more formal than oral ones, always comprise idioms like the greeting of *Salaam Alaykum* (peace be upon you) and *InshaAllah* (God willing). Documents can be modified instantly through Google Docs and one can organise meetings through Doodle and Google Agenda. During events, people Tweet with 'hashtag' trending strategies. Facebook and WhatsApp are more widely used as alternatives to email and texts. Computer presentations are made through PowerPoint or the more interactive Prezi. Mobile phones are only used in case of emergency. More classical charities, such as JMF, communicate more on Facebook. Averroès, a student organisation, gives priority to phone calls and still relies more on face-to-face communication; it is easy for one to miss important news if one is not present, as a large amount of information is shared by word of mouth–the same applies to Amatullah. The Internet could be seen as a remedy to a relatively busy schedule, especially if one is a student at university or works in a nine-to-five shift job or has to take care of children, like many at Foul Express. Dematerialising the office is therefore a tool that maintains some contact between members, cutting through the constraints of a variety of different commitments. Looking at more traditional charities like JMF, Averroes, or Amatullah, the network remains exclusively local (university, neighbourhood, town). However, at Foul Express, one third of the members live far away from Paris in cities like Rennes, Strasbourg, Marseille or even in foreign countries (Gulf states, the UK and Spain). Virtual platforms allow charities to build a considerable network between different organisations: Foul Express is in touch on a regular basis with an illustrator based in eastern France, bloggers from central France and other organisations based abroad (UK). Some of its partners are even scattered around Europe (FEMYSO).[5]

Members are also in touch with a Muslim entrepreneurs' trade union (SPMF), comprising groups working on 'Islamic Ethical finance' or certifying 'Sharia compatible' financial products, which all rely on a board of *shouyoukh* (Muslim scholars) as advisers for important decisions and policies in light of Islamic ethics – for instance, publishing particular articles. Therefore, Foul Express is still able to mobilise important social capital and keep volunteers motivated. Konrad Pędziwiatr (2010, 91) posits that one of the explanations for their attractiveness is that they incarnate for Muslims 'trenches of resistance against dominant society'.

During meetings, Marwan from Foul Express liked to recall the history of Japan when it came to modernity, drawing an explicit parallel between Japan and the current situation of European Muslims:

> There were two clans to decide, for the first one, if Japan resists to the British or, for the second one, if Japan tolerates them. The second clan wins the debate, but they have forgotten from where they came; and this is what gave birth to the dehumanised Japan where the spiritual is asepticised . . . moral of the story: do never forget from where you come and hold firm to your differences.

Marwan often recalled this story as an introduction to the aim of Foul Express: 'Free mankind from the complexes which are being imposed on him by the system.' He advocated a life dedicated to 'love for God and harmony on Earth' and is opposed to 'competition, commercial success and perceiving knowledge as a means, not an aim'. Some volunteers working for multinationals become aware of the mind-set spread in the corporate sector and eventually change their perspectives. Foul Express, however, has a nuanced approach. Although some members work, as Mourad said, for 'big companies making results', there is more a trend of introspection, or a process of learning (or learning again) a certain form of humanity through Islam, inspired by Marwan's journey. In 2006, he resigned from his position as a trader when he realised the extent to which the current financial system was fuelling injustices. As a consequence, he wrote a book and founded his charity. The impulse at the beginning of Foul Express can be expressed with one sentence: decolonisation is a process of questioning and critical thinking.

Individual choices and personal responsibility are continuously questioned: 'Is it good to put my money in a bank that encourages weapon trafficking? Is it good to buy toys made by children?' Although Mourad or Ibtissam found it 'hard to abandon references to corporate culture', perspectives can change, like that of Sofiane, who recently got into an engineering school and realised that preparatory classes were 'some kind of hell. (. . .) I would never encourage my own children to do it.' Mourad recalled how he realised the dangers of the corporate mind-set:

> In a company, you're formatted, formatted, formatted. (. . .) But I only realised how formatted I was after talking to Marwan (. . .) In my opinion, believers who do not realise this (and there are many) they don't realise the evil they do around them to themselves.

Members are generally opposed to the employment policy of some multinational groups, or their selection through competitive exams; they criticise the establishment, the culture of elites of companies or the school system.

As an illustration, the visual universe of Foul Express revolves around icons of resistance. Their manifesto is illustrated by the picture of an anonymous man hiding his face behind a stylised mask of Guy Fawkes worn by V, the main character of *V for Vendetta*, as a reference to the Anonymous movement; next to articles about the *Indignados*, this makes the charity's spirit closer to the ideals shared by these global movements, like the one of the '99 Percenters'. These symbols seem to make the charity part of a transnational, global, universal quest for alternatives and not only a protester. Antoine and his wife Kadidia, once volunteers at Islamic Relief France, engaged in a world tour 'without taking the plane', looking for alternate initiatives in areas like housing, food or social development. One can observe a striking contrast when comparing big NGOs or famous public figures to small-scale organisations such as Amatullah or Averroes and their members. The latter do not have more than a hundred 'friends' on Facebook, their websites are not often updated and their communication strategy does not rely on the latest technologies; however, they still make a noticeable impact in their neighbourhoods and with the civil services, as seen in previous chapters. These charities operate as safe spaces for two reasons: first, they provide a faith-based environment in a secular society where politicians and media often tend to alienate Muslims (see Chapters 3 and 4). Second, they provide an environment free from the culture of ego, possessions and power which define success by material comfort, wealth and fame, elements which most volunteers try to avoid. They offer a nest of resistance to the overwhelming hegemonies of a hyper-modern,[6] white-dominated, secular and neoliberal society. Beyond resistance, they are also powerful mediums of decolonisation.

Emotional theology and alter-system mind-set

In a hyper-modern society characterised by individualism, fragmentation and atomisation of its population, with weaker ties, trust and social solidarity (Elshtain 1995, 5–27), these charities happen to be trenches of resistance (Pędziwiatr 2010). Indeed, as per the elements observed in Chapters 4 and 5, through the omnipresence of Islam as a matrix comprising faith, practices and ethics, they are a resistance to secularisation. Through their collective dimension, they are a resistance to individualisation. Through spirituality, they are a resistance to materialism. Through the celebration of their cultural and historical legacies, they are a resistance to cultural conformation and assimilation. Through their informal modes of governance, they are a form of resistance to corporate culture. Through their emphasis on non-quantifiable elements such as emotions, friendship and love, and values such as patience, gift or forgiveness, they are the core of the resistance to hyper-modernity and neoliberalism. Volunteers do not perceive their charity as a mere working environment but more like a family (see Chapter 4) They are not colleagues; they call each other 'brothers' and 'sisters'. There is no formal hierarchy; everyone is responsible for making the charity work and everyone is free to make suggestions. Decisions are not voted on; the board of trustees is not elected by universal suffrage. These are the result of a process of consultation and consensus inherited from Islamic traditions (*shura*, as seen in Chapter 5). They are not interested in results and do not monitor their actions. They give overall more importance to social bonds, service and conflict resolution than money or fame. The action of these charities are an attempt not to become part of a society functioning on utilitarian efficiency, focused on growth and the merchandisation of human relations through the disappearance of gift and bound-free action and other symptoms of the dehumanisation of modern societies (Caillé 2011a, 11). The members share food, words and stories in a shared space and share times for meals and common prayers. As a result, they form empathetic communities and develop strong ties and trust through primary socialisation (see Chapters 4 and 5). They work for a common good rather than a common interest (Bernoux 2008, 55–9). They are at the polar opposite of result-driven and managerial corporate policies. Many volunteers get involved in charities to distance themselves from a society overtaken by corporate culture, governed by the over-rationalisation of processes and systematic quantification, all having as a consequence the dehumanisation of the human being through the utopian desire of having control over everything, which at the same time makes their actions more socially efficient (Caillé 2011a, 151).

The volunteers also adopt a mind-set in which they focus on emotions and feelings, to associate them with some ritual aspects of Islam – not seeing religion as a set of rules but a theology for emotional well-being. Khadija, volunteer for Islamic Relief, criticised the fact that Islamic sciences are often reduced to the binary of the *halal/haram* narrative (roughly translated as permissible/forbidden). However, for her, understanding and conviction of the heart were essential:

> I didn't come to Islam through the way of *halal* and *haram*. (. . .) And I personally cannot work according to what is permissible and what is forbidden. I want to be convinced I have to do something or to abstain from something. I don't stand people who say: 'if [clothes] are this length, he/she will burn in Hell.' Where is the love, the mercy?

Sana too liked to see emotional aspects in Islam: 'I don't believe in an angry, punishing God. I believe in a God of love and compassion.'

Emre: My most positive experience in life was falling in love, since then I've been trying to find this experience through God.

Buthaina: Sufism was a turning point, I felt very dark, depressed. . . . I used therapy but ultimately finding Sufism helped me. I felt happy every day of my first year.

Faiz: When you do *zikr*,[7] you are more in tune with yourself. I open my chakras. When you say 'Hu', you do it at the right frequency, your heart resonates.

Abbas, from Iranian descent, recalled his experience: 'in my family, they used to do *zikr* when they served drinks.'

Although the practice of *zikr* is often associated with Sufi circles, participants practising *zikr* do not always belong to *tarikas*. Some sessions are organised occasionally at Rumi's Cave and are open to everyone. Whether participants are more inclined to Sufism, or conversely inclined to a more salafi practise of religion, for a large number, religion is interpreted through the lens of empathy and love, and is sometimes associated with a therapeutic experience. God, faith, beliefs and practice become key to the realm of emotions and healing, and, conversely, emotions become key to knowing the ways of God. In this perspective, places like Rumi's Cave aim to offer a comprehensive experience.

Rumi's Cave in London is an anti-colonial space by excellence. The walls are ornamented with Arabic calligraphies and traditional Indian miniatures; people from different cultures sit and chat. Rumi's Cave is not only a mosque, a prayer space where prayers are performed and people break fast during Ramadan. It is a warm, convivial space dedicated to young Muslims, though not only them. Set up by Sheikh Ahmed Babikir in 2011, every month 'the Cave' hosts an open-mic where young people are free to perform music, songs, poetry, storytelling and more. The open-mics have featured Rastafaris, Jews, Sikhs and numerous Muslim celebrities, some coming as far as from California to perform at the Cave. Storytellers such as Jumana Moon and Sef Townsend would present the story of Yusuf and Zuleikha from a Muslim and Jewish perspective; Ahmad Ikhlaas would sing the Night Journey of Prophet Muhammad in Jamaican Patois, Poetic Pilgrimage would sing Hip-Hop mixing Islamic references or Fahad Khalid would play his legendary 'Allahoo' qawwali on his steel-string guitar (see Figure 7.2). Rumi's Cave, as a community hub, is also a place for discussions led by university

Figure 7.2 Musical performance of Fahad Khalid at Rumi's Cave

132 *From resistance to self-determination*

students or researchers about their research on the Muslim diaspora in the Caribbean, yoga workshops, alternative therapies like cupping sessions, philosophical discussions around theories of Carl Gustav Jung (for example) and more. Sana summed up the reasons why she enjoys the Cave as a space: 'There is a different vibe than other mosques. I feel at peace. People can sit, have tea, there is Internet, people can nap . . . I love Rumi's Cave.'

It is also a space for emancipation from traditional conventions. Rumi's Cave audience is curious about themes such as organic *halal* meat (see Corbet 2015), eco-friendly mosques, permaculture or urban gardens (as promoted by MADE), up-cycling, herbal medicine or mental health. Many critically reflect on their life choices, as, for example, Mariha, who explained about the ethics of her choice of trying to be vegan:

> Through what we eat we have an intense relationship with the Earth. There is no difference between ethics and Islam because this is where my ethics come from.

Much more inclusive than traditional spaces, through poetry, songs and discussions they break taboos such as depression and divorce and talk about feminism, gender equality and understanding religion as a general framework for social harmony. The former manager of Rumi's Cave, Abbas Zahedi, is the founder of BARBEDOUN[8] [all in capitals], a pop-up bar offering drinks resulting from a fusion between traditional Iranian Sharbats and cordials from the British Temperance Movement (see Figure 7.3). He also organises events, discussions and

Figure 7.3 People chatting at an event of BARBEDOUN

musical events featuring 'diasporic' artists in a safe, open and intimate setting. His aim is to offer an alternative space for those who do not relate to British pub culture and want a space to socialise with people comfortable with their diasporic identities, but do not fit any traditional community at the same time. Initiatives as these, reviving spiritualities, cultures and tradition in an ever-modernising and secularising society, are cores of resistance, alternatives and continuity at a same time. In a society which tends to be ahistorical, these organisations hold on to their cultural and spiritual roots. They reflect the emergence of a brand new European society which is growing more diverse, colourful and rich.

In an ever-normalising world where the certification of skills is expected, assessed, monitored and controlled, initiatives like Amatullah or Averroès, Foul Express, Rumi's Cave or JMF are exceptional and almost rebellious. Spaces of resistance, they work to bind their members through the transmission of knowledge and skills; they do not simply act but pass over the baton to younger generations. Although opposed to the system, they are not 'anti-system'. Although participating in social and political life, they are not fully 'engaged'.

In Justin Gest's (2010, 50–61) four quadrant model, anti-system behaviour is characterised by violence, clandestine activities in order to undermine, disrupt or overthrow the system (active anti-system) or rejecting or withdrawing from the system (passive anti-system). Conversely, engaged behaviour is characterised by political and social participation (active) or inactivity and complacency (passive). The volunteers in this study sit somewhere in between: although some are withdrawing themselves from mass consumption and industrial food and participating in protests against climate change or the use of fossil fuels, they vote and participate in social works. They are setting up parallel activities, creating something separate, but contributing to the whole society at the same time. Their work starts at a lexical level: do Muslims need leaders? Participants have been invited to reflect on the term 'leader'.

Big conferences and seminars are held to encourage young Muslims to become 'leaders'. FCR uses the term 'leader' extensively, like another French Muslim organisation, RNE, aiming at creating 'Muslim elites' by training students to enter competitive, prestigious engineering schools. 'Elite' is a term which, for Hannah Arendt (1963, 409) implies a form of oligarchic government and the domination of the whole society by a few. Most of the interviewed volunteers are opposed to this very domination. Analysing the semantics, the 'leader' works alone: it is a single man or woman. The term is associated with the idea of one in command of others; with power, the leader rules and inspires others.[9] He is an authority figure, on a superior level or rank than the others around him, operating a dichotomy between him and the 'followers'. The concept belongs to the semantics of war, politics and business. The leader is 'the figure of the president of the United States', the warlord, the only one in command, receiving alone all the rewards for the work of his team. The Western leader is the heir of Hercules, in Greek Mythology, who solves any problem and overcomes struggles through his strength, or a lone (super) hero, like Superman, Batman, Spiderman and other products of pop culture. Perhaps he could be Ulysses the adventurer, taking the Argonauts for a ride. The character of the leader is opposed to the biblical prophets, whose only strength was granted by God. Prophets were rather stewards, as the etymology of the Arabic word *khalifat* (caliph) reveals. Many volunteers and sometimes charities put an emphasis on the term caliph in their communication (especially related to the protection of the environment), such as MADE; Antoine and Kadidia, two volunteers, have given a TED-like talk explaining how their circumnavigation has been motivated by the same idea. The idea of the caliph connotes collectivity as opposed to individuality. The Prophet Muhammad was described in the scriptures as never acting alone but always according to *shura* rules of consultation. In the Islamic tradition, the names of the prophet's companions have never been forgotten (as is testified to by the recent production of a whole television series centred on the character of Umar Ibn Al Khattab, translated into more than ten languages).[10] Whilst the Western leader is the one who shifts the balance, the caliph works towards restoring and safekeeping it. Amatullah and Averroès do not have leaders; everybody is responsible for the charity, and the senior members are 'elder brothers and sisters', only present in order to reassure, guide or suggest in the name of the sense of duty. The herculean executive from prestigious schools holds his strength in his diplomas and his socio-economic rank, obtained through exams and ruled-out contestants. The herculean president is the one who ruled-out his opponents, and the modern businessman is the one who ruled out competitors. The herculean hero is a machine producing results and thinking in terms of problems and solutions. Sermons at Rumi's Cave are often about how the concept of caliph or prophet contrasts with the western 'leader' through various examples, such as when Salahuddine, victorious, let his opponents go back to their homes after the battle rather than killing or capturing them,[11] or when Muhammad was received by stones by the people of Ta'if, and when God offered to destroy them, he declined, saying that perhaps their children would become better people.[12] These examples of patience in uncertain times – mercy, perseverance and resilience rather than competition and enmity – are pillars of the religious discourse at Rumi's Cave: compassion becomes a characteristic of power, and power is to turn one's fiercest opponents into infallible allies. Rabia, giving a talk about 'nature and spirituality' at Rumi's Cave, expanded on the concept of caliph and stewardship: 'There is no dominance of humans. We were given a trust. There is no control, no ownership.' The caliph is the facilitator of skills and energies to achieve a collective goal. He is not an actor of change, he is its medium.

By the critique of current lexicon, current processes, modes of governance, human relations and place of emotions and beliefs, Europe finds itself questioned by the presence of Islam about its past and current posture (Göle 2005, 9, 139). The proudly 'civilising' West (Plaine 1797) is no more. From an eighteenth and nineteenth century led by a division between the 'savage' and the 'civilised' (Lévi Strauss 1962) and a twentieth century operating a binary dichotomy between 'them' and 'us', the world has perhaps come to a time when people realise that by encouraging individual comfort and profit as rules, we found ourselves in a more 'primitive' position than the people described as so in past times. Gandhi wisely said that 'The world has enough for everyone's need, but not enough for everyone's greed'.[13] Undeniably, these charities act as a counterweight. 'The strength of traditional societies resides in their relationship to nature, social relationships and to meaning' (Viveret 2011, 34). These charities are not in a reactionary dynamic; at times people call for a 'degrowth', as opposed to the 'two-figures growth' obsession of corporations and the finance sector. 'Degrowth is a provocation useful to deconstruct the old world, but it is not enough to build a new one' (Viveret 2011, 39). They do not merely criticise the faults of the system, they provide solutions for a sustainable social harmony. They not only free themselves from boundaries and conventions, but revindicate their unique, different identity through their cultural, historical and spiritual roots. The illusion, in the modern collective mind, of thinking that politicians should solve every problem, makes actions like helping the poor, the homeless and the elderly almost look illegal (as feeding the homeless is already a legal offense in some cities in the USA). Somehow, one could draw a parallel with eighteenth century piracy, when sailors outraged by the rigid, unfair discipline and punishments of the Royal Navy broke their chains for a life of freedom and social justice. They are perhaps modern pirates, but far away from the stereotype of murderers and smugglers. Pirates, but more in light of the Ancient Greek etymology of p*eira*, 'to attempt', 'to try', more in the sense of modern Robin Hoods breaking the rules and conventions to walk their own way according to their inspirations, in search for more equitable balance of wealth and power. In the spirit of the mutineers of the HMS *Sandwich* in 1797, they would declare: 'Long have we been endeavouring to find ourselves men, we now find ourselves so. We will be treated as such' (Gill 1999, 300).

Notes

1 Omid Safi. The Disease of Being Busy. www.onbeing.org/blog/the-disease-of-being-busy/7023 [last accessed on 15 Jan. 2017].
2 This section contains elements adapted from a previously published work: Barylo, W. (2016). Neo-Liberal Not-for-Profits: The Embracing of Corporate Culture in European Muslim Charities. *Journal of Muslim Minority Affairs*, 36(3), 383–88.
3 *Foul Express*, Visual Racism, www.foulexpress.com/visualracism [last accessed on 15 Jan. 2017].
4 CCIF Nous sommes la nation, www.islamophobie.net/articles/2012/10/31/ccif-nsln-campagne-communication-islamophobie-nous-sommes-la-nation [last accessed on 15 Jan. 2017].
5 Forum of European Muslim Youth and Student Organisations.
6 See 5.2.
7 Meaning 'remembrance', zikr is a meditative act of worship consisting in the iteration of invocations alone or in a group.
8 BARBEDOUN http://barbedoun.com [last accessed on 15 Jan. 2017].
9 American Heritage Dictionary 2014, Collins English Dictionary 2014.
10 MBC. Omar. www.mbc.net/ar/programs/omar.html [last accessed on 15 Jan. 2017].
11 Friday sermon on the 26 August 2016 at Rumi's Cave.
12 Friday sermon on the 20 January 2017 at Rumi's Cave.
13 Quoted by Pyarelal Nayyar in Mahatma Gandhi: The Last Phase (Volume 10), p. 552 (1958).

References

Arendt, H. (1963). *On Revolution*. New York: Viking Press.
Bernoux, P. (2008). De la Sociologie des Organisations à la Sociologie des Associations [From the Sociology of Organisations to the Sociology of Charities]. In: Hoarau, C. and Laville, J-L. (eds.) *La gouvernance des associations*. Paris: Eres, pp. 55–9.
Caillé, A. (2011a). Du Convivialisme vu comme un Socialisme Radicalisé et Universalisé (et Réciproquement) [On Convivialism as a Radicalised and Universalised Socialism and Reciprocally]. In: Caillé, A., Humbert, M., Latouche, S. and Viveret, P. (eds.) *De la convivialité, dialogues sur la société conviviale à venir*. Paris: La Découverte, pp. 73–98.
Caillé, A. (2011b). Les indicateurs de richesse alternatifs: une fausse bonne idée ? [Wealth Indicators: A Wrong Good Idea?]. In: Caillé, A., Humbert, M., Latouche, S. and Viveret, P. (eds.) *De la convivialité, dialogues sur la société conviviale à venir*. Paris: La Découverte, pp. 141–66.
Corbet, R. H. (2015). Tayyib: British Muslim Piety and the Welfare of Animals for Food. In: Suleiman, Y. (ed.) *Muslims in the UK and Europe*. Cambridge: Centre of Islamic Studies, pp. 67–75.
Elshtain, J. B. (1995). *Democracy on Trial*. New York: Basic Books.
Gest, J. (2010). *Apart: Alienated and Engaged Muslims in the West*. London: Hurst.
Gill, C. (1999) [1913]. *The Naval Mutinies of 1797*. Manchester: Manchester University Press.
Göle, N. (2005). *Interpénétrations. L'Islam et l'Europe* [*Interpenetrations: Islam and Europe*]. Paris: Galaade.
Illitch, I. (1973). *Tools for Conviviality*. New York: Harper & Row.
Lévi-Strauss, C. (1962). *La pensée sauvage* [*Savage Thought*]. Paris: Plon.
Pędziwiatr, K. (2010). *The New Muslim Elites in European Cities: Religion and Active Social Citizenship Amongst Young Organized Muslims in Brussels and London*. Saarbrücken: VDM Verlag.
Plaine, T. (2004) [1797]. *Common Sense* [*With*] *Agrarian Justice*. London: Penguin.
Viveret, P. (2011). Stratégies de transition vers le bien-vivre face aux démesures dominantes [Strategies of Transitions Towards Well-Living in Face of Dominant Excesses]. In: Caillé, A., Humbert, M., Latouche, S. and Viveret, P. eds. *De la convivialité, dialogues sur la société conviviale à venir*. Paris: La Découverte, pp. 25–42.

Conclusion

Venturing into the world of European grassroots Muslim charities, I would never have expected a single question – what motivates these young Muslims volunteers – to bring me far beyond the conventional fields of culture and religion.

Whereas Islam corresponds to the general idea of a religion as *religare* (to rely on God), the fact that a mere smile, which is conferred in a transcendental dimension, blurs the boundaries between sacred and mundane, leads us to look beyond the epistemic and linguistic limitations of classical Eurocentric theories and concepts for describing complex phenomena not rooted in a single cultural cradle. Following a phenomenological approach, when everyday life becomes sacred, we have to acknowledge that beliefs are not just an auxiliary propriety of the subject; it is an environment providing material and immaterial elements which are constantly redefined through a cycle of subjectification and objectivation. As Edgar Morin would say, Islam is a complex system and part of a wider ecosystem at the crossroads between the *anthropos* (human) and the *theos* (divine, transcendental), a matricial frame of reference generating meaning, which is generated in return by the subjective appropriation of its subjects. When these volunteers embed their daily life in a dynamic exchange of gifts with God from a Maussian perspective, God becomes a real social actor (with a relative existence) which has to be taken into account. Their discourse, thoughts and behaviours show that social sciences of religions have to move beyond the usual perspectives of wealth, charisma and power. These young Muslims are driven by a whole array of non-quantifiable and sensitive forces such as emotions, love, fear or curiosity; their actions testify to an emotional economy which requires a frame of analysis that takes into account non-utilitarian motives and factors, such as the one presented by Alain Caillé (2009).

Small, local and dynamic, they break from both conventional mainstream NGO structures and elder generations' faith-based organisations. Run by young volunteers in their twenties, interested in general issues and community works such as feeding the homeless, helping students or setting up an alternative media, they do not aim to make a huge difference but rather do what they feel is a 'duty'. Focusing on quality rather than quantity, they believe in small scale projects, the results of which can only be seen in the long term. Beyond differences of cultures, religions or professional backgrounds, joining forces with groups of all faiths and none, these Muslim change-makers are in line with global movements; they look for more humble modes of governance and more balanced distributions of power and wealth. Fluent in new technologies and the use of social media and networks, holding to their cultural and spiritual legacy, they are Muslim and modern (Göle 2003) at the same time, bringing an alternative way of living into a hyper-modern secular society. Offering volunteers a way of acting concretely and immediately, their attractiveness resides in their alternatives to the welfare state and formal, slow bureaucracy. These charities perform an essential political action in its radical sense, that of the *bios politikos*, 'the life of the City', and are able to even make a tangible difference in areas such as the fight against discriminations.

In a climate of rampant and institutionalised islamophobia, these young Muslim men and women do not just criticise the system or stay stuck in reactive attitudes; they rather bring solutions with themselves, turning public services into supporters. By contributing to their communities at a local level on mainstream issues, they bridge the gap between Muslims and authorities with a sustained dialogue which humanises and de-alienates Muslims as participant citizens and partners and works against perceptions of Islam as an abstract and threatening entity. This young generation effectively removes lexical constructions based on binary distinctions between cultures, ethnicity or religion, such as 'Muslims/non-Muslims' or 'Them/Us'; they generate heterotopias which contribute to the emergence of a pluralistic society and sow the seeds of mutual understanding.

Attractive for people in search of cultural references, a community, spending time in a useful manner or finding a meaning to their lives, they provide a cohesive, safe environment, enabling the building of solid bonds of trust between the various volunteers and stakeholders and developing consequent social capital. In these family-like environments, volunteers from all faiths and none are 'brothers' and 'sisters' to each other. Mixing people from divergent schools of thoughts and opinions, the experience of otherness, of new tasks in a new social environment, provide life-changing experiences which lead volunteers to redefine their place in society and the world and, eventually, make emerge a balanced understanding of Islam. Charities become a powerful, constructive and natural mean to fight against the social frustrations prevalent in deprived areas, making possible the prevention of resentment and marginalisation which could lead to violence. Giving volunteers a sense of duty, these organisations become the cradle of an active citizenship.

As a starting point, these young Muslims have realised the limits of government institutions for solving problems such as homelessness, students' precariousness or poor support in education. Willing to tackle issues which concern their daily life, they have developed through these organisations an immediate opportunity for social action and concrete results. With an outstanding flexibility and adaptability that allow exchanges and mutual construction, the cohesive environment of these charities makes volunteers stay involved for years by giving them a sense of responsibility. Because they value humane interactions, they do not have the rigidity and hierarchy of bureaucratic institutions; they are spaces with infinite possibilities. They are a space for the exercise of primary democracy where innovations, transformations and alternatives to the usual modes of governance are experimented with, such as the informal consensual and consultative *shura*. Through this participative and accessible form of radical politics, Muslim volunteers adopt along their journey an understanding of the role of citizenship (and the role of the believer) as someone responsible and accountable. Not only Islam and citizenship are found compatible, but their set of values is deemed to be common. According to them, any 'good' Muslim is necessarily a 'good citizen'.

Along with an understanding of their role as citizens, they experiment with new ways of fitting in a hyper-modern, secular Europe and try to appropriate elements of mainstream culture for their own development, as with '*halal*' consumer products. In search of methods of growth or management, inspired by the financially effective methods of big multinational companies, some not-for-profit organisations become paradoxically driven by figures and results where money, Facebook likes and followers become means by which to reach happiness. Adapting their interpretation of the Qur'an and *hadiths* for backing their race for success and performance, their idea of a believer comes closer to the *Homo oeconomicus*, a problem solver, a machine which earns, possesses and consumes. However, growing numbers amongst volunteers realise the excesses of the modern social, political and financial systems and, through their voluntary works, try to break from conventions and advocate a more humane lifestyle rather than the result-driven life which seems nonsensical to them.

Like the adoption of a neoliberal mind-set by not-for-profit organisations, the subtle imposition of conventions grounded in a white, secular, hyper-modern society is a form of subtle but tangible colonisation, a 'metacolonisation' (Bulhan 2015), which pushes the non-mainstream to abandon their cultural and spiritual particularities. However, making use of their cultures, identities and traditions, whether they adapt, use or criticise modern methods, these charities become cores of resistance to modern, overwhelming, colonising and enslaving systems, rules and mind-sets. These are micro-societies built on the foundations of love, conviviality and compassion where Islam becomes a theology of emotional wellbeing. They get rid of mottos of 'success' and 'performance', which seep from multinational and managerial companies; they focus their work on the sense of duty, sharing and responsibility, rather than solving problems and creating results at any price.

Because modern societies spread the idea that every problem should be solved by governments or technology (Styrdom 1999; Apel 1993), they attempt to take social issues into their own hands, becoming almost modern day pirates in its etymological acceptation from the Ancient Greek '*peira*', for 'attempting'. They are men and women looking for ways of building their own independence, who decided not to be prisoners of a certain history or culture, but felt free to forge their own identities and 'create themselves endlessly' (Fanon 1967). The entirety of humanity and human identity are both in permanent movement; 'a living being does not have a substantial identity as its substance modifies and transforms itself always' (Morin 1986, 296). The world changes the individual who changes the world in reciprocal return: 'It is not only Humanity that is a by-product of the cosmic destiny, it's also the Cosmos that is a by-product of an anthropo-social destiny' (Morin 1977, 92). Humanity is movement and its dynamic dimension has to be taken into account. It shapes the world and is reshaped permanently . . . by what it has generated.

Beyond belief

The term of interpenetration (Göle 2005) would hardly find a better illustration than one of the Muslim charities and volunteers working across Europe at the dawn of the third millennia. However, at the time of this work, they happen to be in the early years of their foundation; what is to expected from the charities and volunteers in their twenties at the time of writing? The globalisation of social challenges raises a second question; in an ever-diverse world, will the analysis of social issues through the spectrum of culture and religion be relevant in hyper-modern areas?

The young Muslims in this research practise Islam in light of the European context while building a new Europe in light of Islam. They do not only understand Islam as a set of beliefs and rituals, but as an ethics for social harmony. Working with stakeholders of all faiths and none, they together share a common faith which is not necessarily religious: the faith in humanity's ability to be compassionate. For example, in community hubs such as Rumi's Cave, people realise that Islam is no stranger to concepts from Dharmic spiritualities, that Karma and divine justice are closely related. Concepts embraced by this generation of young Muslims, like the trends of veganism, yoga and others, are found in mainstream society (Haenni 2005) and are not necessarily based on a certain spirituality. Conversely, seemingly 'new' methods such as neuro-linguistic programming, co-creative events, art-therapy or consultative democracy are nothing actually 'new'. Most of these elements, viewed as modern and recent, are found at the roots of the Islamic tradition. Thus, it is to be expected that more original initiatives will emerge through a process of interpenetrations (Göle 2005) in which different cultures mutually enrich each other, in order to resist hegemonic patterns of modernity. Rather than opposing modernity and Islam, they simply embrace Islam within modernity (Fadil 2006, 60; Göle 2003).

Beyond the shy attempts of intercultural 'dialogue' blooming on the continent, could one see in future years joint works between Muslims and other charities on universal topics such as education, finance, social inequalities or gender issues? Could one see an end to the dividing dialectics digging deeper gaps between multiple 'us' and 'others'? Or would one see emerging new ways of thinking about the world as a diverse and plural whole, using a new 'We', the one of 'average citizens' comprising men and women who, far beyond their differences, are thinking about common solutions through universal values? These Muslims shed light on more global concerns: race, class, gender, environmental, spiritual, financial and political struggles are becoming less a matter of space and time, but they are all symptoms of a race for power, wealth and ego, which goes beyond any culture, religion, gender or border. It is to be expected that one will see emerging key social or political figures from the men and women who have been volunteering in these charities. Some of the volunteers I have interviewed in this work have become elected politicians now at key positions in their city councils.

During the first two decades of the twenty-first century, the world is undergoing a total and global crisis which is economic, ideological, political, social and cultural, all at the same time. One not only observes a shift in the localisation of centres of power, but also, on a deeper level, witnesses of a change in the targets of social and individual struggles occurring in societies (Duclos 2003). Because feelings, emotions, culture, history and faith are not quantifiable, they are depreciated in the current hyper-modern, neoliberal system – except in niche markets – which focuses on the production of power and the satisfaction of egos. In sum, people are taught to 'achieve' and be 'successful' by conforming to 'prestigious' white, hyper-modern, secular, neoliberal standards, while they sacrifice a basic understanding of their identities and identity in general. And because power, ego and wealth need divisions to survive, the latter had to make the former exist in a more acceptable form. Neoliberalism made acceptable through money the inequalities previously made unacceptable by law. The volunteers in these charities are not a homogeneous group of hippies wanting to change the world; they look for pragmatic solutions (Bowen 2011) at the risk of compromising their religious ethics. As demonstrated through various accommodations and patch-ups of attempting to stick an 'Islamic' label to almost everything imaginable, some run the risk of rendering the human being as a means rather than an aim. Whereas this work focuses on Muslim, local, grassroots organisations, there is a need to answer the question of if these small scale initiatives can be effective on a larger scale or in different, not necessarily spiritual, frames of reference. My focus on the European context also limits the reach of this research; would one observe similar trends in non-'Western' countries? However, whether they embrace or resist the conventions of the modern world, they appear as various and diverse combinations of traditions and modernity in a continuous movement (Vermeersch 2004; Morin 1986; Weber 1965). They embody a new contemporary, modern society, transformed by the world and transforming the world in return (Morin 1977, 92). They become at the same time an alternative rupture and continuity. What they offer to Europe is also a mirror of what Europe offers them: they both redefine each other.

However, observations show that many have realised that what current systems sell as prestigious goals are illusions (as 'prestigious' comes from the Latin *praestigium*, illusion); individual possessions and self-orientated careers are not able to solve the local problems they witness in daily life, such as poverty, lack of education or violence. Becoming 'leaders' of part of the 'Elite' would be tantamount to adding more fuel to the machine which will subjugate them in return. Many came to realise that nine-to-five jobs, conventional studies and modern lifestyles make people willingly (but comfortably) dependent and imprisoned: the collective mind thinks that life 'should be' working for a company, paying bills and a twenty-year mortgage. More dangerously, society thinks that it cannot be otherwise. The culture of mass entertainment has defined 'fun' as a synonym of 'happiness' and 'fun' as the opposite of 'wisdom'. In spaces like Rumi's Cave, young Muslims can have fun and gain wisdom at the same time. They have the opportunity to study traditional crafts, learn about historical texts such as the *Mathnavi*, enjoy music or express their creativity at the same time. Thus, these initiatives are also alternatives to a modern society colonised by corporate utilitarian culture, becoming less humane and more individualistic and focused on 'success' defined as material comfort. These charities share the idea that happiness has to be handcrafted and that such work requires giving time, energy and resources without expecting anything in return. They are in line with other global movements for more equitable forms of justice, governance and wealth.

While data-visualisations issued by the OSCE or Human Rights Watch are flooding Facebook and Twitter and showing ever growing inequalities, people become thirsty for alternatives, whatever their nationality, culture, religion or socio-economic class. I believe that the current decade – and probably the next – is at a major turning point. These are the decades where communities from different cultures, spiritualities and identities, with more skills, more talent, and more ambition than ever, will fully develop their own alternatives to the establishment's systems, will become more powerful, visible and audible than ever, and will gain unprecedented legitimacy in the public sphere. However, the excesses of the modern world – such as managerialism, savage and brutal liberalism, race for wealth, power and ego – will not stop; they are the consequences of the sum of selfish mind-sets inherent to the darkest sides of humanity. The more populated world will become more unequal, resulting in – currently ongoing – more serious damage not only to people's properties, food, security and comfort, but to people's minds. The core topic of Bulhan's (2015) article on metacolonialism is the psychological damage resulting from it; people from ethnic and religious minorities already suffer from more mental health issues than other groups, mainly because of racism and discrimination (Mehmood 2015; Amer 2005; Chakraborty and McKenzie 2002). Having to conform to dominant norms under the pressure of both mainstream society and their own social circles makes young Muslims fight a war on two fronts. More people will realise that society need tools to heal from this society of consented destruction and to prepare the next generation to deal with the sirens' chants. Already present to some extent, concerns will shift more towards feelings, emotions and concepts such as compassion, love, forgiveness, understanding, kindness and faith as much as the current society pays attention to people's incomes and households.

With the emergence of new waves of feminism and decolonial movements – especially when amongst European Muslims, people realise the wounds from previous forms of colonialism – today's keywords in modern societies are conflict, violence and injustice. However, as this generation is growing more qualified, skilled and connected, if we reduce our decade to the scale of a day, this evening's keywords are sustainability, independence and alternative. Spaces like Rumi's Cave, Foul Express or Barbedoun are already developing such heterotopias; a lot is happening and has not been studied yet. If we look further in the quest for self-determination, once these spaces provide enough comfort for communities to reflect on wider issues, tomorrow's keywords will probably be healing and growth.

Rather than suggest any recommendations (I would refer to those suggested in *Muslims in Western Politics* [Sinno 2009]), this present work aims at giving insights and raising new questions. In the field of psychology, further research may be undertaken to explore how faith-aware therapies currently being experimented with in some public health services are practised for healing mental health issues (Betteridge 2015). In the field of media, how will diasporic communities manage to make their voices heard; how will they negotiate the way they are presented? At times when some Muslims are migrating from the UK and the US to settle in regions like Andalusia, what impact will this strategy have compared to that of staying in mainland Europe? How will today's Muslim artists and entrepreneurs impact dominant trends? Eventually, when this generation of young Muslims has children in the years to come, how will they pass on the baton to the next generation, and how these will make use of their legacy?

I have little doubt that some of these currently small Muslim charities, having overcome the challenges of the European experience, will become leading stakeholders in general matters of social justice. Even further, social action-orientated multifaith initiatives such as Association Coexister in France or St Ethelburga's Centre in London show that young generations have a particular interest in making a difference with people from different traditions. Programmes such as Friends for Change or Spiritual Activists show the outstanding potential that have people from different cultures, spiritualities and ethics joining forces and becoming activists, through the celebration of their different backgrounds. It is perhaps only a matter of time before the diaspora strikes back.

References

Amer, M. (2005). *Arab American Mental Health in the Post September 11 Era: Acculturation, Stress, and Coping*. Theses and Dissertations No. 1403. Toledo: University of Toledo.

Apel, K-O. (1993). How to Ground a Universalist Ethics of Co-Responsibility for the Effects of Collective Actions and Activities. *Philosophica*, 52(2), 9–29.

Betteridge, S. (2015). Exploring the Clinical Experiences of Muslim Psychologists in the UK: Religion in Therapy. In: Suleiman, Y. (ed.) *Muslims in the UK and Europe*. Cambridge: Centre of Islamic Studies, pp. 38–47.

Bowen, J. R. (2011). *Can Islam Be French?* Princeton: Princeton University Press.

Bulhan, H. A. (2015). Stages of Colonialism in Africa: From Occupation of Land to Occupation of Being. *Journal of Social and Political Psychology*, 3(1), 239–56.

Caillé, A. (2009). *Théorie Anti-Utilitariste de l'Action et du Sujet [Anti-Utilitarian Theory of Action and Subject]*. Paris: La Découverte.

Chakraborty, A. and McKenzie, K. (2002). Does Racial Discrimination Cause Mental Illness? *The British Journal of Psychiatry*, 180(6), 475–7.

Duclos, D. (2003). *Société Monde: le temps des ruptures [World Society: Times of Ruptures]*. Paris: La Découverte.

Fadil, N. (2006). We Should Be Walking Qurans: The Making of an Islamic Political Subject. In: Jonker, G. and Amiraux, V. (eds.) *Politics of Visibility: Young Muslims in European Public Spaces*. Bielefeld: Transcript Verlag, pp. 53–78.

Fanon, F. (1967). *Black Skin, White Masks*. New York: Grove Press.

Göle, N. (2003). *Musulmanes et modernes: Voile et civilisation en Turquie* [*Muslim and Modern: Headscarf and Civilisation in Turkey*]. Paris: La Découverte.

Göle, N. (2005). *Interpénétrations: L'Islam et l'Europe* [*Interpenetrations: Islam and Europe*]. Paris: Galaade.

Haenni, P. (2005). *L'islam de marché: l'autre révolution conservatrice* [*Market Islam: The Other Conservative Revolution*]. Paris: Seuil.

Mehmood, M. (2015). The Role of Self-Esteem in Understanding Anti-Semitic and Islamophobic Prejudice. In: Suleiman, Y. (ed.) *Muslims in the UK and Europe*. Cambridge: Centre of Islamic Studies, pp. 150–8.

Morin, E. (1977). *La Méthode: La nature de la Nature* [*Method: The Nature of Nature*]. Paris: Seuil.

Morin, E. (1986). *La Méthode: La vie de la Vie* [*Method: The Life of Life*]. Paris: Seuil.

Sinno, A. H. (2009). *Muslims in Western Politics*. Bloomington: Indiana University Press.

Styrdom, P. (1999). The Challenge of Collective Responsibility for Sociology. *Current Sociology*, 47(3), 65–82.

Vermeersch, S. (2004). Entre individualisation et participation: l'engagement associatif bénévole [Between Individualisation and Participation: Voluntary Involvement in Charities]. *Revue Française de Sociologie*, 45(4), 681–710.

Weber, M. (1965) [1904–1917]. *Essais sur la théorie de la science* [*Essays on the Theory of Science*]. Paris: Plon.

Glossary of Arabic terms

abaya	a loose robe-like dress
akhi	brother
alhamdulillah	praise be to God
Allah	God
amana	deposit, faith
attar	oil-based perfume
baraka	blessings
da'wa	propagation of Islamic values
dîn	faith, path
du'a	invocation
Eid	Islamic festival
fatwa	religious ruling
hadith	report of words and deeds of the prophet of Islam
Hajj	pilgrimage to Mecca
halal	allowed for practice or consumption according to religious rules
halaqa	meeting and informal discussion about a religious topic
haram	forbidden, protected
hassanate	rewards for good deeds
hijab	headscarf
hijra	migration to more auspicious lands for religious practice
iman	faith
inshaAllah	God willing
khalifat	caliph, steward
maghrib	sunset prayer
mahram	legal male partner or family member
mashaAllah	God's will
nasheed	acapella religious song
niqab	face veil
nizam	system
qamis	long robe wore by men
qyiam	night of prayers and discussions similar to a halaqa
sadaqa	wisdom or non-compulsory alms
sharia	religious frame of legal references

shouyoukh	religious scholars; plural of sheikh
shura	consultation-based decision making process
siwak	stick for cleaning the teeth
sunnah	according to the words or deeds of the prophet of Islam
surah	chapter of the Qur'an
tarika	Sufi order
ummah	worldwide Muslim community
zakat	compulsory alms
zikr	meditative act of worship consisting in the iteration of invocations alone or in a group

Index

abuse *see* racial abuse
acceptance 61, 69, 109, 114
action 54, 67, 72–6, 93–5, 137; action-oriented 21, 143; anti-utilitarian 6–7, 14, 22–3, 130; collective 99; political 4, 34, 94, 138; religious 11, 13–15, 18–19, 24, 68; social 37, 52, 117, 135
active 3, 6, 75, 90–1, 95, 133; individualism 114; *see also* action; citizenship; participation
activism 19, 33, 37, 51, 117, 143; cyber 1, 126; political 5, 31, 53
administration 59, 62, 93; *see also* authorities
Africa 3, 42, 109–10
alienation 49–54, 62, 79, 129, 138
alternative 4, 7, 85, 92, 119; citizenship 21–3; media 36, 68, 126, 137–41; political 34, 78; space 133, 142; therapies 41, 132
anti-utilitarian 8, 25, 43, 82, 112; *see also* action
apart 54
apophetic *see* identity
appropriation 98, 137
articulation 3, 19–20
assimilation 19–20, 92, 97, 111
atomisation 99, 106, 129
attractiveness 4, 8, 42, 66–7, 82, 117; reasons for 34–7, 73, 85, 105, 126–8, 138; social environment 63, 71, 77
authorities 20, 72, 114, 117, 138; perceptions 45, 49–55, 61–3; relations with 3–4, 7, 36; religious 19, 66, 106

background: cultural or ethnic 20, 33–6, 41–5, 54, 66, 125–6; social or professional 6–7, 137; spiritual 4, 72, 109

balance 6, 49, 69, 73, 126, 134–5; religious understanding 8, 77, 138
ban *see* hijab
banking 7, 106
banlieue 2, 19, 36, 60
belonging 8, 86, 96–7
beneficiary 3, 11, 20, 24, 75, 86–9; perceptions 55, 61–2
brother 108
brotherhood and sisterhood 3, 68, 80, 91, 129, 134–8
bureaucracy 7, 21, 30, 35, 77–8; absence of 81, 105, 138; effects of 93, 99, 117
burkini 1, 50
business 8, 33, 108; businessman 3, 134; methods 110, 116, 133

Caillé, A. *see* anti-utilitarian
caliph 17, 79, 96, 134
Caribbean 3, 42, 132
categories 5, 97–8, 116; conceptual 15–17; ideal-types 19–21, 24, 43; volunteering 41
challenge 5, 35–6, 51, 72, 76, 140
change 21, 52, 76–7, 85, 134, 139; self 66, 75–6, 128; social 7, 54, 56–61
charisma 6, 79–80, 130
charities *see* organisations
citizenship: active 6–8, 13, 21, 82–4, 138; passive 8, 86, 96–9; perceptions of 13, 92, 96–100, 124; practice of 19, 54, 76; *see also* alternative; belonging
city council 3, 52–8, 61–2, 141
civil servant 3, 45, 55, 58–62, 76
class 6, 8, 113, 140
colleagues 24, 60, 74–5, 80, 90–1, 129
collective 89, 93, 129; identity 76; mind 110, 135, 141; practices 16–17, 94, 99;

148 Index

project 77, 134; responsibility 34; *see also* action
colonisation 95, 110–18, 139, 142; consequences of 15, 53; neocolonialism 110
complex 6–8, 13–20, 22, 41–3, 104, 125; systems 17, 24, 137
conflict 86, 91, 93, 100, 127, 142; resolution 4, 79–82, 130
consensus 70–2, 77, 86, 98, 130, 139
consumerism 97, 104–7, 112–17
conviviality 55, 67, 71–2, 80, 105, 124
copenetration 19, 24; *see also* interpenetration
corporate 79, 105–6, 115–18, 123–5, 128–30
counter-space 34; *see also* alternative, space
crime 1, 4, 50–1, 77
crisis 1, 8, 86–91, 124, 141
culture 61–3, 80, 99, 107–12, 116, 130–5; democracy 99; diversity 20, 35–6, 42, 76; modern 100; system 14, 24; *see also* background; corporate; diaspora
cyber-activism *see* activism

da'wa 63, 109
decolonial 9, 53, 142; decolonisation 125, 128–9
de-diasporisation 110
degrowth 135
dehumanisation 54, 95, 99, 118, 128, 130
democracy 77–82, 85–6, 92, 98–9; Islam and 20–2; primary 99–100, 140
demotivation 86
dialogue 16, 53–5, 61–3, 75, 82, 140
diaspora 30, 34, 108, 141–3; cultures and background 6, 36, 67, 107, 124, 133
diversity *see* background; culture
dominant 6, 45, 49; norms 20, 142; society 1, 8, 53, 111, 114, 128

education 36, 55, 63, 75, 111, 138–40; level of 3, 8, 19–20, 37–42, 115; religious 31
ego 9, 106, 117, 124, 129, 140–2
elders 34, 134, 137
emotions 82, 111, 124, 137–42; emotional theology 125, 129–34; in theory 6, 16, 22–5
engagement 4, 6, 19, 33–6, 72, 79; civic 21, 98, 112
entrepreneur 36, 42, 108, 128, 143

environment 8, 21–2, 33–7, 95, 124–5, 134; social 4–8, 49, 63, 66–72, 76–81, 91; in theory 14–18
ethnic 35, 42, 53, 63, 110, 125
ethnocentrism 15
ethnonormativity 111, 113–14
Eurocentrism 7, 13, 15, 110–11, 137
Europe: context 30, 49–52, 72, 95–7; Muslims in 19–20, 31–6, 41, 86; standards 111, 114; *see also* dominant
experimentation 85, 92, 106–8, 112, 114, 118
extremism 1–4, 19, 52, 81

Facebook 35–6, 53–4, 63, 106, 111–17, 126–9
faith: beliefs 11, 15–17, 67, 131; faith-based 31, 36–7, 62, 118, 123; trust 90–1; *see also* background; religion; secularism; spirituality
familiarity 61, 68, 70, 109
family: environment 35, 60, 67–9, 77–80; home and household 16, 22, 70, 85, 130; *see also* background; culture
food 35–6, 56, 106, 125–7, 130; services 3, 37, 55; *see also* halal
France 1, 42–4, 62, 95–7; Muslims in 19, 30–6, 49–55, 92
friendship 91, 105, 111, 124, 129

gender 6, 8, 19, 41–2, 66, 114
generations 4–5, 13, 19–21, 31–5, 108–9
gift 14, 22–5, 89, 130
globalisation 15, 35–6, 53, 114, 140
God 23–4, 90–1, 131, 134
governance 35–6, 67, 77–9, 98–100, 117
grassroots 4, 30, 63, 81

habitus 19
hadith 8, 54, 67, 116
halal 3, 7, 19, 104–7, 125, 130
hardships 88, 90–1
hegemony 110
heterotopia 34, 138, 142
hierarchy 30, 68, 79, 81–2, 98, 129
hijab 36, 51, 55, 66–70, 106–9, 112–13; ban 1, 33, 50, 95
homeless 4, 33, 56, 71, 75, 135; *see also* identity
hub 24, 67, 70, 123, 131
humanisation 63, 99
human rights 1, 50–2, 98
hybrid 17, 34, 108, 118
hyper-modernity *see* modernity

ideal-types 5, 13–14, 35, 43
identity 18, 21, 34, 97, 106–7; apophetic 53–4; building 67, 72–7; homeless 109; Islamic and Muslim 17, 19, 52, 68; passive 133
image 49, 53, 62, 73, 95, 106–7
India 42, 108, 114
individualism 33, 97, 99, 107, 114, 118
inequalities 21, 36, 125, 140–2
informal 4, 33, 67, 79, 92, 98
infrapolitical *see* action, political
institutions 24, 34, 77, 100
interaction: social 22, 62, 138; *see also* attractiveness
interpenetration 19, 140
interpretation 16–18, 70, 72
invocation 11, 71–2, 126
Islam *see* religion
islamophobia 4, 49–52, 124; institutionalised 7, 138

laïcité 20, 50, 61, 95
leader 79, 116–17, 133–4
legitimacy 62–3, 107, 111, 116–17
life experience 16, 20–4, 67, 73–7, 91

mainstream 31, 34–5, 49, 52–3, 63, 107–13, 118
management 34, 116–18, 139
marriage 19, 104, 107
matrix 18, 24, 61, 91, 129
media: mass 124; portrayal of Muslims in 36, 41, 50–3, 92; social 30, 36, 53, 93, 106–8, 112–17; *see also* alternative; Facebook; mainstream
mental health 53, 113, 132, 142–3
metacolonisation 8, 110–11, 114, 125
migration 2–3, 33–4, 41, 109, 143
mobilisation 21, 52, 54, 59
modernity 23, 34–5, 105–8, 114, 125; hyper-modernity 14, 99, 111, 129–30
Morin, E. 14–18, 24, 43
motivation 21–3, 74–5, 78, 86–92
movements 34, 53, 129, 138
Muhammad *see* prophets
multiculturalism 19
multifaith 143
music 41, 68, 70, 107, 131

neighbourhood 33–5, 62, 99
neocolonialism *see* colonisation
neoliberalism 104–11, 114, 117, 124–5, 129

network 62, 115, 117; social 20–1, 35–6, 67–73
NGOs 30–5, 41–2; *see also* organisations
norms 8, 91, 114, 142

objectification 112
organisations 22–5, 30–5; Muslim 20–1, 31–4, 37, 44; *see also* NGOs
orientalism 19, 109

participation 20–2, 96–100; economic 108; political 30, 77, 81; social 74
passive *see* citizenship; identity
performance 16, 94; business 116–18, 139
phenomenology 14, 19, 42–3, 76
pirate 135, 139
pluralism 19, 61, 80
Poland: context 33, 49, 52, 63, 72; Muslims in 41–3
police *see* authorities
politics 30, 33, 62, 74, 92–100; infrapolitical 34; politicians 21, 50–4, 77, 92, 95; post-conventional 33–4; and religion 13, 94; system 110–11, 125; *see also* islamophobia; mainstream; participation; trust
poverty 33, 36–7, 63
power 21, 41, 61–2, 106, 110–14, 129–35; governance 80–1; in theory 6, 14, 22–3
practices 35, 76; prayer 2, 13, 68, 72, 126–7, 131; religious 14–21, 31, 42, 75; rituals 3, 11, 15–18, 68–71, 117, 130
prayer *see* practices
primary democracy *see* democracy
products 8, 104–8, 111–12
professional: background 6–7, 42, 105; skills 35, 4–21, 124–6; *see also* business; entrepreneur
prophets 90, 134; Muhammad 52, 71–2, 116
proselyte 52, 61–2
public: relations to the 36, 55–9, 72, 92–5; services 34, 49–50, 61–3; sphere 34, 53, 58, 86, 99

Qur'an 2, 17, 67, 115–17, 139

racial abuse 13, 49, 51, 53, 67, 72
racism 8, 36–7, 70, 125, 142
rationalisation 22, 99, 104, 116–18, 124–5, 130

religion: as concept 14–19; freedom of 50, 96; lived 13; merchandisation of 105–11; social dimension of 21–4, 91; *see also* background; faith; practices; secularism; spirituality; visibility
resistance 123, 125, 128–9, 133
ritual *see* practices

sacred 7, 11–15
salafi 19, 107, 131
secularism 15, 20, 49–50, 95, 133; in society 33–5, 61, 111–13; *see also* laïcité
sheikh *see* authorities
shura 86, 92, 98, 100
sister *see* brotherhood and sisterhood
skills *see* professional
social action *see* action
social capital 21, 36, 67–8, 72–3, 81, 99
social environment *see* environment
social interactions *see* interaction
social media *see* media
social network *see* network
society *see* dominant; France; mainstream; Poland; UK
soup kitchen 2–3, 36, 41, 74–5
South Asia 2, 108–9
spirituality 17–23, 41, 76, 90–1, 124–5, 129; self-development 72
stakeholders 20, 36, 138
stigmatisation 53, 86, 95, 114
students 11, 36–7, 42, 50, 55–61
subjectification 16, 137

sunnah 3, 11
sustainability 35, 67, 82, 124, 135
symptoms 114, 123, 130, 140
system *see* alternative; complex; culture; dominant; politics; religion

televangelism 106
terrorism 2–3, 51–2
traditions 17–18, 135; Islamic 13, 35, 41, 105–8, 130–4, 140; *see also* background; culture; shura
trust: in authorities 21, 53, 77, 92; bonds 44, 67–70, 78, 81–2, 89, 130; thick and thin 62, 72–3, 80, 99–100; *see also* faith

UK: context 35; Muslims in 30–3
utilitarian 22, 82, 105, 112, 116, 130, 142

violence 51, 133, 138, 141–2
visibility 31, 36, 50–1, 55, 61–3, 95–7
volunteering: categories 19–20, 41, 43; mainstream 22–3; Muslim 21, 24, 30, 35–7, 41–2, 52
vote 92, 97–9, 130, 133

women 13, 81, 107, 112–13; gender mixing 66; image of Muslim 19, 55, 58–9, 63, 95; leadership 52, 72
worship 11, 15, 68

young *see* generations

Printed in Great Britain
by Amazon